A Year in the Edible Garden

A Month-by-Month Guide to Growing and Harvesting Vegetables, Herbs, and Edible Flowers

A Year in the Edible Garden: A Month-by-Month Guide to Growing and
Harvesting Vegetables, Herbs, and Edible Flowers
Text by Sarah Raven / Photographs by Jonathan Buckley

First published in Great Britian 2023 by Bloomsbury Publishing under the
title, "A Year Full of Veg: A Harvest for Every Season"
Bloomsbury Publishing Plc
50 Bedford Square, London, WC1B 3DP, UK
www.bloomsbury.com

First published in the United States of America in 2023 by

Rizzoli International Publications, Inc.
300 Park Avenue South
New York, NY 10010
www.rizzoliusa.com

For Rizzoli
Publisher: Charles Miers
Editor: Klaus Kirschbaum
Assistant Editor: Meredith Johnson
Managing Editor: Lynn Scrabis

ISBN: 978-0847899432
Library of Congress Catalog Control Number: 2022947652

2023 2024 2025 2026/ 10 9 8 7 6 5 4 3 2 1

Printed in China

Visit us online:
Facebook.com/RizzoliNewYork
Twitter: @Rizzoli_Books
Instagram.com/RizzoliBooks
Pinterest.com/RizzoliBooks
YouTube.com/user/RizzoliNY
Issuu.com/Rizzoli

A Year in the Edible Garden

A Month-
by-Month
Guide to
Growing and
Harvesting
Vegetables,
Herbs,
and Edible
Flowers

Sarah Raven

RIZZOLI
NEW YORK

New York · Paris · London · Milan

Photographs by
Jonathan Buckley

Introduction

There are two things I want from my garden: it has to be beautiful— jam-packed with flowers, form, and color—and it has to produce lots of delicious, fresh, homegrown food. I've loved cooking since I was a child and have always known that homegrown is best, so a kitchen garden has been a priority.

Few things give me more pleasure and help me relax and wind down at the end of the day and at the weekend than wandering through the vegetable garden and into the greenhouse—first, to see what's looking good and then to decide what to eat. It feels like a luxury not to have to travel anywhere to buy fresh food, and that's better for me and better for the environment.

Once you start growing your own, you can make sure your easy-to-grow favorites are there week by week, changing as the year goes on. In winter, I adore picking enough leaves for a punchy salad, as well as a basket of kale for dinners and lunches. Then, I'm thrilled when the rhubarb starts in spring, and the early fava beans and peas toward the end of the season. I love being able to dig new potatoes and pick zucchini and pole beans as baby vegetables—tiny and tender and at their absolute best in summer—and then by midsummer, enjoying tomatoes for breakfast, lunch, and dinner. By autumn, meaty eggplants are on offer, and finally the squash, before we're back around to the salads and kale again. Having this ever-changing freshness keeps my cooking on its toes, with a hand picked harvest there whenever I want it.

If we grow too much for us (that's Adam, my husband, and I, plus sometimes a grown-up child or two, home for the weekend), then the team at Perch Hill get first dibs and pick what they like to eat. Anita Oakes is in charge of growing the vegetables here, with Josie Lewis overseeing all parts of the garden. They have their favorites, as do the rest of the team, which all make it into the garden. Together, we grow colanders and colanders of fresh edibles, which we also integrate into our lunch menu in the Perch Hill café when the garden is open. Pretty much nothing goes to waste.

Abundance and ease

Previous page The central pot features dahlias, salvias, and lemon verbena for edible flowers and tisanes. These tender perennials are brought in for winter and planted again the following spring.
Below The vegetable garden at Perch Hill in spring, with rhubarb in the foreground.
Next page Perch Hill, a garden in the middle of a 90-acre organic farm in the densely wooded Sussex Weald.

In the parts of Perch Hill given over to vegetables, I have concentrated my efforts (over what is now 30 years) on trying to ensure that we get the maximum amount of delicious produce from every corner throughout the year. That's my number one driver as far as edibles go: year-round, square-meter productivity. It's why most of the vegetable garden is devoted to cut-and-come-again plants, which we can harvest on one day, only to find that a week later we can do so again. These cut-and-come-agains provide us with efficient productivity. That's why classics such as cabbages and main-crop potatoes don't usually

make it into my plot, while salad leaves, plenty of herbs, and leafy greens always do.

We tend to grow one or two difficult-to-buy and exceptional-tasting potato varieties such as "Pink Fir Apple" and "Ratte", but the large main crops (such as "Maris Piper") are easy to find—even organic ones—in supermarkets, produce stores, and through local vegetable-box schemes. They are true space guzzlers, so I'd say don't waste your precious garden beds on these.

For the sake of culinary completeness, you might think it crazy not to grow Brussels sprouts or cauliflowers for winter. No matter how handsome they are, unless you have lots of space, I'd leave them to the farmers. They sit in the ground for a good 6 months before harvest and then, after all that waiting, give you only a small amount of food per square meter. And, as a brassica, they need netting protection against cabbage white caterpillars, which can add fiddle, time, and work.

The plants we do grow must be both productive for a long time and easy to look after. I want to have a good range of crops, which means that no single plant should require too much attention. I've tried growing ginger and sweet potatoes, for example, but wouldn't recommend either. They require a lot of fuss, or at least more heat and better light than we can give them naturally in the UK. Even with those essentials, they produce rhizomes and tubers that are only half the size we're used to seeing in the shops.

Instead, I want the things I grow to germinate reliably and progress fast to harvestable size. Once there, they should be slow to bolt and sit at just the right picking stage for ages, offering kitchen ingredients with minimal TLC.

Abundance and easy growing is about finding crops that give you a great return, even when resources are limited. Each and every one of the edibles I recommend are life-enhancing and generously productive in any space. Anyone with a bit of garden, a yard, or even just some pots or window boxes can grow at least a few of the crops I recommend in this book. You don't need great skill, knowledge, or space to harvest fresh, healthy food.

Since my mid-twenties, I've grown something edible wherever I have lived. No matter how small my home, I've managed to prop a few pots on my doorstep. When I lived in a an apartment in London, I used to sow things to eat into long, narrow boxes that were made by my now-husband Adam to fit our window ledges. Our window boxes were supported by a couple of plant theaters

mounted on either side of the back door to give us more growing room. All of these containers were densely planted with easy-to-care-for crops like parsley, lettuce, Swiss chard, and herbs—all available for simple snipping right outside the kitchen door. There are so many benefits to growing in this way. First, when if picked the correct way, these crops regrow, even in winter. And second, growing in containers is often done well out of the reach of neighborhood cats.

A two-season system

What I've found from our trials and experiments here at Perch Hill is that there are plants that can provide you with great things to eat for 365 days a year.

Most traditional approaches divide vegetable gardening into four seasons, but it's simpler and more successful to stick to two. A useful general principle is to consider the 12 months to be split into two halves: early October to April, when it's colder, greyer, and rainier here in the UK, and May to September, when temperatures and light levels rise. That gives us two seasons and lots of edible plants that will fit into each. You just need to know what does well in which and select from the right group. There are a few must-haves (such as parsley and chard) that do well in both seasons, but these sorts of plants are rare.

It's safe to say that the hardy plants (mainly annuals) are the all-important givers for the October to April season: think kale, leeks (though these are not, of course, cut-and-come-again), chard, salad arugula, and any of the mustards. The half-hardy or tender varieties, such as tomatoes, basil, cucumber, zucchini, pole and French beans, are the crops to concentrate on between May and September. This two-season system will help you hugely in growing food if you are a beginner grower.

Opposite, clockwise from top left
A summer harvest; a pot with
Hyacinthus orientalis "Anastasia"
growing up through kale in March;
dwarf French bean "Speedy";
a potato trial.

Flavor, color, and life

Although abundance is a big motivator for me, outstanding flavor is right up there too. To this end, we continue to repeat trials at Perch Hill to establish which forms have the most distinctive taste. I love a trial. It really helps to work out which are the best varieties for flavor and for our growing conditions here in the UK, so we can be confident in our recommendations when speaking to other growers and offering advice. You'll see I've mentioned the results of various trials throughout the book.

Our kitchen garden grows on a slope that wraps around the flower garden and cookery school building and is therefore very prominent as you come into Perch Hill. Being so visible, this whole area needs to be more than just productive; it's important that it's also full of interesting plant combinations that offer color, form, and shape. If you're growing food in your garden rather than in formal rows in an allotment, you'll learn that these things matter. Throughout the book, I've highlighted the plant combinations and forms that bring character to the garden.

Finally, it makes sense to me on all levels that we garden according to organic and no-dig principles. The garden here is run entirely without the use of chemicals. We're lucky to have plenty of well-rotted manure available from the organic farm next door, but even if that wasn't the case, organic we would be. There's increasing evidence that organic food is better for you than nonorganic food, and that grown slowly, without the use of lots of extra water and chemical fertilizers, food tastes better. While there's nature and biodiversity to attend to above ground, there is equal richness below ground, with mycorrhizal fungi, earthworms, and millions of other invertebrates that need to be nurtured for healthy soil. With that in mind, we moved to a no-dig system years ago, more or less retiring our spades and opting to leave the soil structure undisturbed.

I am a great believer in encouraging natural pest predators into the garden (most garden birds, frogs, toads, and beneficial insects) as well as companion planting (using one plant to help another remain healthy and free from pests). It's a satisfying way to garden that brings so much life to the vegetable plot.

The main pillars of our Perch Hill kitchen garden are abundance, ease, flavor, color, and nature. They're what you'll find advice on in this book. Now on to what I'd suggest you grow…

What to Grow

Deciding what to grow in the time and space you have available is one of the main pleasures and challenges gardeners face. I use a method that divides edible plants into five categories to help me decide what I'm going to grow and how much of it. If you have lots of time and space, you could choose something from each category. If you're short of either, you should stick with just the plants in category 1. These are the generous producers that will keep giving on minimal TLC, though you could add in a few things from category 2 if you have room.

The labor/reward ratio should be at the forefront of your mind. Concentrate your time and energy on the easy and generous producers, particularly where space is limited. I always think it's best to grow something you really love, and to grow enough of it to transform a meal once or twice a week, rather than go for small, not-very-useful quantities of a wider range of plants. For me, this means an emphasis on salads and herbs any time of year. Use these pages to make your own selection, and then use the rest of the advice in this book, which is based on 30 years of trialling here at Perch Hill, to grow what you love efficiently, well, and with joy.

Category 1: Big producers

In this category, you'll find the cut-and-come-again plants that offer a harvest that appears to be almost limitless. To ensure this reliability, you need to keep picking to keep them producing. You should not leave fruit and pods on the plants or allow the leafy ones to get too big and struggle, as that's when they bolt or concentrate their energy on ripening only a few bumper-sized fruits rather than a new crop.

We work to two seasons at Perch Hill: the first in the colder, greyer October to April, and the second in the lighter, warmer May to September. We adjust the varieties we grow accordingly (see p. 12).

For the latter, warmer season, we select varieties bred for greater heat and drought tolerance—for example, kale "Red Russian" replaces kale "Scarlet", which is harder cropping and has better flavor in the summer season. And the prolific chard "Lucullus" is the one to go for in the hot, dry months. Bred in Australia, "Lucullus", is much more able to put up with our average summer conditions and it is also slow to bolt.

The selection in this list are all worthwhile, even if space

Previous page **Rainbow chard, which we can pick year-round.**
Opposite **Harvests from category 1, the big producers.**

is limited, and most are ideal for growing in pots. The most prolific producers are at the top of the list, which moves down in order of square-meter productivity, so if you have very limited space, select from the salads, herbs, and leafy greens only.

Salads
- Lettuce
- Salad leaves
- Edible flowers

Herbs
- Annual salad herbs (such as parsley and coriander)
- Perennial herbs (such as mint, sorrel, chives, fennel, tarragon)
- Tender perennials (such as scented-leaf pelargoniums)
- Woody evergreen herbs (such as bay, sage, and, to an extent, rosemary)

Leafy greens
- Kale
- Annual spinach
- Spinach beet
- Chard

Summer squash and zucchini

Beans
- Pole beans
- French beans

Rhubarb
Great for shade.

Peas
- Sugar snap peas
- Snow peas

Both more prolific than shelling pea varieties.

Tomatoes
A key crop, but not pick-and-come-again. See categories 3 and 4.

Cucumbers
Large varieties and small, Persian cucumbers.

Peppers
Chilies and sweet peppers.

Eggplant

Productivity table
To make clear how productive some edibles are compared with others, see the table below, which shows the results of a small patch of garden given to Savoy cabbage compared with the same-sized bed of asparagus and purple sprouting broccoli, as well as the same surface area given to Swiss chard and a salad leaf like mizuna "Red Knight" (You'll see why the latter is my take-to-the-moon plant.)

	Savoy cabbage	Purple sprouting broccoli	Asparagus	Swiss chard	Mizuna
Sowing to harvest time	7–8 months	9 months	3 years	8–10 weeks	4–6 weeks
Harvest duration	Single	4–6 weeks	6 weeks	6–8 months	6 months (if sown Sep/Oct)
Quantity from sq.m/year	2 colanders	6 colanders	4 colanders	40–50 colanders	40–50 colanders
Square-meter productivity	Very low	Low	Low	Very high	Very high

From category 2, a four-color beetroot harvest.

A note on growing in pots

For growing in pots and large containers, I recommend the following selection (taken from the main category 1 list).

- All the cut-and-come-again salads and herbs
- Compact varieties of kale such as "Red Russian"
  If picked regularly, it becomes sort of bonsaied.
- Swiss or rainbow chard
- Climbers such as pole beans
  To make use of vertical space
- Chilies
  These are particularly suited to pots as they look great, need little room, and can be grown inside on a window ledge if necessary.

Category 2: Easy edibles

Easy edibles are the plants that can be thrown in and ignored. They thrive on their own and don't need much attention. They are ideal if you have limited time or you grow vegetables on an allotment and can't make it there every day.

Annuals

Even in drought, annuals will just about be okay without regular watering. They don't need constant harvesting to stop them running to seed.

- Beetroots
- Fava beans
- Kale
- Kohlrabi
- Leeks
- Purple sprouting broccoli
  This helps bridge the "hungry gap" in spring.
- Squash
  These admittedly take up lots of space but are happy on minimal TLC if you add plenty of well-rotted manure when planting.

Perennials and shrubs

You can plant these perennials in spring or autumn, and they should keep producing for years or even decades without requiring much attention.

- Asparagus
  I think asparagus just about makes it into this category, but it's a borderline case. It's so tasty, and is best eaten straight from the garden, but it crops for a short time and doesn't properly provide a harvest until 3 years from planting. It's only for those who have lots of space and can keep on top of the weeds long-term. If you have an asparagus grower near you, you are better off filling your space with other plants from categories 1 and 2.
- Bush and cane fruit (such as black currants, blackberries, and raspberries)
  Note that I don't cover fruit in this book.
- Evergreen herbs (such as rosemary and sage)
- French artichoke
- Perennial kale, such as sea kale
- Rhubarb

Tubers

- Jerusalem artichokes
- Potatoes
  These are ideally sprouted and earthed up, which is a small amount of work. Even if you only manage to get them into some rich soil without doing either of those things, you will probably end up with a worthwhile harvest.

Category 3: Flavor first

We've all experienced tasteless tomatoes or bland carrots from the supermarket or even produce store (often because commercial growers put productivity and ease of storage before flavor). It's true that buying organic, locally grown vegetables in season matters (increasing your chances of tasty produce), but it's even better to grow them yourself, focusing on varieties that pack a flavorful punch. In this category, you'll find the edibles that especially benefit from being homegrown.

Varieties and time
Growing excellent varieties slowly and with care means better flavor. A lot of commercial varieties are not bred for flavor, and growers flood their crop with nutrients and water to speed up harvest.

- Tomatoes
  If you have a greenhouse (where they crop longer and harder than outside and aren't prone to blight), you will find that

tomatoes are one of the most worthwhile plants to grow.

Sugar content
Vegetables with a high sugar content (which rapidly converts to starch after harvest) are much nicer when freshly picked or pulled.

- Shelling peas
- Sweet corn
- New potatoes
- Carrots
- Asparagus (less so)

Water content
Some plants grown quickly with lots of heat and water (as they often are commercially) have a fraction of the flavor of those grown more slowly in the home garden or greenhouse.

- Many herbs (such as tarragon, basil, and chives)
  Homegrown, these herbs have twice the flavor as those you find in supermarket bags.
- Lettuces
- Peppers (chilies and sweet)
  Until you've grown a pepper yourself, you won't really know their true sweet smokiness.

Texture
The texture of supermarket vegetables is often impacted by over-refrigeration and long transport times. Getting from plot to plate can really impact the flavor of the produce. Homegrown, right at your back door, is an utterly different and much better experience.

- Beans (particularly French and pole)
  When fresh, they're squeaky on your teeth!
- Purple sprouting broccoli
- Radishes
  These are best when just picked and crunchy.

Size
Finally, in category 3, I've included the vegetables that taste much better harvested as baby vegetables—something you can control yourself when growing at home as you can pick them whenever you like.

- Baby Florence (bulb) fennel
- Beetroots
- Fava beans
- Zucchini
- Pole beans

A selection from categories 4 and 5, the unbuyables and the lookers.

Next page The vegetable garden in late summer. There's always lots of flowers as well as vegetables, which help to attract pollinators, keep the good and bad insects in balance, and add color to our plates.

Category 4: Unbuyables

This category focuses on the edibles that are generally not easy to find in shops. I include here unusual colored varieties of some readily available vegetables.

- Beetroots (multicolored)
- Cranberry beans
- Chard
- Zucchini (multicolored, climbing, and crookneck)
- French beans (purple and yellow)
- Onions (green)
- Tomatoes (green, black, yellow, and orange)
- Unusual herbs (such as chervil and summer savory)

Category 5: The lookers

I recommend this final category, which includes plants that are both edible and ornamental, bringing life and color to the garden. I used to include flowering parsnip in this category because their flowers are beautiful, acid-green umbels. I loved picking them for arranging, but have found the flowers, stems, and leaves can burn the skin on a sunny day, so parsnip flowers are best avoided.

- French artichoke
- Herbs (such as oregano and sage)
- Kale (particularly "Redbor" and "Scarlet") as well as kalettes
- Leeks (purple-washed varieties such as "Northern Lights" and "Saint Victor")
- Rainbow chard
- Scented-leaf pelargoniums

A note on growing in a greenhouse

In the practical sections of each chapter, you'll find jobs "in the greenhouse", which really means any space that's protected under glass or cover. I rarely recommend buying additional equipment; however, if you want to grow a plentiful supply of vegetables through the year, I suggest working out how to include even a small area of under-cover space.

If you possibly can, include a greenhouse in the garden. It is a fabulous way to extend a garden's potential—particularly if there's room in it for soil-filled troughs or beds, as well as a bench for propagating.

A polytunnel is also a great space for growing almost any plant, and is often easier to integrate into small spaces. Offering all-round light and a bit of frost protection, it makes certain crops like tomatoes much easier to grow.

If you don't have space or budget for a greenhouse or polytunnel, you should consider a small cold frame, which will offer cooler and brighter conditions than any spot in a house. And if you don't have space for a cold frame, even on a balcony, you might consider buying seedlings from a good nursery rather than trying to grow more than the odd thing on an indoor window ledge. In my experience, plants in these conditions really struggle, which can become pretty discouraging.

January & February

I love being able to walk outside in January and February and pick something delicious for lunch or dinner. Cropping tomatoes, and the heady smell that goes with it, is a luxury in summer, but leaving the house to harvest a colander of peppery salad, pick a bunch of herbs, or snap some stems of kale when the weather is properly cold is just as rewarding. You can grow vegetables for storing through the colder months (and even make yourself a storing box in the autumn, see p. 336), but freshly picked produce is even nicer.

Over the years, it has been a surprise to me how hardy lots of edible crops truly are. With all the wind and rain we usually have in these months, along with the days being so short and light levels low, it's hard to believe that there's anything that will grow and self-replenish, but there are plants that actually prefer the cool and grey months.

Given a bit of heat, even just a couple of warm days in April (and a month earlier under glass), lots of the annual salad crops—arugula, mizuna, mustards, and hardy green herbs like chervil—bolt pretty instantly, running up to flower, setting seed, and dying within just a week or two. That doesn't happen at this time of year.

There are more possibilities in the milder south but, wherever you are, it's well worth experimenting with a range of frost-resistant edibles. It's true that in winter, your options widen if you have an under-cover area—even just one cold frame—but if that isn't possible there are things that do okay outside (as long as you're not in deep snow for weeks on end). And the milder winters we're now experiencing mean some plants keep growing, albeit slowly.

We all know about Brussels sprouts, cabbages, parsnips, and leeks, but these all need to be in the ground for ages before you can pick them. And once harvested, that's it. We do grow leeks because they look good and we love to eat them, but the rest don't usually make the grade in our garden. Luckily, there are plenty of edible plants that give an abundant winter harvest.

Mizuna, which originates from China, has long been grown through the winter in Japan and even survives outside in the country's snowy highlands. We've found it stands up well to frost and snow in the UK, as do the mustards. Salad arugula also performs well in the cold, as do the reliably productive kales and recently bred kalettes. They're still cropping slowly into January. With a bit of protection, chard does pretty well in Sussex, as do some of the soft-leaved spinach varieties.

Next are the early-season edible flowers. My birthday is at the beginning of February, a dour old time of year. I love picking bowls of salad to eat with family and friends, decorated with violas and polyanthus, of which there are surprisingly plenty.

Between all these, you've got regular and repeatedly pickable plants that are delicious to eat and easy to grow, with decent square-meter productivity. You can cultivate them in the garden or greenhouse, and many are great for pots.

I recently made a winter visit to West Dean Gardens in West Sussex, where they have an array of ornamental and delicious edibles lined up in pretty terra-cotta pots displayed on tiered plant theaters in one of the Victorian glasshouses. It's a very cheering sight: beautiful crops of winter-hardy-herbs, salad leaves, dwarf kales, and pea tips all growing strongly.

In the early autumn, we gather many of the small pots we have around the garden and fill them with cut-and-come-again salads, herbs, and leafy greens. Before I had collected so many pots, I used to use polystyrene boxes from the fishmonger with holes pierced through the bottom for drainage (pictured on p. 337). They are both deep and insulated, making them ideal for winter growing (in fact, better than terra-cotta). Single varieties of salads and herbs, as well as mixes, work well. We still use them, or lengths of guttering pipe, to grow early crops of pea tips and radishes.

In winter, just as in summer, regardless of space and with minimal TLC, you can produce a whole range of good things to eat.

Salad

Even if it's just a small bowl of leaves, I love to eat a salad most days, January and February included. I might not feel quite the same if it was a supermarket bag, but freshly picked winter salad is delicious. There are so many possible flavors, textures, and colors that no bowl need be the same.

What I aim to grow, pick, and combine in a salad has evolved over the years. I want a base of crunchy lettuce to give bulk and texture, enough to fill about 40 per cent of the bowl, while the next 40 percent provides the main flavor, and that comes from different cut-and-come-again leaves. If I want something gentle, I include the earthy flavors of baby beetroot leaf, chard, and/or spinach. If it's a strong flavor I'm after, I go for hot and peppery leaves (including arugula, mustards, and cress), or perhaps the cabbagey ones (mizuna, komatsuna, or baby leaf kale). I might also add a touch of bitterness from dandelion or chicory. The world divides on bitter flavors—you'll either love or hate these—but I find they can brighten a salad if used sparingly. The final 20 percent is mainly salad herbs, plus some extra items like pea tips, radishes, or Florence fennel, and a topping of edible flowers.

The soft-leaved herbs include flavors of aniseed, such as fennel, dill, sweet cicely, and, my favorite for summer salads, young tarragon leaves (though that's not up and ready yet). A citrus burst comes from sorrel, the invaluable lemon queen, which starts to reappear in February. Soon, you can add an oniony flavor from chives or a celery taste. Finally, there's the clean, grassy notes of parsley. I quite often add the leaves from a stem or two of flat-leaved parsley to my winter salad. Whatever the weather, even in snow, you'll still be able to pick parsley. I also class coriander as grassy, with an overlay of aniseed. Certainly, if it has been grown in the glasshouse, we're picking coriander now too.

Grouping the flavors in this way helps you to plan what you want to grow and then mix your leaves in the right proportions to get a good balance. Bear in mind that, as the seasons change, you may want to adjust that balance. For example, as winter moves into

Spinach "Rubino" hardly falters in frosty conditions.

spring, I crave hotter, stronger salads that feel cleansing. By summer, I go for the fresher, lighter flavors of aniseed and lemon.

You'll also need to bear in mind the food these leaves will be accompanying. The robust flavors of cheese, red meat, or root vegetables (beetroot is the classic here) need equally mustardy, strong flavors to balance them, whereas with fish, chicken, or mild-tasting vegetables such as Florence fennel or cooked celery and peas, bright, perky salads with an aniseed or lemon zing are ideal.

When I pick, I also think of the look of the salad in the bowl. With leaves in greens, pinks, crimsons, and whites all there for the harvest, you can make sumptuous color combinations, even without edible flowers (which we almost always do add).

Whatever I've picked for our salad, I serve it with just a fruity, cold-pressed, extra-virgin olive oil, plenty of flaky salt, and a squeeze of lemon or splash of tarragon or red wine vinegar. That's how winter salads taste best in my view: clear, crisp, and clean.

It's not just the taste, but also the goodness that makes growing salad worthwhile, and we all tend to need a bit of this after Christmas and New Year. Eating raw leaves gives us plenty of vitamins and minerals, particularly the B vitamins, including folate (B9), as well as a boost of vitamin C. The stronger-tasting winter leaves, such as arugula, watercress, the mustards, and mizunas, are all super nutritious. As brassicas, they contain plant compounds called glucosinolates, the antioxidant phytochemicals that make broccoli so good for us. Glucosinolates appear to reset cells to self-cleanse, thus helping to protect us from an array of diseases.

Health aside, even in winter, good salad is exceptionally easy to grow. Christopher Lloyd was the first person who inspired me on the salad front. He was an acquaintance of my father's. After a summer internship working in the garden at Great Dixter, he became a friend of mine too. I remember having dinner with him in February, 20 years or so ago. Christo justifiably boasted about the sixteen different leaf varieties he'd picked for that evening's salad, presented as a course in itself in a huge, shallow wooden bowl.

Thanks to him, I started experimenting with anything salady that was said to be winter-hardy. This resulted in our first edible trial, with twenty cut-and-come-again salads, herbs, and leafy greens put on aesthetic and taste parade.

Harvesting Salad

I've found there are lots of things that crop well in East Sussex in January and February. Success will depend on where you live and how cold it gets in the winter, but if you can offer some protection, it's so worth having a try. Here, sown in September, we can pick repeatedly from the same root systems, with each plant cropping much longer at this dark time of year than the same varieties sown in spring, which gives us plenty to eat for months. With chard and mizuna, we often harvest from 6 to 8 weeks after sowing, and keep picking regularly until April, or even longer in the case of chard.

There is a fashion now for eating microgreens, the just-germinated seed leaves of lots of salad varieties and herbs. This makes good sense if you only have indoor window ledges on which to grow your edibles, as microgreens are best grown inside. They do taste fantastic and look great on the plate, but I find using a generous quantity of seeds for only one or two cuts a bit wasteful. Instead, I tend to start harvesting when most plants have more like ten leaves, not one or two.

Bunched salad leaves and flowers.

Thinning out and kerching

To harvest young salad plants and any cut-and-come-again salad, I advise you cut or, even better, pick just the outer leaves stem by stem. Be careful to leave the heart of the salad intact to allow the plant to fill out slowly again. This technique is called picking round.

We do this with all the leafy plants through autumn, winter, and early spring. If we picked salad (and soft green herbs or chard) by cutting the leaves in one go, almost down to ground level, we would be forcing most of the plants (even hardy varieties) would struggle, if not die. The cold and damp in these cooler months to rot the base of each plant.

In late spring and summer, when growth rates increase, we stick to picking round most of the time. Every so often, when the plant threatens to run up to flower, we cut the heart as well, which is what I call "kerching". I use scissors or a kitchen knife and slice at least a good 5 cm (2 in.) from the ground, so the root will hopefully regrow. It doesn't always work, but it can stop bolting. In a hot, dry spell, many of the salads remain set on running up to flower whatever we do, but it's worth a try.

These two techniques for picking most obviously apply to plants with a distinct heart such as lettuce, including the loose-leaf kind. It's also true of the slow growers, such as mizuna and mustard "Red Frills." For illustrations that show the techniques, see p. 63.

Binding and preparing salad leaves

In hot weather (even on a sunny February day if picking in a greenhouse), pick little salad leaves straight into a plastic bag; otherwise, they can wilt in 10 minutes.

As I pick my salad ingredients, if I'm harvesting quite a few to keep us in salad for several days, I bind them variety by variety into bunches with elastic bands. When back in the kitchen, I place everything into a sink full of cold water for a couple of hours to wash and condition the leaves. I repeat this once or twice to ensure that no earth or animal surprises appear in the bowl. Then, I compile my salad, pulling out the leaves I want from their bunches and drying them gently with a tea towel or salad dryer. (Wet leaves don't hold dressing.) Finally, I dress and toss them and add a smattering of edible flowers and perhaps some toasted seeds. The rest, rubber bands still in place, go into a plastic bag or box in the bottom of the fridge for another day.

Best of the lettuces and salad

Most of the varieties included here are exceptionally hardy and are cut-and-come-again, so are suitable for harvesting leaf by leaf all the way through winter. Many are also good beyond winter, coming into their own in spring. Some, such as wild arugula and rainbow chard, are even available to harvest throughout the year.

Lettuce *Lactuca sativa*
I start off almost any bowl of salad with a base of lettuce, and I can vouch for the first five here as winter-hardy. They've all survived outside sitting under a couple of inches of snow. They were knocked back but didn't die. Within 3 weeks of the thaw, we were picking from them again.

1 "Black Seeded Simpson"
This is my favorite large, crunchy, and tasty hearting lettuce. It has done very well in our trials over the years. You can grow this and harvest it as a baby leaf, which is the best option for October to April. In the summer, leave it to develop to its full size and make huge hearts. When it resembles that classic old variety "Webbs Wonderful," you can pick it all in one go. This is one of our year-round stalwarts.

2 "Cancan"
One of the hardiest lettuces, this has a robust, endive-like texture and shape, and looks pretty growing in the winter garden. It is lovely picked leaf by leaf for winter salad bowls.

3 "Cerbiatta"
This is a new variety that has superseded other green oak-leaf lettuces, with good winter hardiness and an excellent, long, light cropping pattern. The stems have a nice crunchy texture and sweet taste. It's good all year, slow to bolt, and even after pruning (see p. 39), will regrow. So don't pull out this one by the roots.

4 "Merveille des Quatre Saisons"
This is an old French variety in the so-called "round" or "butterhead" group, with a soft texture and open structure and crumpled, bronze outer leaves around a loose heart. The color is more intensely crimson-bronze in the cold months. It lives up to its name. We repeat sow this in early spring and autumn to cover pretty much all seasons. We also love the bright green "All The Year Round," which is similar. Both are stalwarts.

5 "Red Salad Bowl"
We used to grow the upright and excellent "Solix" but this is now unavailable. Instead we grow the easy and reliable "Red Salad Bowl" (or the very similar red oak leaf) pretty much all year. It has crimson-bronze leaves, which become richer in the cold; a loose-leaf lettuce structure; and tall, upright crunchy stems. It's bolt-resistant with good flavor. It's useful for bulk leaves and a real trooper, whatever the season. "Salad Bowl" is equally good.

6 "Reine des Glaces"
We grow this mainly for spring and summer for its crisp texture, but I recommend it in winter too—particularly if you have space under glass. It may not grow hearts as quickly as it does in summer, but even the outer leaves have a bit of "Iceberg" crunch, which can be lacking in continental loose-leaf varieties. This variety is a bit more slug-prone than others.

Salad leaves

Each one on this list is a joy to grow and eat. These leaves are where most of the flavor in our salads come from.

1 Chard *Beta vulgaris* subsp. *cicla* var. *flavescens*
Brilliant stem and leaf color are the main reasons to include baby leaf chard in your winter salads. It won't produce huge amounts unless grown under cover, but it is worth having and truly gets into its stride in spring. At this time of year, we grow Swiss chard and rainbow chard (see p. 146), "Rhubarb Chard" is pictured.

2 Chicory *Cichorium intybus*
This is bitter when raw—less so if blanched in situ with a plate over its crown. The odd leaf mixed in a bowl is a good sharpener. If you're short on space and want high production, grow leaf chicories rather than hearting types, which must be sown in June/July for harvesting now. Leaf chicory "Variegata di Castelfranco" (pictured) has crimson-splotched leaves and comes into its own in spring; we pick it lightly for months.

3 Corn salad *Valerianella locusta*
With a gentle, fragrant taste, corn salad (or lamb's lettuce as it's known) is an integral part of many a French salad. (It's particularly good with hazelnuts.) It has a nut-crossed-with-violet flavor. We find it slow to produce outside; however grown under glass, it's worthwhile for a February to April harvest. Then, it usually bolts. We also find it tends to succumb to botrytis.

4 Cress
American cress (*Barbarea verna*), also known as land cress, is a winter favorite, thriving even after a hard frost (pictured). It's like watercress in taste, but even stronger. Crop regularly to perpetuate the formation of new leaves. If left unpicked for a couple of weeks, it becomes too hot for salads. Slice the top off your plants and make soup. The cress will grow back for a more mild harvest.

Garden cress (*Lepidium sativum*) is a different kettle of fish, with a much more delicate flavor. Varieties "Bubbles" or "Greek" are prettier versions of what you get in an egg and cress sandwich. Sow it densely, pick it once, and if you're lucky twice, sow it again.

Watercress (*Nasturtium officinale*) is perennial. It crops when there's less around in early spring and autumn. You don't need running water—any vegetable bed will do—but you need to water copiously through the growing season. Growing it on the side of a polytunnel so it's watered with runoff is nifty.

5 Kale *Brassica rapa* (Perviridis Group)

We grow most kales to full size and crop right through the winter. But we also grow some to pick as baby leaf for salad. They add a mild cabbagey taste (in a good way) and fantastic color and substance to mixed salad bowls. I go for "Emerald Ice," which has grey-green leaves and ivory hearts, and "White Peacock", for colored leaves in pink, purple, and white.

6 Komatsuna *Brassica rapa* (Perviridis Group)

One of my favorite winter salad leaves, it has lush, juicy, water-filled leaves and a gentle brassica taste. We use it as our midwinter spinach replacement. It's easier to grow than baby leaf spinach but is similar in texture and taste. It is delicious raw in a salad, wilted as a Chinese-style green, and excellent in a stir-fry. The plants are hardy enough to grow, particularly under glass, through winter. Also good under glass in winter, though better to grow and slow to bolt in spring and summer, is the delicious bok choy. Try "Golden Yellow," plus the crimson and green forms (pictured).

7 Mizuna *Brassica rapa* var. *nipposinica var. laciniata*
This is a slightly spicy Japanese leaf that comes in green or crimson. I love both, and we often grow them alternating in a checkerboard pattern. The standard green mizuna has feathery leaves that look lovely in the bowl. "Red Knight" is the crimson, fuller-leaved form.

8 Mustard *Brassica juncea*
It's the mustards that tend to garner the most interest when I do tastings. The leaves look good, have a varying intensity of flavor and are oddly little-known and grown. For winter in particular, I couldn't recommend them more strongly. New varieties come on the market regularly, but there are a few stalwarts.

"Red Frills," (pictured), for example, is the mildest, with the distinctive taste of new potatoes. "Golden Streaks" is the next one up in strength. This is a brilliant green with a highly cut, almost serrated leaf edge. "Red Giant" is hot and delicious. It can get up to horseradish strength when fully grown, so it is best picked little and often if you want to avoid it taking your head off. It's definitely best used as a scattering among other things. It's also a strong grower, whatever the weather, so grow it in a container or in the ground on its own rather than in a mix. Once the leaves become large, use them for a stir-fry or soup. And finally, "Wasabina" is another powerful one that crops longer than the rest. It seems to be the slowest to bolt once the late spring heat arrives.

9 Arugula
Traditionally, this is one of the most widely foraged winter plants throughout Turkey, Greece, and Italy. It has different names according to where you are: ruchetta or rucola in northern Italy, roquette in France, rocket in Britain, and arugula in the United States. One tends to think that because wild and salad arugula taste the same, they are the same but, in fact, they're not closely related. They're both brassicas but wild arugula (*Diplotaxis tenuifolia*) is a hardy perennial that originates from the Mediterranean and Asia, whereas salad arugula (*Eruca vesicaria* subsp. *sativa*) is a hardy annual.

For salad arugula, "Serrata" (pictured) and "Dentellata" are my current varieties of choice for winter. They have quite generous, fleshy leaves and strong but not head-removing pepperiness. New ones come on the market all the time. Both have good cold-weather resistance. We sow and grow them from September to April.

Wild arugula has narrower, bonier leaves. We grow this in the winter, but turn to it in summer when, as a heat-tolerant perennial, it is slow to run up to flower. This forms almost perennial clumps in our garden. It grows back again and again if we continue picking. It is our arugula stalwart from April to October. If it runs up to flower, try cutting it back hard. It should regrow.

10 Spinach *Spinacia oleracea*
The hardiest of all soft-leaved spinach varieties that we've trialled is "Rubino" (pictured), which survives outside even in a frost. For more on spinach, see p. 148.

11 Winter purslane
Claytonia perfoliata
This is a wild annual that is often seen growing in churchyards. It is originally from North America, where it's called miner's lettuce (miners ate it during the California Gold Rush to prevent scurvy). It has water-filled mini-waterlily pads topping each thin stem. It's very hardy and used well in winter in Turkey and Greece to replace cucumber in tzatziki. The leaves are good in a mixed-leaf salad, but a bit slimy in texture on their own. The edible flowers are also pretty for late-winter and early-spring salads.

Summer purslane (*Portulaca oleracea* subsp. *sativa*) is very similar, but half-hardy. It is best sown under cover in March, or outside in April.

Salad herbs and extras
These all work great scattered over a salad. For more on herbs, see p. 74.

1 Florence fennel *Foeniculum vulgare* var. *azoricum*
Florence fennel, also known as bulb fennel, shouldn't be confused with the leafy fennel (see p. 83). It is best sown early in the year: March or even February if you have space under cover, or any time from June, so that bulbing starts as the weather cools. If sown in April or May, it will bolt rather than bulb. If you have frost-free under-cover growing space, you can also sow this in August/September for a winter harvest. A sunny day can still make it bolt.

2 Pea tips *Pisum sativum*
There are certain pea varieties bred to form more axillary buds (such as "Serge") that are often used commercially. We find any of the sugar snap or snow peas varieties are quick growing and ideal for pea tips. Also, a box of cheap marrowfat peas, which are popular in the UK, gives you as good a crop of pea tips as any. We sow these into crates or guttering (see p. 305) and harvest straight from there. They don't go out in the garden. Sow and grow closely for cropping once or twice, then add to the compost heap.

3 Radish *Raphanus sativus*
These are a quick crop, taking just 4 to 6 weeks from sowing to harvest (as roots). We pick the odd leaf after 2 to 3 weeks for salad. Sliced radishes are a great addition to a sandwich, and I love them as a crudités dipped into something like anchovy mayonnaise. My

favorite is the deep pink globe variety "Caro" (pictured).

4 Wood sorrel *Oxalis*
There are a few good ornamental, container-suitable wood sorrels that have become available recently, such as so-called shamrock (*Oxalis tetraphylla* "Iron Cross"), which comes from Mexico. These have the incredible, zesty taste of all sorrels. They thrive in dappled shade and tend to emerge in autumn/winter and crop until it gets hot and dry. Then, it tends to die back for a dormant period.

Edible flowers
In winter, it's violas and polyanthus we use in abundance, with the edible flowers we harvest changing from one season to the next. For more on edible flowers. see p. 188.

January & February

There are things to do inside—or at least under cover in the shed or greenhouse—when the weather is dire. If you get the odd bright day, you can do a few tasks outside too.

January is a month for plotting and planning, but once you get past the first week or two of February, there are also some specific things to sow. It's particularly the slow-growing plants such as tomatoes that benefit from being started off before the end of winter. We also do the first substantial sowing of hardy annuals, including salads, herbs, edible flowers, and spinach, which are so important for harvests later in spring. The previous generation of these crops, sown in

September (see p. 304), are cropping hard now, but they tend to bolt if you get the odd patch of warm weather, so it's good to have a new posse of plants ready to take over.

Super-hardy crops such as fava beans and spring onions need to be started off now if you haven't planted them already. And early potatoes need to be sprouted. Setting this up takes minutes and helps to maximize your harvest.

You may think January and February are months for armchair gardening, but don't succumb entirely! Get out there, and do at least a bit of growing and harvesting.

Planning and Preparation

In January, collect all the printed and online catalogs you can get your hands on and make sure you've got your orders in for seeds and tubers of all your stalwarts and favorites, as well as a handful of new things to try.

Plot design

Once you've got your growing list, you should create a seasonal plan. Make a bold, black-line drawing of your plot on white paper, which you can clearly see through tracing paper. (Baking parchment works fine.) In pencil, draw on to that what you think will work together, bed by bed, season by season. I use cut-outs from catalogs to make sure things look colorful as well as providing abundance. This is also a good moment to plan the sites and distribution of your frames and structures for maximum upper-storey drama. Extrapolate your sowing and planting plan for the year from the plan.

Source pea sticks and hazel poles

Source and order silver birch pea sticks and hazel poles to support your edible climbers. I think they look nicer and are better than imported bamboo canes. Harvested now, when they're not in leaf and the sap is rising, the smaller branches of these trees are pliable and easy to weave into shapes and teepees. You want them pre-leaf because otherwise all the new foliage curls up and browns and makes the frames look a mess. The stakes will grow again

after being cut. For making structures, see p. 128 and p. 208.

Have a clean up

Clean the greenhouse and get everything ready for sowing. Insulate it if you need to (see p. 363). I'm naturally untidy person, but having a declutter and sort out at the beginning of the year makes sowing so much nicer.

Mice and voles

Now is a good time to make sure your greenhouse or potting shed is free of mice and voles. Mice love all sorts of things, not just peas and fava beans. We have a stray cat who has made her home in our polytunnel (we call her Polly-cat), and we've encouraged her to stay.

You can soak seeds in liquid seaweed fertilizer overnight to make them unpalatable, or soak a rag in paraffin and crumple the seeds around in that before you sow. It's better to set a mousetrap or a live trap baited with peanut butter, which is a mouse (and rat) favorite.

Making a Propagator

Consider investing in a propagator or better still make your own with a horticultural electric blanket. This can be laid on top of any greenhouse table with a layer of capillary matting over the blanket. The matting cuts down the watering requirement, slowly releasing water to the roots as it's needed, and the basal heat improves growth rates. We germinate almost everything for the vegetable garden on heated benches in the polytunnel. Our propagator is homemade. You can create something similar with these layers.

1   Use a sheet of black plastic or an empty compost bag that has been split open for the germination stage. The plastic keeps moisture and warmth in and light out, which creates ideal germinating conditions for most seeds. A few seeds need light to germinate (the packet will tell you), so don't add this layer if you're sowing those.
2   Seed trays or equivalent
3   Capillary matting or Hortiwool (a new sustainable product); both hold water well, which means less watering
4   Horticultural electric blanket (to provide basal heat)
5   Polystyrene insulation tile
6   Wooden bench

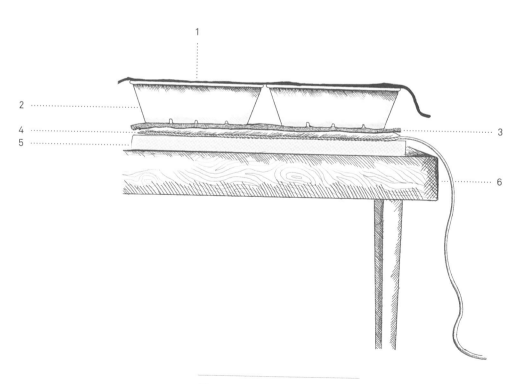

Sowing Essentials

March is our main sowing month, but January and February are an excellent time to ensure you have all the essentials you need before you get going in a few weeks.

Sowing media

For all our sowing, we use a peat-free, sustainably produced potting compost and place pretty much everything on our heated propagator mat. Warm up your compost or keep your bags of compost inside to help speed up germination. We put ours on the heated bench. At this time of year, we also water the compost in the trays from watering cans that have been sat on the hot bench.

Labels

The other thing I never fail to do is label everything as it's so easy to forget what's what. Make sure you have plenty of labels on hand and, when it comes to it, always start writing at the blunt end of your label, otherwise you'll be constantly taking the labels out of the pots to read them.

Storing seeds

Have a place to store seeds. For any leftover seeds, secure the seed packet and place in an airtight box—ideally with a silicone sachet, which helps to keep the seeds dry. Store somewhere cool until next year. We have a special slot in a fridge.) This process ensures that even pea and bean seeds remain weevil-free and you get decent germination (for most things) for several years to come.

Sowing systems

Different plants suit different sowing systems. As a rule, we go with the following:

- For expensive seeds, such as tomatoes, we sow into half-sized seed trays (see p. 54) or trays divided into smaller sections by a green cane.
- For medium-sized seeds, such as coriander and brassicas (which don't like their roots to be disturbed), we sow into modules or Jiffy-7 coir pellets (see p. 60).
- For large seeds, such as peas, mustards, parsley, beetroot, spinach, and chard, we sow into lengths of guttering. It's the quickest and simplest system for these easy-to-handle seeds (see p. 57).
- For large seeds, such as zucchini and cucumbers, sow into individual pots with one or two seeds in each. Some cucumbers are expensive, so plant one to a pot to avoid any waste (see p. 89).
- For beans of all types, we sow into root trainers. As legumes, these suit a long, deep root run (see p. 58).

In the Greenhouse

Sowing in Seed Trays

Around the middle of February, we start sowing a few things in seed trays. We start with peppers and eggplant and move on to tomatoes (which could be safely done in March too). If you don't have a greenhouse or polytunnel, you should delay sowing.

Peppers Both chilies and sweet peppers are best sown into half-sized seed trays and should germinate within 10 to 14 days, but they can take longer. Don't lose heart. You only want a few seedlings of each. We've found that the smaller tray size stops us getting too carried away. Peppers like a lot of moisture, so keep the compost well watered, but never dripping wet.

Eggplants These are also slow-growing. Germination can take anything up to 3 weeks. We want half of the seedlings to be ready for planting in the glasshouse in May, so now is the time to sow. The rest we want ready for early June for planting in the garden. In their native habitat, they're short-lived perennials, which explains why they're on a slightly slower time frame than other vegetable seed we grow.

Tomatoes These are slow to grow and benefit from being sown early in the year. They take 7 to 10 days to germinate (if sown into warm compost) and then another 4 weeks or so before they're ready to be separated. Then they need 4 weeks growing into their pots before being planted where they are to fruit. So if you want tomatoes as early as possible and you have a greenhouse to grow them in, mid- to late February is ideal.

Edible flowers For spring harvesting, sow violas now. Most varieties will flower in 8 to 10 weeks. Varieties include "Green Goddess" and "Sorbet Phantom." Also sow marigolds, cornflowers, and *Salvia viridis* "Blue."

How to sow in seed trays

We only do a little traditional sowing into rectangular seed trays these days. With all that separating seedlings and potting, it is too time-consuming and fussy, so we only use this method for a few specific things, including very tiny (and therefore difficult-to-sow) seeds and expensive seeds. This system is good when we want to keep trace of almost every seed and seedling and only want a handful of plants of one variety.

- Fill the tray with soil-based, peat-free compost, breaking up any lumps as you go. Tap and firm.
- Water the trays before, not after sowing. This avoids displacing the tiny seeds to the edges. Or you can place the tray in a watertight container to soak from the base.
- For valuable seeds (like tomatoes), you can divide a seed tray into sections with green canes. We sow five or six seeds of at least five or six varieties. Ideally, we want a range of flavors. If you have limited space, sow at least two or three varieties.

- Sow a small pinch, not a palmful. Treat the seed (however small) like gold dust. Sowing as thinly as possible is the route to success. Save the leftover seed for next year (see storing seed on p. 52 and p. 88).
- Aim to sow individually placed seed in neat, well-spaced rows so they can germinate and grow for a few weeks without competition from neighbors before being separated.
- Place the number of seeds you want on the surface of the compost and, only when complete, press the seeds in a little with your finger to cover. This method allows you to see where you are and keeps you from oversowing if you get distracted.
- Cover with a dusting of sieved compost and label. Peat-free compost tends to have twigs and bits in it, so it's good to sieve these out.
- As jungle climbers, tomatoes and warm-climate natives like chilies, sweet peppers, and eggplant all need a bit of basal heat to give them a kick start, and then the seed will germinate quickly. Use a propagator or heated bench if you have one. Tomatoes and eggplant like temperatures of 18 to 24°C (64 to 75°F).

Sowing in Guttering

These hardy annuals will all germinate quickly and consistently. Keep them cozy, somewhere light and warm. Transplant outside while it's still quite cool, once the growing season really gets going. Most of the annual herbs and many of the salads crop well for 2 to 3 months, but they then need replacing. From mid-February, serial sowing every 8 weeks into guttering is a perfect, time-efficient way to grow salads and herbs for picking all year.

Salads Leaves including mizuna, arugula, and mustards can be sown now, together with lettuce—particularly the smaller and fussy seeds.

Herbs Sow some hardy cut-and-come-again herbs including chervil, coriander, and parsley. Parsley seeds germinate quicker if they're soaked overnight in water (pictured opposite, top left).

Spinach and chard With quite large seed, spinach is ideal for gutter sowing, as it allows for good spacing of the seed. Try varieties "Medania" and "Rubino."

Pea tips I recommend successional sowing of pea tips. Try to sow some in a gutter or crate every 4 to 6 weeks (see p. 305). We use cheap marrowfat peas for this. Sow evenly spaced down the whole gutter or use the "station sowing" method (see p. 91).

Radishes Aim to sow at least once a month into guttering for the first few months of the year.

How to sow in guttering
This sowing system particularly suits medium to large seeds. I'm a huge fan of sowing into half-moon gutter pipes. We use gutters that are 112mm (4 $\frac{1}{2}$ in) wide and usually sold in 2m, 3m, or 4m (6 $\frac{1}{2}$ to 13 ft) lengths. Black is best for warmth from solar gain. It's time-saving, yields great germination, and minimizes root disturbance. In trials, we have repeatedly gotten more than double the germination rate when compared with sowing direct into the garden, yet it takes hardly any more time. And our seedlings can be planted at a decent size when they are better able to resist slugs. I heartily recommend this method, unless you have perfect, alluvial, rich, but well-drained soil (and few slugs).

- Don't bother to drill holes in the bottom of the gutters. Simply leave the ends unblocked, so the water can drain away.
- Fill the gutter with peat-free potting compost.
- Water the compost from the top.
- Place the seeds about 3 to 4 cm (1 $\frac{1}{2}$ in) apart on the top of the compost. Don't push them in until you've laid all your seed—that way you won't forget where you've placed them.
- Push each seed in lightly with your finger, so it's just under the compost surface. Cover with a thin layer of sieved compost and label.
- Water every few days when the compost starts to dry on the surface. The one downside to

gutter sowing is you need to be careful with watering. Compost dries out quickly in the sun, but it is not usually an issue until April or May, and hardy annuals will be planted by then.

- For rapid germination, put them somewhere warm if you can. Once the seeds start to sprout, move to a cool spot with excellent all-round light to help promote root growth.
- Once the seedlings are 3 to 4cm (1 $\frac{1}{2}$ in) tall plant them out. This should be at the end of March or early April (see p. 120).

Sowing in Root Trainers

Root trainers are made from quite robust plastic, which will last a few years. To be more sustainable, you can get some of the same effect using toilet paper tubes.

Fava beans Fava beans are cold-weather plants. They perform best if they get their deep roots established when the weather is cold and damp, which will cut down the likelihood of pests and diseases when they crop in early summer. I love fava beans and aim to sow them three times in the year (as described below). We are currently trialling varieties to sow in June for an autumn harvest.

1   January/February for planting in early March in a mild spell.
2   October for planting in November and overwintering outside. If the winter is severe,

this lot may not survive. If they do, it means beans in May. Use a polytunnel if you have one.
3   December for planting in January/February, in case the second lot doesn't make it.

Sow and put in a cold greenhouse or cold frame. Don't overprotect them, which is the most common mistake. No heat is key. Heat can inhibit germination. With it, you're likely to get more seed rot. So put the root-trainer trays somewhere cold. Fava bean seeds are frost tolerant and will germinate even at 2°C or 3°C (36°F). A bit of frost seems to do them good, but severe winds will do damage—particularly when it's frosty.

Sweet peas I love growing sweet peas with edible peas. They look good together, and sweet peas are great pollinator attractors. In theory, they can increase the harvest.

How to sow in root trainers
Root trainers give a deep, narrow root run, which is just what all legumes, including all beans (and sweet peas) thrive on.

When they first germinate, they put down one long root. This breaks off when it hits the air at the bottom of the pot, and like snapping off the tip, the root then throws out lots of side roots farther up. When these side roots reach the side walls of the root trainer, they slot into a groovelike channel and are directed straight to the bottom of the pot. They then break off and produce side roots, so you get a virtuous cycle of root development, with a root system forming quickly. The initial root will be shorter and will branch out less if you sow it into a short pot. Essentially, a longer root means more root branches, which means a bigger plant, faster.

- Sow one seed to each root trainer cell (there are 32 cells to a set). Use a loamless compost with an open structure (such as a peat-free potting compost). The plant roots need air, as well as moisture and nutrients.
- Dampen the surface.
- For fava beans, push each large seed in with your finger to about 2 ½ cm (1 in) below the surface of the compost. Ensure it's on its edge, not lying flat. Water again. Label.
- Both sweet peas and fava beans seem to be equivalent to mouse, squirrel, and rat caviar. If you have the root trainers in a cold greenhouse, put them on a sheet of wood or ply (not hardboard), resting on upturned large pots. Make sure that there's a good overhang from the side of the bench so that the mice can't climb up.
- Check for germination every few days.
- Don't water again until you see seedlings start to come through (usually 10 to 14 days).
- Once the seedlings appear, keep them cool at about 5°C (41°F). This promotes root growth, rather than stem growth, which is exactly what you want.
- Every week, check your plants. Water them lightly if they are dry.
- In a mild spell in March, plant them (see p. 121).

Sowing in Modules

There isn't much to sow in modules yet, though if you're sowing very few tomatoes, or just want two or three chili or eggplant, you will want to use this system instead of the seed tray.

Spring onions We do our first sowing of spring onion seeds now—a tiny pinch of seed in each module. These are hardy annuals, so plant in April (about 5 to 6 weeks from sowing). They will be ready to harvest in 10 weeks from sowing if

sown now. This reduces to 8 weeks if you wait to sow in April.

Coriander Sow now and in August/September.

Edible flowers We sow borage—one seed to a module. Borage is a bit of a thug, but we love it. You only want a few plants of both the blue and white. It is a prolific self-sower. You will find it pops up anywhere you've had it before once the soil starts to warm. Sown toward the end of February, it's ready for planting a few weeks later and will be in flower for the end of April or early May.

How to sow in modules

This sowing system suits seeds that are happy to grow in a little clump together, with seedlings able to push each other apart but not outcompete each other. This system is also good when you have large seeds and don't want more than a few seedlings. In this case, sow one seed to a module.

- Fill the tray with peat-free compost, breaking up any lumps as you go.
- Water the trays before—not after—sowing.
- If using Jiffy-7s, you will need to rehydrate in a watertight barrel or plastic crate for a few minutes before you sow.
- Plant one set, clove, or seed per cell (or in the case of Jiffy-7s, into the dimple that's on top of each one). If sowing spring onion or onion seed, sow a tiny pinch (3 to 4 seeds) per cell.
- Label.

- For hardy annuals, place them in a cool, light, frost-free place. They do not need heat.
- Check twice a week to see whether they need water. Keep their compost well watered, but never dripping wet.
- Allow them to germinate. It can be tricky with small seed to sow every cell with just one seed. If two or more germinate, remove the weakest-looking one after the first has been showing for about a week. Just pull it/them out and throw away. This avoids the need to separate seedlings.
- Once roots appear at the base of the tray, if hardy, they are ready to be planted (see p. 121). If half-hardy, pot them.
- Whether planting or potting, make sure you remove the Jiffy-7 net from each pellet to allow the plant's roots to run free. It's important you do this, as leaving the net on really holds the plant back.

....

Sprouting Potatoes

Sprouting means laying the seed potatoes out, eyes upright, in a light, cool but frost-free place at about 10°C (50°F) to bring them into growth early.

There is great debate about the necessity of sprouting potatoes. In our comparison tests at Perch Hill, sprouting does seem to ensure a quicker and slightly larger harvest. With early varieties, such as the first early "Foremost," it gets them off to a flying start. We can begin the harvest by the end of June (or early June if forced inside).

We also sprout blight-prone main-crop potatoes such as "Pink Fir Apple." Sprouting makes them grow faster and form larger potato tubers once planted. We can get a crop of potatoes in August or early September, before the worst of the blight takes hold.

- If we only have a few tubers to sprout, we line up our seed potatoes in egg cartons. If we're doing a lot, we put the seed potatoes in shallow, open boxes, like the slatted-bottomed ones you get at the produce store. We divide the boxes up with sections of folded newspaper to keep the tubers upright and slot them in.
- The potatoes need to go somewhere light but cool. Light is important, so don't shove them at the back of a shed. A garage or porch, slightly warmed by the house, is ideal.
- Keep an eye on the potatoes while they sprout and wait for strong, short shoots to appear in 4 to 6 weeks. These should be about 2 to 3 cm (1 in) long from the eyes of each tuber. You don't want the white, spaghettilike things you get when potatoes are kept in the dark, but stout green and pink shoots.
- If you want to maximize the size of your potatoes, rub off all but three or four of the shoots at the top end of the tuber before planting. If you leave all the shoots intact, you'll end up with lots of small potatoes. It's up to you. To save money, you can leave all the sprouts on and cut a potato tuber in half as you plant, but you may find a few rot off.

In the Garden

Forcing Rhubarb Outside

Now is a good time of year to force rhubarb. We don't always do this at Perch Hill, because forcing the same crown repeatedly eventually tires it out. If we need lots of early rhubarb for an event, we will force them. If you want low-maintenance rhubarb, you don't need to force them. Simply wait until they naturally start to shoot. Go for early varieties like "Timperley Early." If you do like having a go, you should force rhubarb the traditional way, which is under a terra-cotta forcer or, more prosaically, an upturned chimney pot or trash can packed with straw for insulation. You can also force it inside (see p. 362).

- Ideally, you would begin this process the previous autumn, selecting a healthy, 2- to 3-year-old plant. Allow the crown to die back and clear away any debris once the leaves are brown and withered.
- In January, if there's been little rain, water your selected crown(s) well.
- Cover the crown with straw and put a tall rhubarb-forcing pot over it.
- Then wrap with recycled bubble wrap or clad the outside of the pot with burlap stuffed with straw. If you have access to fresh farmyard manure (which gives off heat as it rots), surround the pot with this too.
- In 5 weeks, take a look. Traditional rhubarb forcers have removable lids for exactly this reason. Even packed around with manure, you can remove the lid, have a look, and pull some stems through the hole. The rhubarb may have started to grow, but usually takes 6 to 8 weeks.
- If you know there's going to be a hard frost, pick all your forced rhubarb whatever its size. Frost splits the stems and makes them translucent and not good to eat.
- Inspect once a week and keep an eye out for rot, which can be encouraged by the lack of air circulation. Also keep an eye out for slugs.
- When ready, pick all the stems off every week until your unforced plants begin to take over in late spring. Remove the forcer and the straw and give the plant a good mulch of compost. Do not take more from this plant for the rest of the year, and do not force it 2 years in a row.

Picking Lettuce

Picking the outer leaves of young salad plants and the cut-and-come-again lettuces will promote the heart to go on creating new ones, often into spring. This technique is called "picking round" (see p. 39, and the illustration opposite, top). It's ideal for leafy edibles with a distinct heart, but it also works for salads such as mizuna. If you sowed lettuces and salads in September, you can thin them out until the weather gets warmer. Once your plants are at risk of bolting, cut them off about 5 cm (2 in) from the ground (see kerching, p. 39, and the illustration opposite, bottom). Only pull them up by their roots when bolted as some varieties (like "Cerbiatta") resprout well.

Supporting Garden Birds

Last, but most certainly not least, we make sure that we're feeding the birds in January and February. The more you feed your garden birds in these lean months, the more of them will survive to breed and eat the slugs and snails, as well as the aphids, which may otherwise motor through your precious seedlings in April and May and transfer potential diseases (such as mosaic virus and fungal tomato blight) later in the year.

We have some sturdy, shop-bought bird feeders, but we also make our own to hang from trees (see p. 368).

Nesting boxes

I want to attract as many wild garden birds into our patch as possible. I am a nature lover anyway, but have also noticed that since we started consciously helping our birds, the number of aphids, slugs, and snails has been hugely reduced. It's a win-win.

We are lucky to be surrounded by farmland and woodland with lovely old trees—particularly ancient oaks that provide natural nesting sites—so we have a large blue tit and great tit population. These, along with coal tits, marsh tits, and nuthatches, all visit our feeders. We try to encourage them to stay by providing extra nesting boxes in quiet, hidden areas of the garden. When we first arrived, we planted one quarter of a mile of hedges, all of which are used as roosting sites at other times of the year.

In the vegetable garden, we have a wooden nesting box on the back of the shed. It's best to site your boxes away from the prevailing wind, but as this west-facing wall has a hawthorn hedge beside it, it's nicely protected. The hole is 3 cm (1 in) which is ideal for great tits, blue tits, house sparrows, and even nuthatches. A metal plate helps to protect the entrance from predators.

We also have open nesting boxes spread at regular intervals throughout the rest of the garden. There's one in an evergreen climber on the wall of the Oast Garden. Robins and wrens are attracted to this type of planting. A robin's nest will be made by the female, using leaves, moss, and dried grass. A wren's nest will usually be made of leaves, moss, lichen, wool, hair and feathers, with the male making several nests and then the female taking her pick and further lining it with hair, and feathers. We hang out sheep's wool to help them with this.

When we break a teapot lid (which seems to happen quite a bit in our café), we use the teapot for the wrens. We hang them in the hedge so that the spout is low and will drain away any rain.

The quantity of nesting sites is key. You can never have too many nesting boxes. We aim to add a few more in sheltered, hidden places every January and February, and are always thinking where we might be able to add hedges in good time for nesting (see p. 97).

March

The smell of plants, seedlings, and their compost in the greenhouse or polytunnel at this time of year is one of the vegetable gardener's life enhancers. Open the door of the greenhouse or lift the lid of a cold frame on a bright and sunny day, and you're hit with that rich organic smell. At Perch Hill, it is soil mixed with something reminiscent of chocolate high in cocoa solids, plus a sharpness from scented-leaf pelargonium cuttings, which are growing en masse. That's our particular blend. I love it, and it's good for the soul.

There's a huge practical advantage in having even a minimal type of under-cover growing system, but I'd say it's worth it for this smell alone. There's a rarely used English word—petrichor—which describes the smell of rain falling on dry soil. But it's not just this earthy "perfume" that's so uplifting. It's the warmth and humidity that goes with it. This immediately reminds me of holidays. Working or simply being in a greenhouse or polytunnel at this time of year makes spring feel close. As well as being useful for growing, it's a mood lifter, which many of us—including me—can certainly use after a long winter.

It's easy to see why March is the great month of sowing. The new season's growth is truly on the move, and we want to make the most of that. Pick up any pot of overwintered cuttings you will find a miniature fuzz of white roots starting to poke out of the holes in the base, and where the old leaves branch from the main stem, axillary buds will be developing.

Tomato seedlings sown last month are getting into their stride and will soon need separating, while the fava bean seedlings are in need of action. Their roots are bursting out of root trainers and they should be planted as soon as possible. Then there are the hardy annual salads and herbs that were sown into gutters a few weeks ago. It's easy to think luscious, newly grown seedlings will be far too soft and sappy to survive cold nights outside, but these truly hardy annuals will be fine. We quite often get snow in March, and under a flurry (rather than standing snow), they survive.

It's time for sowing zucchini and cucumbers (for early crops in the greenhouse), leeks, peas, and beetroot, and you can get going with the winter brassicas too. We try to do some now and leave others to the slightly less jam-packed April.

Out in the garden, spring starts more slowly. The hearts of the cut-and-come-again salad crew that have provided us with all important ingredients through the winter are increasingly nudging up and out as the weeks go by, their rate of leaf production nearly doubling from the start to the end of the month. And these leaves are joined by an ever-increasing range of herbs and edible flowers as the weeks progress. Our salad bowls have lots of exciting new components.

Parsley has been a stalwart provider through the winter, but its growth and production rate climbs steeply as light levels increase

Previous page Hardy salad and herb seedlings sown in guttering in February are now ready to be planted in the garden.
Below Arugula, mustard, and oak-leaf lettuce are all ideal for a March harvest.
Opposite Edible flowers including fava bean "Crimson-flowered" and polyanthus.
Next page The petals of *Primula* "Stella Scarlet Pimpernel" match the stems of "Rhubarb Chard."

and the days get longer. Chervil and coriander, plus the early-emerging perennial herbs—sweet cicely, French sorrel, lovage, and chives—all join in, with mint lagging a bit behind. By the middle of the month, they're mostly pickable by the handful here in Sussex.

Sage falters in the winter and doesn't really start growing until April, but bay has new growth and rosemary is at its peak. Most varieties are covered from top to toe in blue flowers, buzzing with wild and honey bees as soon as the sun shines. For instant cheer, I love these aromatic flowers scattered over rice or roast potatoes, as well as the odd stem of winter-flowering pansies and primroses. They're all blooming away strongly now.

Purple sprouting broccoli, picked fresh and perky, is at its best in the next couple of months, as is the more tender "White Early," which is a rare find in a produce store but easy to grow. It gives invaluable harvests that start a couple of weeks earlier than the purple form. You need to have a large vegetable garden or allotment to justify growing these two. Like many of the brassicas, PSB and WSB (as they're known in the trade) take up a lot of space for many months. I'm so grateful to have them out there in March and April, when there tends to be rather little homegrown produce.

Our leeks, kalettes, and spigariello have been picked almost bare by now, just as the sprouting broccolis become available to harvest. They are so much more delicious when picked moments before they hit the pan, so they are truly best homegrown. And, within reason, the more you harvest, the more they will grow. Side shoot form if you take out the central nascent floret.

We are also just beginning to harvest our early rhubarb. We grow "Timperley Early" and "Red Champagne" for harvesting now. Some years, we cover our mid-season rhubarb "Stockbridge Arrow" with forcers, also for picking this month.

Between this posse of edible things, our plates and bowls are increasingly filling with delicious homegrown possibilities.

Herbs

Producing baskets of food from the garden is all very well if you have tons of space, but I know this is increasingly rare. Many people now live in towns or cities. That's made me really think about the best edible plants to grow to give the best value per centimeter from the garden, pot, or window box.

In this regard, I'd say herbs are the front runners for March. In a window box or a series of pots on a doorstep, you can produce delicious flavor-enhancers for countless meals and, unlike newly sown annual salads, neighborhood cats tend to leave these pungent leaves alone.

You don't need great volume with herbs. I always think if one family of homegrown ingredients can easily transform a rather bad cook or a standard meal into someone or something incredible, it has to be herbs. Fresh herbs are so much more effective than dried, and homegrown more than shop-bought. Growing slowly outside (rather than hydroponically, like many supermarket herbs) and picked from your own pots, the flavor is more intense. We've done taste comparisons between shop-bought and homegrown. With tarragon, coriander, and mint in particular, the difference is huge. If I think about cooking a roast chicken, a spring salad, or a bowl of pasta, I turn to herbs that I turn for an easy, reliable, dish-transforming ingredient that only needs inches of growing space.

Evergreens

Although evergreen, thyme is a no-no for harvesting early in spring. It sulks through the winter and needs to recover with a bit of sun and warmth. Sage has not yet picked up its growing pace either.

Of the reliable evergreens, rosemary is the top of my list. March is the moment for rosemary, which is flowering right now, and there's no better plant for spring pollinators. Rather than choosing the standard grey-blue-flowered rosemary, I go for a named variety with more interesting colored flowers and definite habits.

Bunched chives (both garlic and ordinary), mint, fennel, and lovage.

I'd also be lost without bay now, even though it can get huge. Given a regular trim so that is sort of bonsaied and kept compact in a pot (or as we have it, planted in a yard with its roots surrounded and restricted by hardcore), it makes a good evergreen tree for a small space. A few fresh leaves thrown in with a tin of tomatoes, some capers, and olives make for a simple pasta, or add it to the cooking water with chickpeas, cranberry beans and butter beans. For me, bay is a March essential. It perks up almost any flavor.

Perennials

On to the March herbaceous perennials. The good thing about most of the perennial herbs is that they thrive in the most terrible spots in the garden. Plant them in builder's rubble and you'll still get a harvest. French sorrel, my favorite of all salad herbs for its unique, sharp, lemony flavor, grows happily here in damp shade. It's already growing at full tilt now, and we can harvest handfuls a couple of times a week. It's only when you don't harvest sorrel that you get problems. In the same genus as wild dock, it similarly tries to flower and set seed.

Sweet cicely is unusually early among herbaceous perennials too, its leaves appearing here in midwinter. I first came across this while botanizing in Yorkshire, where it grows wild on the roadsides. With soft feathery leaves and white umbellifer flowers in spring, every part of this plant is good to use: the baby leaves in winter salads, the flowers for decorating spring desserts and the seedpods for a fresh, aniseedy tea.

Chives are fully up by the middle of the month here. We grow two varieties (see p. 82) and lots of them for their edible leaves and flowerheads, and because they're loved by pollinators who feast on the nectar-rich flowers. Plus, we use the leaves to make a natural fungicide (see p. 207).

The feathery plumes of fennel are core to the look of our garden in spring, quickly filling out to form puffy clouds between all our crocuses, narcissi, and tulips. We grow it as much for its looks as its taste. We have a little of the standard green fennel, and more of the bronze variety, which forms a beautiful carpet through lots of our borders in spring. One word of warning about leaf fennel: it's a prolific seed producer and can become a bit invasive. We cut back most of it to the ground before flowering to help contain it.

Then there's lovage. This fleshy-leaved umbellifer with a smoky, celery taste is one of my favorite herbs for early spring.

Clockwise from top left
Bunching curly-leaved parsley;
a jug of spring herbs (if kept cool,
they'll store well in water); crocus
and French artichoke seedlings
growing up through a carpet of
bronze fennel in my friend Arthur
Parkinson's garden; spring herbs
French sorrel and coriander.

Annuals

There is a good posse of soft-green annual herbs for March cropping. Parsley (strictly speaking, a biennial) is a winter stalwart, with the flat-leaved "Gigante di Napoli" just as hardy as the curly, English-leaved form. Both will have emerged through the winter unscathed from an autumn sowing and will be putting on tons of new growth as the weeks go by. A spring salsa verde, with this as its base, is one of my favorite March things to eat. Pair it with a roast chicken, almost any fish, or a pile of griddled purple sprouting broccoli.

Into this list can also go chervil (we grow the robust "Vertissimo") and one of my favorite all-time herbs: coriander. Now is just its moment. One tends to think that, because coriander is used in Asian food, it must love it hot and humid, but it bolts straight away in those conditions. It's much better sown in September or February for harvesting in the next couple of months. With more moisture and less light intensity, it forms great leafy plants from now until May.

Harvesting Herbs

If I'm picking more than just a sprig of any of the soft green herbs, I pick with elastic bands on my wrist as with salads (see p. 39). I leave the heart of the plant intact as I cut the herbs and bind them, a single species at a time.

Once inside, with the elastic bands left on, I refresh them in cold water, soaking them for half an hour or so, before drying gently in a lettuce dryer or clean tea towel.

I also often chop them with the elastic band left on the stem. If the herbs are bunched together, it makes the cutting task quick and easy. Herb scissors with multiple blades are handy for cutting, though I rather love using a mezzaluna.

Any herbs that I don't use I leave on the stem and put in a jug with a little water. In March, I leave them somewhere cool. In summer, they go into a jam jar chosen to fit in the door of the fridge. Stored cool and in water, they'll usually last 5 to 7 days.

With rosemary—particularly, at the start of the month while it is still growing slow—I avoid breaking off the side shoots down to their main branch. Instead, I aim to mimic a grazing animal and snip off single tips. That way, the plant will bush out again a little faster.

Best of the herbs

After salads, herbs are the largest group of plants we grow at Perch Hill. They are a must-have, no matter how small your productive garden. They both look good and add flavor to almost anything you cook.

Woody perennial herbs

These are the evergreens that have a woody structure above ground all year and keep at least some of their leaves. They thrive in well-drained soil in sunny, Mediterranean-like positions.

1 Bay *Laurus nobilis*
Crush a freshly picked leaf in your hand and you'll realize this is the herb often used to flavor salamis and preserved meats. In winter, I love using this with tomato instead of summer basil.

2 Myrtle *Myrtus communis*
An elegant, aromatic shrub, and unusual among herbs in that it likes moisture. In the Mediterranean, it is often a marker of riverbeds. It is semi-tender and so ideally needs the shelter of a south-facing wall. The leaves are delicious and used in much the same way as bay. We use the black berries like juniper and black peppercorns in preserves and marinades.

3 Oregano *Origanum vulgare*
This is not always hardy here in East Sussex, so we tend to sow seed or propagate it from cuttings for new plants every year. It's a classic herb to add to Mediterranean food and tomato sauces (either fresh or dry), or to scatter fresh over a Greek salad.

4 Rosemary *Salvia rosmarinus* (syn. *Rosmarinus officinalis*)
I love rosemary. We grow six different varieties at Perch Hill, starting with "Miss Jessopp's Upright" (pictured, C), which has tall, straight stems and is great as a hedge in a sunny area.
At the other extreme, we have several plants of rosemary Prostrata Group (*S. r.* Prostrata Group) around our Dutch Yard (pictured, D). It cascades, softening the straight edges of the red brick in that part of the garden. We also grow this in a decent-sized pot by the back door, from which it tumbles in relaxed and elegant green and blue folds. I can go out and harvest from this plant all year.

We grow four others that I'd recommend. Firstly, I love "Foxtail" (pictured, B), which has a perky silver underside to its rich dark green leaf and an upright habit that gives it great presence. We plant it with the similarly colored French artichokes in the central beds of our herb garden. They make a handsome pair.

We also have "Green Ginger" rosemary there, which doesn't look unusual, but

smells and tastes of ginger beer. It's great for drinks, desserts, and cakes. It will transform a gin-based cocktail when added to a simple syrup.

We've just started growing a soft-pink flowered form, "Rosea." It seems to be a little slower-growing than others and less hardy, but in a sheltered spot, it makes a pretty change.

Last, but absolutely not least, is "Tuscan Blue" (pictured, A).

This is my all-round favorite rosemary with its glamorous deep-blue flowers. We have three plants of this romping up through the base and back of an open-slatted wooden bench on the south side of our barn, with a lemon verbena plant at either end. Mixed up with self-sown bronze fennel, it's one of the best things in the garden in March. Surprisingly, like thyme, it doesn't seem to

mind being sat on. We pick it lightly so it doesn't drown the seat completely (it's a vigorous grower); otherwise, it's left to its own devices.

5 Sage *Salvia officinalis*
Delicious, handsome, and productive for months on end, sage is ideal for growing in a border or in a pot right by the back door. As an evergreen, it's particularly valuable for picking lightly right through winter and into spring. Loved by pollinators, its tubular purple flowers are wonderful for late spring and early summer, and great for scattering over savory dishes. As the flowers go over in midsummer, cut them back and they will flower again and crop hard right through the autumn for use in squash dishes.

6 Thyme *Thymus*
Thyme is one of the herbs that struggles most in heavy clay soil like ours, so we've trialled several thymes at Perch Hill over the years to see which grows well and will take pretty heavy harvesting. Our top three are: "Jekka," which leafs up and flowers early for spring picking; white-flowered creeping thyme (*T. serpyllum* var. *albus*), which thrives in a container (pictured); and common (or old English) thyme (*T. vulgaris*). If plants get a haircut after flowering, they quickly produce fresh leaves to harvest and flower again. These three give us a succession to pick all year, except in the depths of winter. We grow the first two from cuttings and the last from seed.

Perennial herbs

This group includes things you can plant one year and then harvest from for years to come. They are good for a low-intensity productive garden, and for people who have little time for sowing but like to pick a bit from their own back yard.

1 Chives *Allium schoenoprasum*
We grow two varieties: ordinary chives (pictured) with a round leaf cross-section, purple flowers from early May (which the honey and bumblebees love) and an oniony taste, and also garlic chives (*A. tuberosum*), with a flat leaf cross-section, white flowers from July and a more garlicky flavor.

Ordinary chives emerge early in the year, pickable here from March or even February, whereas the garlicky type comes a couple of months later. That's useful, as if you have both, you have good succession. Cut them to the ground after a week or two of flowering and they will quickly regrow. You can do this several times in one year.

There's another reason I'm happy to see our chives reappearing in March: it means we can think about making a barrel of chive spray, our treatment of choice to help keep other plants mildew-free (see p. 207).

2 Fennel *Foeniculum vulgare*
The leaf and stem fennel I'm talking about here is different from Florence fennel, also known as bulb fennel (see p. 46). We grow both. In March, it's the leaf form—both bronze ("Purpureum") and green—that is doing its thing. Before you add raw leaves into your spring salads, have a good look for aphids. They are very effectively camouflaged and can coat every stem and leaf in spring. When you look closely at the feathery leaves, particularly in May, you'll often notice they're moving!

3 Lovage *Levisticum officinale*
Growing to more than 6 feet when in flower, this spectacular umbellifer is widely used in eastern-European cooking (it's the key ingredient in Hungarian goulash). It is a large plant, so it is only suited to gardens with plenty of room. It's often grown in an herbaceous border as an ornamental. Its baby leaves have the flavor of smoky celery. The taste quite quickly becomes unpalatably strong (apart from in stocks, where one leaf is useful), so either stop picking it and enjoy its elegance, or repeatedly cut the plants to the ground to encourage more baby leaves to form.

4 Mint *Mentha*
Our most recent taste trial of sixteen different mints helped us to determine which we liked best for teas (see p. 238), for eating raw (that was spearmint, *M. spicata*), and for pairing with other ingredients like potatoes in the kitchen (Bowles's mint and spearmint). It's *M.* × *villosa* var. *alopecuroides* Bowles's

mint that's pictured here.

Mint has a bad reputation as an invasive plant. It can take over a little. Grow it in pots or in out-of-the-way places where you can leave it to run riot and then happily pick regular handfuls. If growing it in pots, divide and repot every year or its flavor diminishes.

5 Sorrel *Rumex acetosa*
I love both common sorrel
(*R. acetosa*) and French sorrel
(*R. scutatus*, pictured). If you
want to harvest leaves most
of the year, choose French
sorrel. Cut it back at least once
a month and put the stems,
nascent flowers (which look
like wild docks), and leaves on
the compost heap. This is one
of the most prolific plants we
grow—so much so that this
was the plant I harvested once
a week to give our hens a treat
during the chicken lockdown
caused by bird flu. It will grow
in most sites and situations.

6 Tarragon *Artemisia
dracunculus*
It's key that you get the
green-leaved French tarragon
(*A. dracunculus* French)
rather than the silver-leaved
Russian tarragon, which
has a bitter flavor. Tarragon

is my favorite herb (along
with basil "Sweet Genovese")
and is so worth growing at
home as it has many times
the flavor of supermarket
(often hydroponically grown)
tarragon in bags. Honestly,
two sprigs of this from your
garden has the flavor of five
supermarket stems, slightly
anaesthetizing the tongue
when eaten raw. It's the best
herb to eat with fish and
chicken, and also added to
vinegar for the best salad
dressing. Protect from
hard frosts, and mulch in
autumn. It also grows well
in containers. We find it loses
flavor year on year, so take
cuttings any time from late
spring if you can.

Hardy annual herbs (or biennials grown as annuals)

These are all fine to be grown
in pots, but we find them easy
to look after, with less watering
and greater bolt resistance, if
grown in the ground.

1 Basil *Ocimum*
"Sweet Genovese" is the classic
variety, but see p. 270 for my
favorites, as well as p. 236 for
use in teas. The key with basil
is not to sow it too early. Our
first batch is sown in April, and
then a second sowing in May for
all-summer picking. It hates cold
nights and turns black if planted
too early (or too late) in the
season. A couple more tips: sow
into modules or gutters as basil
doesn't like root disturbance;
and water in the morning,
not the evening, to help keep
botrytis at bay.

2 Chervil *Anthriscus cerefolium*
This is a British native
wildflower that you sometimes
see in undisturbed ground in a
churchyard. Chervil only grows
in the wet and cold, refusing to
germinate in the main growing
season. It's an invaluable winter
and early spring herb with
a gentle aniseedy taste. It is
delicious in salads and omelettes
when folded in last minute.
It's 100 percent hardy and will
happily grow outside through
rain, snow, and hail. We sow this

in September for picking lightly in winter and then heavily until late spring when the heat and light make it flower and seed.

3 Coriander
Coriandrum sativum
Coriander does well from an early autumn or late winter sowing, thriving in the cooler weather with decreasing hours of daylight. It's at peak production from March to May.

4 Dill *Anethum graveolens*
This is an annual herb with so many different roles. We aim to successionally sow it so that it is available to harvest from spring to the end of autumn. The leaves are invaluable in the kitchen. (It's a key ingredient of Scandinavian dishes such as gravadlax.) The flowers make a brilliant, acid-green cut-flower filler that lasts 10 days in the vase. We also use the flowers for decorating salads. Finally we use the seeds for baking, tagines, and teas. It self-sows freely, readily crossing with closely related fennel. Dill doesn't like root disturbance so we sow it into a gutter, or sometimes directly where we want it to grow.

5 Parsley *Petroselinum crispum*
This is a biennial grown as an annual, because it's not the flowers but the leaves we grow

it for. We grow mainly flat-leaved "Gigante di Napoli," which has a soft texture and huge productivity for 6 months. We use curly-leaved parsley as border edging. Wash your parsley seeds in warm water the night before sowing and dry on kitchen paper overnight. This washes off the germination inhibitor in the seed coat to give you a quicker harvest.

March

In terms of preparation and sowing for the kitchen garden, March is the busiest month of the year. It's full-on sowing time, and from around the middle of the month, planting also begins.

Last month, we started sowing the hardy edible crops, such as fava beans, along with salads, herbs, and the first edible flowers. They will need potting or planting into the vegetable garden now.

The fruiting half-hardy annuals (tomatoes, eggplants and peppers, both sweet and hot) that were also sown early in the year will now need separating. March is also the month we pot dahlia tubers for edible flowers and start to plant our sprouted potatoes.

With the warmer, dryer weather we usually have in Sussex, late March is the perfect time to reactivate the compost heap. We flip ours into a new bay. If you're making compost on a smaller scale, you should turn whatever you have into a new bin. I recommend watering on a compost activator such as comfrey fertilizer (see p. 206) or liquid seaweed, which will hopefully start it steaming again. For more on making and maintaining compost, see p. 244.

Planning Your Sowing

We do a huge amount of March sowing under cover in our polytunnel. It seems like every length of guttering, seed tray, and root trainer tray is in use. Almost everything is sat on heated propagator benches enjoying basal heat to speed up germination and assist speedy root growth (see p. 51). To help stay on top of it all, here are some helpful tips.

Sow or buy

It sometimes feels hard to draw breath in March with so much to do, but remember you can always skip the sowing stage (at least for some plants) and visit a garden center in April to buy hardy edibles, and then visit again in May for the more tender crew. You can buy your seedlings online too. If you don't have any under-cover space, you should be doing that anyway. The main downside to buying rather than sowing is that you are choosing from a narrower, pre-selected range.

Organizing seeds

So as not to feel overwhelmed by all this March sowing, I've devised a simple successional seed-sowing box. You can use a CD or shoe box and divide it into sections for a similar effect.

My box has eleven compartments that I've labelled with the months. November and December are together as there is not much to sow then. When I get my seeds, I put them in the slot corresponding to the month they are best first sown. If the packet has a generous quantity of seeds, I never sow all of them at once. If they are things that I want to repeat sow—carrots or lettuces such as "Black Seeded Simpson" or "Merveille des Quatre Saisons"—I put the packet back in a slot a month or two on from that first sowing month.

With this system, I never forget that these edibles need to be sown again. Keep the box cold and dry, and the seeds will be fine from one year to the next. You'll get prolonged reliable germination (see p. 52).

In the Greenhouse

Sowing in Pots

The seeds we sow into their own individual pots are the whoppers and difficult to fit individually into a cell. Their large surface areas mean they can rot easily in compact coir pellets.

Cucumbers We usually sow cucumbers in the middle of March, placing them on the heated bench in the polytunnel. If maintained at a temperature of 21°C (70°F), they will germinate within a week. They can take a couple of weeks if it's cooler. When you see the first white roots at the bottom of the pot, pot them on into 1-liter pots to grow on. They can be planted into greenhouse beds in late April. Any that are being planted into the garden should wait until late May when the frosts have passed.

We always sow a Middle Eastern cucumber that's the size of a big, fat cigar (our current favorite is "La Diva"). We also sow "Petita", which produces lovely sweet cucumbers in huge quantities.

For Perch Hill's school kitchen or for the lunches we host on our garden open days, we grow a highly prolific, supermarket-style variety called "Marketmore." Children tend to love the round, sweet cucumbers like "Crystal Lemon" and "Crystal Apple," which is great for crudités as they are nice and crunchy.

Zucchini I recommend a mix of three zucchini—one plant of each: "Romanesco,"
"Bianca di Trieste," and "Soleil"—for good colors in the garden and on the plate (see p. 184). I also love the climbing summer squash "Tromboncino" (to eat like a zucchini), but as this is not one for forcing, we wait to sow it in April for planting in the garden at the end of May.

How to sow in pots
- Fill a 9 cm (3 ½ in.) individual pot with a peat-free potting compost.
- Water the compost.
- Push the seed in to the depth of your finger's first knuckle, about 2 ½ cm (1 in.) deep. Push it in vertically, rather than flat. The compost usually folds over the seed and buries it, but you can cover it with compost if this hasn't happened. Label.
- There's no need to water again straight away. If necessary, put on a heated propagator until the seeds germinate. Once germinated, water every few days, when the compost starts to dry.
- Keep half-hardy annuals protected inside until the chance of frost has passed. Depending on the plant, you can plant seedlings in greenhouse beds in April if you have the space. If you keep them (or some of them) for planting in the garden, you will need to pot the seedlings once before planting.

We do two sowings a year to get year-round picking. For autumn and winter kale harvests, we aim to sow in March. To harvest the following spring and summer, it's best to sow in May.

Guttering

We sow as much as we can in gutters. With this system, there's no separating seedlings or potting, so it's brilliantly time-saving and, well spaced. You can just push out one seedling at a time. Focus on large seeds that are easy to handle (see p. 57).

Peas These are a top priority at this time of year.

Leeks These are also essential for March sowing. I love these for their vertical shapes and winter hardiness. We sow them in gutters three times a year: first, in March (these can be planted in April and harvested in summer as finger leeks; next, in May (planted in June for eating in autumn; and finally, in July (planted in August or September for a winter crop). The main one we grow is the beautiful, purple-washed variety "Northern Lights." "Saint Victor" is very similar.

Onions If you are growing onions from seeds not sets, you can sow them now. This applies to varieties such as "Rossa Lunga di Firenze."

Seeds to Sow Now

Modules

For medium-sized seeds that prefer not to have too much root disturbance, we use a modular cell system (such as a tray divided into small cells) or Jiffy-7 coir pellets (see p. 60).

Kale and kalettes Brassicas don't like root disturbance, so they're ideal for Jiffy-7 pellets We tend to sow into guttering for closely planted cut-and-come-again salad leaves.

Salads Any salads you've not got to in February, such as lettuce, plus sea beans, saltwort, and summer purslane, can be sown now in March. Sow the seed well-spaced at 5 to 6 cm (2 in.) apart.

Herbs Sow any herbs that were not sown in February, such as dill (which is slightly less hardy).

Station sowing in guttering

Station sowing is when you sow a mini-pinch of three or four seeds at each station spaced roughly 5 cm (2 in.) apart. Remember to sow the seeds all the way down the gutter before pushing them into the compost—that way you can see your spacings at a glance and know how much gutter you have left. Beetroot and pea tips can also be sown using this method.

Beetroot Most beetroot have multi-germ seeds, which means they already have a little clump collected in a sort of nugget. We sow them well spaced, 2 to 3 cm (1 in.) apart. We usually sow a tricolor mix, including a standard purple such as "Boltardy," as well as a stripy pink and white, such as "Chioggia", and finally an orange, such as "Burpee's Golden."

Rainbow chard If it is to be harvested as baby leaf, rainbow chard is also good station-sown.

Spring onion As well as sowing a pinch into a module (see p. 60), we also station sow into gutters every 6 weeks or so.

Pea tips Station sowing is ideal for pea tips. We sow some in February and a second lot 4 to 6 weeks later in March.

Root trainers

We don't start sowing the bulk of the beans until next month, but we do one last sowing of fava beans in March (see p. 58). Left any later, we find our plants are blighted with more black bean aphid and fungal diseases than if they're sown and settled into the garden before the warm, dry weather begins. They really benefit from a deep, moist root run, which they'll still get if sown early and planted by the middle of April. As well as a last sowing of fava beans, sow sweet peas now as companion plants, if you haven't done so already.

Separating Tomato, Eggplant, and Pepper Seedlings

We do very little traditional sowing into small rectangular seed trays in March. In February, we sowed tomatoes, peppers, and eggplant into trays, and now it's time to separate the seedlings.

Tomatoes Separate the seedlings once they each have their pair of seed leaves and one pair of true leaves.

Eggplant and peppers These tend to be a bit slower, but they usually need attention by the end of March.

- Fill individual 9 cm (3 ½ in.) pots with peat-free potting compost. Use a dibber or pencil to create a deep dimple for each seedling.

- To lift out each seedling, get as much root as you can by pushing a dibber (or use a rigid label or pencil) right down to the base of the tray. Lift the seedling from there. Avoid touching the stem; instead, lift it out by the roots or leaves. You may need to tear the roots of one seedling from another a little, but don't worry. As long as there are some roots, the seedlings will be fine. You can be firm.

- You can bury the stem a bit as it makes it stronger and encourages more roots to form. This applies particularly to tomatoes, which thrive buried down almost to their seed leaves. This part of the stem has the potential to form extra feeding roots, which makes the seedling more vigorous, quick growing, and ultimately more productive.

- Firm the seedling into its new pot and water. Label. Place the pot back on the heated bench.

- It's important to give them plenty of space and light. They must also be kept frost-free and at a temperature that's as even as possible between day and night. The temperature shouldn't go below 10°C (50°F) or the plants will be stunted. Aiming for 14 to 16°C (57 to 61°F) is ideal.

- Give them a nitrogen-rich foliar feed such as nettle fertilizer (see p. 206) every couple of weeks to keep them growing well. Always keep them moist.

- Once the seedling roots have filled that pot, usually by April, repot them into a larger pot. At this stage (usually 2 to 3 weeks later), you'll need to put a stake at their side and tie the plants in as they grow.

Planting Tubers

Potatoes and dahlias are both tubers that originate from warmer climates. To get them cropping faster in our cooler temperatures, you can force them into growth a little early by planting them in late March or early April.

Potatoes

There's lots of potato action in March. First thing is first: to ensure a quicker and slightly larger harvest, you need to sprout your potatoes early in the month if you haven't done so already in early February (see p. 61). Ideally, you need to use seed potatoes that have been sprouted for 4 weeks before planting. Then, move quickly on to forcing early potatoes inside. We try to get some early crops planted outside by the end of the month and into April (see p. 122 for instructions). This will give you new potatoes in early June.

Forcing potatoes inside

It's such a bonus getting crops early. If you have a greenhouse or polytunnel, this is a worthwhile way to use some of that under-cover space.

You can even force potatoes in August, which is outside of their natural growing season (we use the delicious "Anya" and "Charlotte" sprouted in July). This guarantees potatoes for Christmas. We plant ours in baskets and crates, bringing them inside once the nights become cold again and frosts threaten in the autumn.

At this time of year, we make quite a thing of forcing potatoes. Over the years, we've collected large zinc buckets and willow baskets to do our potato forcing in. They look so much nicer than plastic bags (or green fiber forcing bags). We have them along the main greenhouse path. We line them with pierced empty compost bags, which helps to keep the compost from spilling out and also helps to retain moisture.

- Line buckets or baskets with old compost bags that have been turned inside out. Like that, the bags are black and absorb any heat.
- Roll down the sides of the compost bags to about half their height and pierce the bases a few times for drainage.
- Half-fill with compost mixed with one third molehills (or a soil-based compost such as John Innes No. 2) to about 30 cm (1 ft.) deep. Earth from molehills will give you lovely crumbly loam where the moles have done the hard work for you. They create the most friable grass-free soil from a depth usually below the worst of the weed seeds, and soil enhances flavor. Avoid mushroom compost with potatoes as the lime in it promotes the proliferation of scab.
- Push the tubers into the compost/soil mix in the bases of the bags. Make sure the tuber is well covered. We did a trial in which we planted some baskets with one tuber and others with two to see if it made any difference to the harvest weight. With most varieties, single tubers produced more than double the harvest, so just go for one.

Earthing pot-grown,
forced potatoes.

- Carry on earthing them up, bit by bit every couple of weeks until they reach nearly the top of the bag.
- Feed once a week with seaweed fertilizer from May. Keep the compost damp but not sopping wet.
- The shoots will come up to flower in May.
- Harvest at the beginning of June, when flowers appear (see p. 169).

Dahlias

For edible flowers, we only need a few dahlia plants. We usually leave them in the ground and mulch them to protect them through the winter in situ. If you're starting afresh, follow these instructions for planting your tubers.

- Plant into a 3-liter pot. A 2-liter size is often too small for bigger tubers. You don't want to force them in and damage the root. A big pot also allows the tubers to grow happily until the frosts are finished and they can be planted in the garden.
- Plant each tuber in peat-free, multipurpose potting compost. Plant just under the compost surface; do not bury deeply. Plant them stem up, with the tubers (which remind me of a bunch of sausages) hanging below.
- Water well.
- Place on a heated propagator or somewhere under cover, light and frost-free until they start to shoot (which may not be until the end of April). Water only when the compost is dry.

- Water them in well. Grow them somewhere light but frost-free. We keep ours on the heated bench in the polytunnel to give them a helping hand for a couple of weeks, and then we bring them up to the unheated greenhouse.
- Once they have about 20 cm (8 in.) of growth (usually after 6 weeks or so), roll up the sides of the compost bags and earth up the haulms (the top growth of potatoes) by adding more compost around the leaves and stems to partially cover. Allow some of the leaves to remain exposed.

- Different varieties shoot at different rates so
  don't despair if they don't all shoot at the same
  time. Once you see shoots and roots appearing
  in the holes at the bottom of the pot, plant
  them in the garden, but only if the risk of frost
  has passed.

Cutting Care

The polytunnel here is full of cuttings we have
taken the previous autumn, with rosemary,
scented-leaf pelargoniums, and sage all sitting
on the propagator bench. They need to be potted
individually.

Check the bottom of each pot for new white
shoots. If you can see a few emerging, knock
out the whole contents gently onto the potting
bench, separate each rooted cutting, and pot
them into their own pot of gritty compost.

It's a good idea to give those that have
grown rapidly, and been moved on already the
previous autumn a tonic of something like
SB Plant Invigorator, an environmental-friendly
pesticide, milewcide, and nutrient, to help them
with their March growth spurt. We use this a lot
at Perch Hill. It is classified as nonchemical and
nonbiological. It contains sodium lauryl ether
sulphate, which is a surfactant that gets rid of
pests and washes spores from the leaves.

In the Garden

Sowing Direct

It's still too cold for most things to be sown directly outside. If we sow here before the middle of April, we find the seed tends to rot or get eaten by birds before it germinates. With the soil slowly warming up and light levels increasing, you'll see a few weeds beginning to germinate in the garden. That is always a good reminder that you can start sowing your own more desirable seed out there too.

Fava beans For now, it's still only the truly hardy things such as fava beans that we can direct sow. My favorite variety by a street for March sowing is "Stereo," which has small pods and beans that never get tough.

Summer savory Direct sow a swathe of summer savory next to the beans. This hardy annual herb has a thymelike flavor and is cut-and-come-again, so invaluable for bunches of green herbs early in the year. It's a companion plant to fava beans, helping to protect the crop against black bean aphid.

How to sow direct

To help the soil warm and dry enough so that it's ready for sowing, we aim to cover at least one area with a sheet of reusable, thick, black plastic (which absorbs heat) or clear plastic. This encourages weed seeds to germinate, which cleans the bed. You can quickly hoe them before sowing.

- For fava beans, sow the seed so that it is vertical, not flat. Sow about 2 ½ cm (1 in.) deep, spaced 15 cm (6 in.) apart in a staggered double row. Sow six extra seeds at the end of the row as insurance for nongermination. Water.

Hedges

On a rather different scale to seed-sowing, March (or October) are ideal times to plant hedges. If you're gardening on heavy clay, as we are, March seems to be the best moment to plant hedges.

We have added lots of hedges at Perch Hill since we've been here, and it's something I'm really proud of. They play a key part in creating shelter here on our windy site. A wind-permeable barrier is much better than a solid fence. Hedges are also key to the biodiversity of the garden and crucial nesting and foraging sites for our ever-increasing population of garden birds, who help us to keep on top of pests (aphids, slugs, and snails) in the vegetable garden.

Hawthorn, in particular, is quick-growing and thorny, so it provides perfect nesting habitats for lots of the smaller birds. The thorns offer good protection for the young against predators such as foxes, cats, and dogs. Consider including an evergreen so birds have cover in winter.

Remember to trim your hedges in August, once the baby birds have all fledged. Cut off all whippy new growth first and then trim to a good shape or frame. We cut them back hard on the top to prevent them growing too tall and shading out plants at their base. You don't want too much new growth on evergreen hedges before winter, so only cut back hard in spring. With a well-established hawthorn hedge like ours (planted 25 years ago), we have to prune in winter too.

April

My aim is to have a colorful, productive patch for as many months as possible, and April is the kitchen garden's first paintbox peak. Spring's edible flowers now mix with an array of hyacinths, followed by tulips and the showiest of the salads and leafy greens (such as rainbow chard and kale "Redbor"), as well as purple leeks and the foliage of French artichokes. Together, this gives us full-on color razzmatazz, which I love.

Central to all parts of the garden are tulips. As with dahlias, we scatter tulip petals over salad. In November, we plant hundreds of bulbs through the vegetables, selecting varieties we've found to be most perennial, so they come up reliably year after year. We like varieties such as "Green Wave," "Spring Green," "Ballerina," "Mistress Mystic," and "White Valley" (syn. "Exotic Emperor"), to name a few. We aim to get them buried to a depth of 15 cm (6 in.). Deep planting makes these bulbs more perennial, which allows us to fill the space on top with patterns of vegetables, salads, and herbs.

We have tulips weaving through the perennial French artichoke bed at the eastern edge of our kitchen garden, purple tulips with purple leeks, as well as tulips lining the main grass path up the vegetable garden alongside colorful chard and kale. We have also recently created a new bed using a layered principle—not in the sun but in light shade, with rhubarb crowns surrounded by a range of bulbs including highly scented narcissi (see p. 106).

The patterns can be both beautiful and bountiful. For much of spring, we have a double cropping. We can enhance our meals with homegrown food and our vases with flowers from the same square meter (see p. 364 for advice on planting).

The idea of layering works in large pots too. We have kale above our hyacinths in a huge pot on our doorstep, salad leaves over the top of tulips in the deep long-tom pots in the Oast Garden, and parsley with narcissi in the Dutch Yard. Again, it means we can crop the edible leaves for much of winter before the foliage and flowers of the bulbs emerge, and it doesn't deplete either harvest or show.

Key to the grace and beauty of our productive garden are the woven silver birch and hazel arches and frames that start to fill it in April, creating the kind of architecture that can be lacking when you only have repeated lines of vegetables.

April is a contradictory month though. The vegetable garden is bright and apparently abundant, but not yet giving us a huge range of food. March, April, and May are the so-called "hungry gap" months, when vegetables stored from last year have usually been eaten and this season's crops have yet to appear. Nineteenth-century parish records reveal that when the poorer villagers had to rely on homegrown food, these were the months with the highest death rates.

The salads that have been cropping through the winter are still going—that is, until we get a stretch of warm, dry weather.

Previous page Rainbow chard with a punchy array of tulips.
Below *Tulipa* "Ballerina" growing up through oak-leaf lettuces to give a double show and harvest.
Opposite *Tulipa* "Caviar" growing up through mizuna "Red Knight," which we harvest pretty much all winter.
Next page The herb beds in March with rosemary at its best. Our French artichokes are also perky by this early stage of the year.

Purple sprouting broccoli takes
over from kalettes and kale in April,
to give us an invaluable harvest.

Then, even if you remember to water the plants at their roots, the mizunas, mustards, and arugula tend to run up to flower and stop producing. On top of that, there's the beginnings of flea beetle infestation, which peppers brassica leaves with tiny holes. We usually start to notice this damage toward the end of April (see p. 159 for how to tackle it).

The leaves of our winter kales have become a little tough and bitter now, with the plants pushing up determinedly to bloom. Their pretty yellow flowers are edible (and much visited by pollinators), but their appearance means it's time to start again and resow. Even chard, if sown the previous August or September, tends to bolt in a hot, dry spell. It's to the February-sown chard and spinach that we increasingly turn.

We also rely on purple sprouting broccoli, which is at its best now. This is a classic hungry-gap crop and, to a degree, cut-and-come-again. Once the central, largest floret is ready, pick it. This will help promote the formation of smaller ones lower in the plant. If you then take the head floret off these stems as they expand after a couple of weeks (rather than cutting right down to the main plant stem), the buds below develop too. Purple sprouting broccoli's white cousin, "White Early," tends to be a little earlier and has a more tender texture, a little like minicauliflower.

The sprouting broccolis are a crop ideal for an allotment (or large vegetable garden), as apart from needing a stout stake to prevent them toppling over and a net against cabbage white butterflies in summer, they require minimal maintenance. But a word of warning: each plant grows to a whopping 60 cm (2 ft.) in width and needs to be planted in early summer (at the latest). That's a lot of space for a long period of time before you get anything to eat.

Even though we have plenty of room at Perch Hill, we don't grow the sprouting broccolis every year. If we do, we only grow a few plants. We tend to give more space to the broccoli-kale spigariello, which offers leaves that can be picked through the winter.

Also in the garden now are lots of herbs: parsley, chives, sorrel, and coriander—with tarragon, summer savory, and mint well on their way, and more and more edible flowers. Next month, we have the largest range to choose from, but autumn-sown calendulas and borage are starting to open and to supplement our pansies and polyanthus.

And then there's rhubarb. Rhubarb is *the* April edible and should be included in every garden if you have the room. It is a large plant, with crowns needing about a meter between them, and thrives in light shade. We harvest from our plants for a good 4-month stretch. Plus, in summer and autumn, rhubarb's huge elephant-ear leaves look good. They are big, bold, and jungly in just the right way.

To start spring off with a bang, we plant our rhubarb with a succession of bulbs that also tolerate dappled shade. For March flowers, we intersperse it with grape hyacinths, followed by perfumed narcissi, and then the odd tulip. These are selected to flower in succession throughout rhubarb's cropping time, starting with *Muscari armeniacum*, then *Narcissus* "Avalanche" and "Cragford," through to mid-season *N.* "Actaea" and finishing with *N. poeticus* var. *recurvus* and *N.* "Rose of May." For April into May, we also use white tulips such as "White Valley" (syn. "Exotic Emperor") and the new viridiflora tulip "Orange Marmalade." Both do okay here in light shade.

We'd fail in April with homegrown meals if we didn't have rhubarb. It's lovely to look at and lovely to eat, giving us some of the most delicious desserts of the year at a low-production moment. You have to crown rhubarb as the indisputable April garden queen.

Opposite Grape hyacinths (*Muscari*) start off the bulb show in our shady rhubarb bed in March. Below By April, the rhubarb bed is full of perennial bulbs: *Narcissus* "Stainless" and "Silver Chimes," *Tulipa* "Orange Marmalade" and *Allium* "Globemaster." These add to the show and harvest.

Rhubarb

We quite often think of rhubarb as a fruit, using it in more sweet than savory dishes, but it is in fact classified as a vegetable that is (sort of) cut-and-come-again. Unlike with bush or tree fruit, keep pulling rhubarb and it keeps producing.

With the right varieties, you can eat rhubarb all the way through spring and summer, but it's for its initial appearance that we treasure it most. An early bird, it starts producing lightly (when forced) in February, more in March, and then in easy armfuls (without forcing) by April. We have a large rhubarb patch here in dappled shade, stocked with three rows, each of a different variety. "Timperley Early" is the first, followed by "Stockbridge Arrow," which breaks ground about 3 weeks later, and finally "Victoria." We are always on the look out for new varieties, and have just added "Poulton's Pride" to our trials — it's a newly bred variety which is said to crop for ten months of the year, from February to November. It has not been in long enough for me to give a verdict, but it sounds promising!

The whole idea of forcing rhubarb came from a chance discovery at London's Chelsea Physic Garden in 1817. Although outdoor-grown rhubarb was eaten in the UK—and had been since the late-eighteenth century—it was not very popular. Rhubarb was mainly grown as medicine. At the Physic Garden, men were working in an area where the rhubarb crowns were growing and, as part of their excavations, they piled a heap of earth over some dormant winter roots. The job took a while to complete, so the rhubarb was kept out of the light and protected from the frost through the winter. Once the soil was cleared in spring, the gardeners saw lots of pink shoots emerging, and these were particularly tender and sweet. And so began a great rhubarb-growing and early-eating trend that has continued since.

Rhubarb is incredibly long-lived. Once established, it grows happily in the same spot year after year, just needing the occasional mulch to keep it happy. My family has a cottage in the Highlands on the west coast of Scotland, and the one thing we are guaranteed to be able to harvest without any attempt at creating a garden is rhubarb. The cottage was built in 1880 next to a Victorian walled garden.

Armfuls of forced rhubarb harvested on a visit to some rhubarb growers in West Yorkshire.

Sections of the walls have collapsed. You'd hardly know a garden had been there, apart from huge and healthy clumps of rhubarb.

In fact, rhubarb is used by archaeologists as a marker of cleared villages in the Highlands. The buildings were often razed to the ground by the landowners. Under the canopy of bracken so common in that part of the world, it's now tricky to locate former dwellings, but a good bank of rhubarb is a good indication to investigate further.

Rhubarb is also a very cold-tolerant plant. There's a long tradition of growing it in Carlton, near Wakefield in West Yorkshire, where it's chilly in spring and overall quite wet. Nestled at the side of the Pennines, the rhubarb fields are in a frost pocket and the hills provide a heavy rainfall. Rhubarb loves that, and the plants thrive.

On top of that, rhubarb is good for us. It's particularly high in vitamin C and it's high in fiber too. Some people worry about the buildup of oxalic acid (which can be poisonous in high doses) that you reputedly get in rhubarb. Indeed, there is an old wives' tale that encourages you to stop eating rhubarb in summer for just that reason. The oxalic acid is, in fact, concentrated in the leaves rather than the stems, so there is nothing to worry about.

Rhubarb forcing sheds in West Yorkshire, where harvesting takes place by candlelight. Daylight rapidly turns the stems green, less sweet, and less tender.

Harvesting Rhubarb

The key thing with rhubarb is to keep pulling it. This promotes more shoot formation below ground level and a self-perpetuating harvest. Plus, it means there's no stub left to rot. This stub end is the tastiest and sweetest bit of the stems, so don't cut it off, just peel away the brown scale part. The best way to harvest is to run your finger down the groove of the stem until you reach the root. Give a gentle tug and it will come off in your hands, leaving any buds forming just below your mature stem to develop into the next crop.

For the plant's sake, it is important to know when to stop picking rhubarb. This depends on variety. If it's an early one that you have been picking since March, then stop in late June so the plant has time to replenish itself for next year. Later varieties such as "Victoria" can be picked until August, after which the stems tend to get a bit woody, stringy, and tough.

It's also worth knowing that rhubarb sometimes shoots great towering flower plumes. This is usually a sign of stress, either from lack of food or water. The plant is determined to reproduce before it disappears. This rarely harms the plant, but it might reduce your crop. We remove these flowering shoots if we get them, and I use them in a great decorative urn inside. You need to cut them down before they set seed.

There are two patterns of harvest from which you can choose.

System 1
Crop only half the stems on a plant at one time. You'll find this recommended in most books and by the Royal Horticulture Society (RHS).

System 2
This is the harvesting pattern favored in West Yorkshire, the center of rhubarb growing in the UK. It is also the system we use at Perch Hill. Once the plants are in their second summer (about 14 months after division), start picking everything you can. New growth will be produced all the time. Pick it, even if it's a tiny stick. If it's not worth cooking, put it on the compost heap. Don't leave it on the plant. This makes the crown put energy into producing better-sized stems. Harvested like this, you'll need to replace your crowns every 6 to 8 years, or rest them for a couple of years and then start again.

Best of the rhubarb

One garden rhubarb variety looks much like another, but it's worth growing more than one to make sure you have successional cropping times. These rhubarb plants (all Rheum × hybridum*) are listed in order of cropping.*

1 "Timperley Early"
This is a good variety for the earliest outdoor crops. It's suitable for gentle forcing for harvest as early as February. Left to its own devices, it crops heavily from March to May.

2 "Red Champagne"
This one is very similar to "Hawke's Champagne," with long stems that are a deeper shade of red than other rhubarbs, and with a good, sweet taste. Though an old variety, it is easy to grow, reliable, and early. It crops from March to June.

3 "Raspberry Red"
This is a recent rhubarb cultivar, originating from the rhubarb triangle of West Yorkshire. This gives high-quality, deep-red, thick stalks with a sweet flavor, without the need for forcing. It is a relatively early cropper, offering stems from April to June.

4 "Stockbridge Arrow"
This is a mid-season variety of rhubarb for an April to June harvest. It produces long, thick stems with a good color and sweet flavor. The leaves are arrow-shaped (hence its name) and more elegant than most. This is a good choice for growing in ornamental borders.

5 "Victoria"
A late cropper, with one of the sweetest and least tart flavors, "Victoria" rhubarb was first available in 1837, the year Victoria became queen. And it's still with us. It has crisp, tender stems from late May to August.

April

If March is the month of mass sowing, April is the moment for planting—not the half hardies—which can't go outside until the frosts are over, but certainly for the hardy edible plants such as onions, fava beans, and evergreen herbs. It's out-into-the-garden time for them. According to traditional garden folklore, Good Friday (usually in April) is the day for planting potatoes. We also make sure our indoor growing beds are well fed and ready for our mass tomato, eggplant, and pepper planting in May.

April is our second mass-sowing month, and the seed box is bursting with vegetable seed to tick off, week by week. We sow some edible seed varieties this month: the quick-growing stuff like pole and French beans, as well as pumpkins and squash. Then, we move on to brassicas, which are so crucial for next winter and spring, as well as the most tender of the edible plants we grow: basil. This will struggle if nighttime temperatures plummet, so mid-April is the safest sowing time.

We're also busy making supports and climbing frames. That's one of the April jobs we tend to fight over. We all love making tuteurs, arches, and frames using locally harvested silver birch, hazel, and willow.

If you live in sheep country, you can gather wool (not all, leave some for the local birds) from brambles in the hedges and hang that in bundles from trees in your own garden. Birds will love using this as nesting material. You'll be amazed at how quickly it disappears.

And one last thing! It's key to keep on top of the weeds now. Do so and you'll save yourself hours of work later in the year. It's particularly the early flowerers and self-sowers that you need to hoe and rake up before they spread themselves around willy-nilly.

In the Greenhouse

Seeds to Sow Now

If the weather is still not great, start with sowing under cover and separating seedlings, and then move on to potting and planting a few things in the greenhouse.

As a useful rule of thumb, if plants have large seed leaves, they are likely to germinate and grow quickly. The large surface area of photosynthetic food factory (i.e., the leaf) makes them romp. This applies to pole beans (and sometimes French beans, which can be a fiddle to germinate), as well as zucchini, squash, and nasturtiums. We sow all these at the start of April, with just 4 to 6 weeks before our last expected frost. We've already done one zucchini sowing for forcing inside, but do another one for planting outside.

We then move on to the tenderest half-hardy herbs and edible flowers: basil, oregano, and marigolds, which dislike cold nights, so they're best left until last.

Finally, in April, we do our main brassica sowing: the slow-burners: kale, kalettes, and purple sprouting broccoli for cropping the following autumn, winter, and spring.

Root trainers
See p. 58 for instructions.

Pole beans We grow several varieties (see p. 224) and harvest the flowers as much as the beans. They taste deliciously beany and are good sprinkled over the top of rice, potatoes, or salad.

French beans If I had to choose just one bean to grow it would be "Blue Lake." We also trialled "Limka" recently and loved the not-at-all-stringy flat pods (see p. 226 for other varieties).

Pots
See p. 89 for instructions.

Zucchini and summer squash For outside planting go for "Tromboncino." We also repeat sow the other varieties already sown in March (see p. 89) for planting inside. From the middle of the month, as soon as they've unfurled the first of their elephant-ear leaves, we plant a few zucchini in the greenhouse. If you don't have one, you can do this under a cloche in the garden. It's amazing how they'll rocket and you'll be picking zucchini in about 6 weeks' time.

Squash We grow four or five varieties (see p. 324).

Guttering
See p. 57 for instructions.

Basil Don't rush to sow basil. It hates a cold night, so toward the end of the month is best time to sow basil. We tend to trial different varieties every year, but our three stalwarts are "Sweet Genovese" (delicious in pesto), bush basil for table center pots, and lemon basil for tisanes (see p. 270).

Marigolds We sow *T. lucida* (with a tarragonlike flavor) and *T. patula* "Burning Embers." We use lots as a companion plant and edible flower.

Oregano Go for the true Greek *Origanum vulgare* subsp. *hirtum*, which is more intense than perennial marjoram (*O. majoram*). This is an evergreen subshrub, so it does not reliably overwinter. Depending on where you live, you may need to sow it again.

Peas We do successional sowing of "Nairobi," our favorite sweet sugar-snap pea variety. "Alderman" is the tallest of the readily available shelling peas with a long, light cropping pattern. We also repeat sow marrowfat peas for pea tips (see p. 305).

Modules
See p. 60 for instructions.

Nasturtiums "Bloody Mary" is our favorite for salad. It really stands out. But I also love "Empress of India" and the even darker "Black Velvet," both are beautiful and rich in their flower color. Alaska Series is also good for our tuteurs.

Brassicas We sow lots of kale here at Perch Hill, including "Redbor," "Scarlet," and "Cavolo Nero," as well as kalettes (see p. 356).

Purple sprouting broccoli We sow this twice: once in early April (for a February crop) and once in late May (for a succession that goes through April and even into May). We grow a variety called "Cardinal," which is prolific, very tasty, and crops for ages.

All sprouting broccolis are very hardy and look beautiful when dusted with frost or snow in the winter garden. Because they are in place for many months, only grow them if you have plenty of room. You will also need to protect them from cabbage white butterflies and wood pigeons with fruit nets or mesh.

Once planted, stake and/or build up the soil around the stem to support each plant. Remove any yellowing or fallen leaves to prevent fungal diseases from setting in. As with kales, leaving one or two to flower at the end of the season results in beautiful yellow flowers for the bees and a delicious and pretty addition to your salads.

Potting

It's time to pot a few things sown in late February and separating seedlings in March.

Tomatoes   It's tempting to think you can move tomatoes from a module or seed tray straight into their final, large planting pot, but this slows their growth. Tomatoes like to feel contained and cosy. Their roots can't cope with a large volume of compost and tend to rot. I think of tomatoes like children; they need to go through all of their developmental stages to do well. You will have hopefully separated your seedlings into a 9 cm (3 ½ in.) pot in March. The roots will fill that 2 or 3 weeks later.

- Pot them on into a 2-liter pot.
- As they grow, support them with a cane and twine.
- Snap off all the side shoots in the leaf axils.
- Once they've filled the pot, they're ready for final planting into a 5-liter pot, greenhouse beds, or a grow bag.
- If you're only able to grow tomatoes outside, wait until the end of May or early June to plant them. We have a greenhouse but, even so, we don't plant ours there until early May.

Chilies and zucchini   You need to pot chilies and zucchini one more time before you put them in the greenhouse or outside.

Greenhouse Jobs

Tomato beds

If you grow tomatoes in a greenhouse as we do, think about preparing their bed now. Outside, we follow no-dig principles, but in the greenhouse, we do dig in manure to integrate it. I recommend getting plenty of well-rotted manure to add. We spread 7 to 10 cm (3 to 4 in.) over the bed.
As well as being very fertile, farmyard manure is better than anything else at helping with water retention, and it enhances the flavor of tomatoes.

Pests

While we're on the greenhouse, now is a good time to clean down the glass inside and out. It's key to make sure you wipe out all the nasty pests and potential problems—mite, molds, whitefly, and aphids—that could have overwintered there. We've had some years where whitefly has become like confetti in our winter greenhouse. Light a "garlic greenhouse" candle (which does the same thing as a sulphur candle) and leave it burning as you close the greenhouse up one evening. It should have done the deed by morning. Unlike with the sulphur candles, you don't have to take all your plants out of the greenhouse first.

In the Garden

Planting Hardy Crops

As soon as the clocks have changed as a marker of light levels, we start planting the hardy seeds sown after Valentine's Day. Don't let your salads, herbs, and edible flowers get rootbound. They never quite recover.

When spring starts in March, it's tempting to get planting with rooted cuttings of rosemary, sage, and thyme, along with mint, French tarragon, and sorrel. Because many of these herbs hail from Mediterranean climates, it's safer to plant them in the garden in April to avoid the danger of newly planted cuttings sitting out in repeated frosts or snow, which we can still get even here in Sussex. As it's still properly cold at night, harden things off by moving them out for increasing hours each day.

Remember, of course, that at Perch Hill we are a few weeks behind the warmer county of Cornwall in our planting times and a few weeks earlier than anywhere geographically higher or farther north. So do adjust these timings depending on your location.

Early in the month, you can plant salads, herbs, chard, spinach, and hardy annual edible flowers. Later in the month, you can plant peas, beetroot, and radishes; however, in colder parts of the country, you may need to add a cloche.

Planting from guttering

Once hardy seedlings are growing well, with seedlings reaching 2 to 3 cm x 2 to 3 cm (1 in. x 1 in.), they're big enough for the garden.

There are two systems for planting seedlings from guttering, depending on whether they are well spaced or closely packed. In both cases, water the planted gutter well before planting. On completion, water the plants in well and think about pest control. Also, don't try to swipe out the contents of the whole gutter end to end, as it tends to collapse and the seedlings will come out in an unruly mound.

Well-spaced seedlings These seedlings will be about 10 to 15 cm (4 to 6 in.) apart (examples include lettuce, herbs, and salad leaves). See both illustrations pictured opposite.

- Lay the gutter on the ground alongside the planting line. Dig a seedling-sized hole.
- Push your hand into the compost between seedling 1 and 2 along the gutter. Push seedling 1 into its planting position.
- Move roughly 12 cm (5 in.) along the planting line and dig another seedling hole. Slide out seedling 2, and so on, working your way down the line until all the seedlings in the gutter have been pushed into individual planting holes.
- Note that mustards, in particular, grow large, so you'll need to either separate the seedlings or increase the spacing between planting holes to 30 cm (1 ft.).

Closely packed seedlings Seedlings will be hard to separate. This includes peas and radishes.

- Using a rake or hoe, scrape a gutter-shaped shallow trench in the garden bed. Lay the gutter on the ground alongside the trench.
- Push your hand into the compost about 40 cm (16 in.) along the gutter. Push this section out as one into its planting position in the trench.
- Move along the trench to a spacing of 40 cm (16 in.) and push the next block out, and so on.

Planting from root trainers
Fava beans Space them at 20 cm (8 in.) apart with 30 cm (1 ft.) between the rows, leaving plenty of room for pea sticks or some form of support to hold them up as they grow.

Planting from modules
Onions and shallots If you've forced onions under cover in modules earlier in the year, start to plant them now. If you have yet to get round to this, you can still plant shallot or onion sets straight into the garden (also see p. 306 and p. 342).

- To avoid the potential of onion white rot, choose a place that has been onion-free for the last 3 years. They need sun and well-drained soil.
- Space 10 cm (4 in.) apart, with 20 cm (8 in.) between the rows if you need to walk between them. Note that spring onions will grow quite closely packed. You can harvest one or two from each clump, leaving the rest to continue and bulb up.
- Keep weed-free, especially early on.

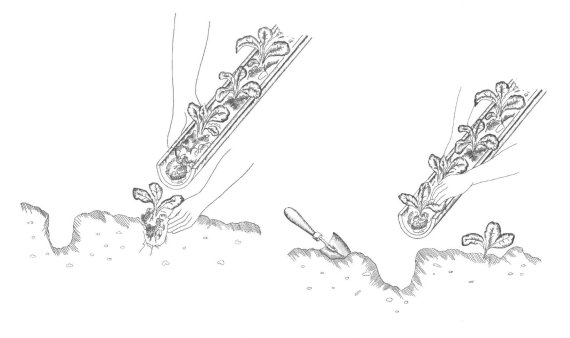

Planting potted / bare-root plants

Buying bare-root plants is often the most cost-effective way to buy quite expensive edible perennials such as asparagus. If the weather isn't frosty, you can plant them straight out.

Perennial and evergreen herbs These include rosemary, sage, and thyme, as well as perennials mint, French tarragon, and sorrel.

Asparagus If you have tons of space (as you might on an allotment), then you should consider asparagus. Whether the plants are bare-root or pot-grown, April is a good time to plant.

- Prepare the bed by removing all perennial weeds. That's key. Bindweed, ground elder, and mare's tail can soon take hold of an asparagus bed and become a nightmare to control.
- Add plenty of well-rotted manure to the planting area. Asparagus is a coastal plant and likes a very freely drained soil, so add grit if gardening on heavy clay.
- Dig a trench about 20 cm (8 in.) deep and 30 cm (1 ft.) wide. Leave 50 cm (20 in.) between.
- Form a ridge of soil down the center of the trench, about 10 cm (4 in.) high.
- Plant crowns 30 cm (1 ft.) apart. Place the crown on the ridge, draping the roots either side.
- Cover with about 5 cm (2 in.) of soil.
- Add more soil as the stems grow, aiming to completely fill the trench by autumn.
- Keep well watered.

Tubers

The beginning of April is a good time to start planting early potatoes here in Sussex. We've experimented with March planting and find we don't get crops any earlier. We do force potatoes inside in March (see p. 93), but our main growing time is April.

Potato tubers, though tender, are safe if they're planted well below the soil surface, which protects them from frost scorch. By the time their haulms emerge above ground, the frosts are usually finished. If a cold snap threatens, you can always earth up their lines for instant protection.

Planting potatoes outside

Once your potatoes have sprouted (see p. 61), you can plant them in the ground. The soil preparation is important, as it loosens the soil/manure mix ready for earthing up.

If possible, in October, mulch the area for potatoes with at least 20 cm (8 in.) of manure before the cold winter months. This feeds the soil and gives an insulating layer for earthworms. If you've not managed that, incorporate plenty of well-rotted manure into the planting area before the tubers go in. They are hungry crops and will always benefit from lots of manure.

If you want your plants to produce larger potatoes, carefully remove some of the sprouts, leaving three or four shoots on each tuber. We like lots of smaller potatoes, so we leave all the growing shoots on. For earthing up, see p. 167.

The vegetable garden with lots of hardy vegetables planted (peas and fava beans), sown direct and germinating (including carrots, radishes, etc).

First early crop

- Plant them in the second week of April; the traditional day to do this is Good Friday (unless Easter is late in April, or it is too cold).
- Make a trench 20 cm (8 in.) wide and 15 cm (6 in.) deep, putting the spoil to one side. This should be easy if you've dug in enough manure.
- If you're digging multiple trenches, space them 30 to 45 cm (12 to 18 in.) apart, and do the same with the spoil so that you have lines of spoil and trenches. Up this spacing to 60 cm (2 ft.) if you want bigger potatoes.

- Break up the soil that's at the bottom of the trenches and add in a spade or two of additional well-rotted manure.
- Plant the sprouted tubers (majority of sprout facing up) in the trenches, about 15 cm (6 in.) deep, spacing them 30 cm (1 ft.) apart.
- Ideally, sow a so-called catch crop of mustard over the top. You can eat this in your salads, and it's a good green manure that improves your soil. The mustard also acts as a biofumigant and helps to control eelworms and wireworms, which can both burrow into the tubers and create a network of holes.

Preparing a fine enough tilth
for direct sowing.

Second early crops and main crops

Plant these in the middle and end of April and early May, respectively. The same instructions apply as for first early crops, but increase the spacing to 40 cm (16 in.) between tubers and 75 cm (2 ½ ft.) between trenches. They are in the ground for a long time, and the extra space is needed for a larger crop.

Sowing Direct

April is the month when direct sowing starts. The soil in the garden is now warm enough and the hours of daylight have increased week by week. That's just what you want for regular and reliable germination outside. You can tell the moment has arrived by the sudden appearance of weeds. They're popping up all over the soil surface. It's a cue for you to get going with direct sowing. We start with carrots, radishes, lettuces, and the summer-cropping, heat-tolerant leaves.

Fava beans It's our last sowing of fava beans that can be made outside. "Stereo" is my favorite. It makes small beans with soft skins.

Peas On fertile and friable soil, you can start sowing peas outside from April. Sow in lines, but zigzag the seed in a pair of double rows, allowing room for pea sticks or a line of vertical netting to be added to support the peas as they grow. It's key (certainly in my garden) to cover the peas that you've sown with chicken wire tucked well in to enclose the lot, or the mice have a field day. My favorites are "Nairobi" and "Alderman."

Carrots If your soil is heavy, sow carrots into raised beds. In both cases, use carrot tape when sowing carrots. This is pre-sown seed attached to a paper tape that biodegrades quickly. All you do is make a shallow indentation in the soil, about 1.5 cm (½ in.) deep, roll out the tape, and cover lightly with fine soil, then water. It ensures nice, even seed distribution, less need to thin, and therefore less chance of drawing in carrot fly. Even so, we usually grow our carrots surrounded by Enviromesh to ensure a pristine harvest. Excellent varieties to sow now include "Early Nantes" and "Flyaway."

Annual salads For sowing summer salads—the more bolt- and heat-resistant crew such as lettuce "Reine des Glaces," "Black Seeded Simpson," and "Merveille des Quatre Saisons." Also summer purslane, saltwort, and sea beans.

Annual herbs Parsley is there for the picking, but it's now time to sow again, either direct or in a gutter (if you've not already done so in March). Sow dill direct from now onward too.

Edible flowers Tougher, hardy, annual edible flowers and companion plants can be direct sown now. Start with calendulas, *Salvia viridis* blue-flowered, borage (white and blue), nigella, and cornflowers.

Spinach and chard "Medania" is the best soft-leaved spinach we've trialled for April sowing. It's not quite as hardy as the red-stemmed varieties such as "Rubino," so it is ideal for sowing now.

Beetroot We grow three different varieties for their three different colors: "Boltardy" (purple), "Burpee's Golden" (orange), and "Chioggia" (stripy pink and white, known as candystripe), see p. 332 for more on these.

Parsnips and radishes Parsnips are one of the slowest vegetable seeds to germinate, which makes them a debatable vegetable to grow in my view. They do, however, make a good companion with quick and easy radish. Mix the parsnip seed in your hand with a pack of radish ("Cherry Belle" or "French Breakfast"). The radishes will germinate within a week or two and will mark your parsnip row. You can pull the radishes and eat them in 6 weeks, by which time the slow parsnips will just be beginning to show.

Tips on sowing direct

There are a few useful rules to bear in mind when sowing seeds directly into the garden. They all begin with "T," which makes them easy to remember.

Timing Get the timing right. And that's now. In most parts of the UK, the soil is now warm enough and not too wet or too dry.

Thin Sow seed as thinly as you can. Fava beans and beetroots have large seeds, while spinach has medium-sized seeds. Space the beans at about 20 cm (8 in.) apart and spinach and beetroot at 5 cm (2 in.). Carrots and most of the salads and herbs have small seeds, so you can't individually place these, but don't pour the seed straight from the packet or the palm of your hand. This creates a clump of seed in one place with too many tiny plants competing for light, food, and water, followed by a bare patch. For tiny seeds, take a small pinch from the palm of your hand and sow while moving your hand quickly down the drill. This will give you a thinner distribution of seed than if you are meticulous and slow. You need to mark the point where you get to so as not to miss a bit or go back over the same spot. I make a line with my finger across the drill to mark the point I have reached.

Thinning Most seeds start to germinate outside after a couple of weeks (parsley can be slower), and small seedlings will appear. When they are about 2 $\frac{1}{2}$ cm (1 in.) tall, get brutal. Thin them out, checking the back of the seed pack for exact distance. Water before and after thinning.

Dividing Perennials

April is the month to lift and divide perennial edibles such as all the hardy herbaceous herbs (chives, mint, sorrel, lovage) and toward the end of the month, the less vigorous ones such as French tarragon.

And this is the moment to take offsets from French artichokes. Taken in autumn, artichokes and tarragon will struggle if the winter is severe, so April is the ideal time, just as their growing curve starts to lift.

I had thought, with their Mediterranean roots, French artichokes weren't hardy enough to grow reliably here, but that's not true. I've got big French artichoke beds. In the south of England, they are usually evergreen, remaining bright and silvery through the winter.

You can also grow French artichokes easily from seed, but the problem is that they won't all come true. Propagation is best done by division. Most books advise you to get offsets from a friend. That's ideal if you only want two or three plants, and you have a generous friend.

Dividing perennial herbs
For evergreen and herbaceous herbs such as chives and mint, now is a good time to divide a congested clump.

- Dig up the whole clump.
- Slice off chunks from around the edges of the plant, discarding the center of the plant if it looks tired.
- Add plenty of organic matter to their new positions and replant.

Propagating French artichokes
With French artichokes, you do things differently, taking offsets from the mother plant, rather than digging the whole thing out of the ground.

- The middle of spring is the ideal time, when the mother plant has started to grow actively after a dormant season, but before it has started to fruit.
- Leave the main plant in the ground. The offsets are the distinctive satellite plants around the crown base. Slice one or two of these off from the outside of the plant, making sure there are some roots attached.

Artichoke offsets taken
from the edge of the mother
plant, cut down, and potted.
These will be planted once
the roots have reached the
bottom of the pots.

- Some gardeners advise planting these new
  plantlets straight into the ground but, in my
  experience, it's worth potting them to give
  them a bit of TLC under cover first. Cut the
  foliage right back and let them grow on in
  a greenhouse, well-watered and kept above
  freezing for a month or so before planting.
- Add plenty of organic matter to the planting
  hole before planting.
- Do not let plants younger than a year old come
  up to flower. Remove the flower buds as they
  form. This encourages the plant to put energy
  into root development and surviving winter.

Mulching

Our final garden job for April, once everything we want to get out is planted, is mulching deeply around and in between everything.

We garden on heavy clay at Perch Hill. When we arrived, we only had a small garden, but even that had a minimal topsoil of only a couple of centimeters on top of deep seams of yellow clay. We dug over, or tilled, our cultivated beds religiously, adding lots of grit as well as organic matter to try to improve soil depth and drainage.

Our soil structure is pretty good now. We don't want to go on disturbing life below ground any longer, so we moved to a no-dig system more than 5 years ago (see Charles Dowding's website for excellent advice on the no-dig technique).

These days, we mulch on top of our beds and around seedlings rather than digging it in. Even when we plant tulips below the winter salads for extra color, we have moved from trench planting to using a soil-corer bulb planter to minimize soil disturbance (see p. 364).

We cover the bare soil thickly with well-rotted farmyard manure or homemade compost. The key thing is not to use any mulch that might be full of weed seed, because it's going to sit on the surface of the beds. If you're using homemade compost, and your compost is turned regularly and your heap produces enough heat to kill the seed, you should be okay. Alternatively, you can use green waste compost.

People will say you shouldn't mulch if the weather is cold, as you'll be trapping the frost into the soil. We do wait if the ground is frozen solid, but then swiftly complete this major job before the weeds truly get going.

Making Frames

Making our own vegetable climbing frames and brassica cages from natural materials has a huge effect on the look and feel of the vegetable garden. We use tuteurs for many different climbers and arches for climbing zucchini, as well as upright hazel aisles for stronger-growing pole beans.

We use locally sourced silver birch or hazel for the supporting posts and a bit of bendy willow for arches. If the birch or hazel wood is harvested in February or early March, the sap is rising, which means the smaller branches will be pliable and not yet in leaf. That's ideal.

As well as the drama and beauty you can get with these instant frames, there's also their practical role. Climbers need climbing frames, and the more I grow vegetables, the more climbing varieties I seek out.

Many people choose dwarf varieties when they're short of space, thinking that small-growing things will allow them to pack more in, but I find the opposite is the case. If you grow climbers such as climbing (not dwarf) beans, climbing squash (such as "Tromboncino" and "Serpente di Sicilia") and tall, cordon tomatoes, they fill the space in the air, not at ground level.

Even if you're a container vegetable grower, with nothing in the ground, this principle applies.

And there's something else. Tall-growing climbers have a long-cropping advantage. If you chose tall-growing forms of things like peas (for example "Alderman," which gets to nearly 2 m / 6 ½ ft.) rather than small forms (such as "Lincoln," which is less than half that height), and also tall cordon varieties of tomato such as "Sungold" (rather than a bush-type like "Tumbling Tom"), then the plant continues to grow, climb, flower, and fruit or crop for much longer. This gives you a long, drip-drip harvest, rather than a sudden oversupply. I'd recommend climbers all the way.

Tuteurs can be made from bamboo canes, but they are nicer made from hazel or silver birch. The supporting canes or branches, referred to as uprights, need to be at least 2 m (6 ½ ft.) tall, but taller ones at around 2 ½ m (8 ft.) are even better, as you can secure them well by pushing them 30 cm (1 ft.) into the ground.

You can supplement these with smaller sticks pushed in between each upright around the base. With bamboo canes, you need to add a network of twine between the uprights to create an efficient

climbing frame, which doesn't look as good but does the job. For hazel and birch, you can use bundles of thinner side branches to wrap around the uprights. The twiggy nature of the thinner birch branches makes them the best climbing frame, giving the plants plenty of handholds on which to climb.

To make your own brassica cage, see p. 208.

How to make an aisle

- For aisles (pictured, p. 129), we use hazel. Go for branches that are 3 to 4cm (1 ½ in.) diameter and about 2 m (6 ½ ft.) tall.
- Uprights are placed at 1m (3 to 4 ft.) intervals and hammered a good 30 cm (1 ft.) into the ground. We do this from a ladder using a rubber mallet.
- Shorter hazel struts are added to strengthen the frame at each corner with some diagonal and/or horizontal bars for bracing and extra frame space for the plants.
- Jute netting is then attached, stretched taut over the hazel frame and secured with twine or flexi-tie.

How to make a tuteurs

- Whether using hazel, birch, or bamboo, push a circle of eight uprights into the ground, sinking them a good 20 cm (8 in.) deep. It's key to secure the tuteurs well into the ground. The inner circle should be about a 1 m (3 to 4 ft.) diameter. In a windy spot, we put another pole in at the center, and it seems to hold them even better.

- Gather the uprights together and tie with a robust flexi-tie or piece of twine at the top.
- If using birch, wrap the smaller branches around the structure. Start at one upright in the circle. Gather all the thinner side branches about 45 cm (18 in.) from the ground, and hold them together in your right hand. Twist the stems horizontally. Carry on twisting until you get to the next upright and twist the second bundle, binding and weaving it in with the next and so on until you get to the beginning again, reversing back on yourself to tie off any loose ends.

- Next, move 45 cm (18 in.) upwards and do another layer in the same way. For tall tuteurs, you may have room to add a third layer.
- We also make teepees with one long spiral from the bottom to the top, so the whole thing looks like a spiral slide. To do this, keep twisting in a spiral motion, gathering as you go, until you reach the top. Toward the top, you'll probably need to work from a stepladder.

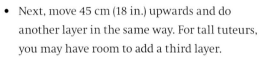

May

Early in the month, there's not much in the way of produce to bring into the kitchen but, within a week or two, things start looking up. We now have plenty of rhubarb, new salad leaves, and the lettuce that was sown in March, along with an array of herbs, early onions, and our number one productive crop: leafy greens. It's a top moment for a couple of different spinach varieties, plus Swiss chard. This is a plant that keeps on giving at almost any time of year, but it's now in May—and then again in September—when it is at its peak.

Toward the end of the month, we also have radishes. You need to eat these quickly once they're ready or the roots get too big, hot, and a bit spongy in texture. We grow "Caro" for its fresh, crunchy pepperiness (great for adding bite to a sandwich), and I also love "Cherry Belle" and "French Breakfast," the latter a classic with long, columnar roots ideal for dipping into anchovy mayonnaise. It's fun growing a mix of colors and shapes to serve as crudités. Radishes are at their best when the nights are a little cool, as they are now.

In the herb garden, I love to harvest thyme and some of its flowers. There are many different varieties. We start picking thyme "Jekka" first, one bred by Jekka McVicar, a herb expert like no other. It's invaluable for coming into active growth and flower early in the year and the perfect planting partner to lemon thyme or white-flowered creeping thyme, which perform later for a neat succession. They are robust and quick growing, which is rare—particularly, on heavy soil like ours. You can harvest it regularly and reliably through most of the May to September growing season. We cut all our plants back after flowering, and "Jekka" in particular, grows back quickly to flower again.

May is also about asparagus—a crop we all eagerly anticipate. When I'm teaching my day course, Year-Round Veg, more people ask me about growing asparagus than any other plant. We seem to particularly love it in the UK. I think this is partly for its exceptional taste but also because it comes at a time when there's a slight lack of exciting things to pick. It has become a vegetable garden classic that anyone with productive beds seems to feel they must grow. My view on asparagus is that, while it's lovely, it should not make it into a small garden. It doesn't earn its space. You need lots of crowns to supply enough for a decent meal, so it's better grown on a field scale. I'd say only consider it if you have surplus ground.

This is a time we use our indoor space to help us to force some crops a few weeks early. Night temperatures can still plummet, and any nascent warmth in the soil is spirited away. And there's still wind chill in May at Perch Hill. We find that with just minimal protection, everything grows at almost twice the rate in the first two or three weeks of May. As with Beaujolais Nouveau in the old days, and the fanfare around the arrival of the first Jersey royals, we can celebrate our own early, edible glamour parade by growing a few crops under cover.

Zucchini "Bianca di Trieste" (excellent for forcing a bit early in the greenhouse); pea "Nairobi" (a new must-have for forcing in the greenhouse in spring); carrot "Early Nantes" (grown from seed tape in the greenhouse); and radish "Purple Plum."

I know many of us don't have inside growing space, but even if you don't have a greenhouse, you can create a makeshift cover. Use a cloche, an extendable mini-polytunnel, or put something together that's a bit more makeshift. Before I had a greenhouse with enough space for indoor growing and propagating, I used to use straw bales covered with an old window (taken from a reclamation yard) laid over the top. It worked well. You'll find it's worth it when you come to pick baby zucchini, sweet salad potatoes or your first small carrots by the end of the month, a good 4 weeks early.

We seem to live in the greenhouse at this time of year. We have vertical space (not possible with a cloche), so we are also able to force peas in there. I love pea tips. We grow them throughout the year, but harvesting sugar snaps from the greenhouse is a new thing. We grew our first row of peas inside during the first lockdown in spring 2020. They were sown in a gutter in February and planted in the greenhouse in March. By early May, we were picking handfuls of sugar snaps almost every day. I've been bowled over by the variety "Nairobi." Its pods and peas are so sweet; they remind me of those minty, buttery petits pois you get in a French restaurant. They've shot into my top ten list of vegetables to grow for as long and as often as possible.

A tip for forcing spring greenhouse crops is to make sure that you have a clump of early-flowering salvias such as *S. viridis* (or *S. algeriensis* or *S. fruticosa*) in there too. These attract bumblebees, the vegetable gardener's best friend. Bumblebees fly out at about 5°C or 6°C (42°F), while most other bees (including honey bees) wait for temperatures to reach 10°C (50°F). If you watch them at work, you'll see that bumbles are thorough. They pollinate every flower—much more so than other bees. That's a good, natural way to increase your early indoor harvest.

As well as cropping from inside, we are busy planting in the greenhouse too. Zucchini go in first, then tomatoes by the middle of the month, finishing with chilies and eggplant. With all the half-hardy crops usually set to go outside by the middle of the month here in Sussex, May is also a busy planting time in the main kitchen garden.

Chard and Spinach

There's no doubt that if I was cast far away from my kitchen garden, and only allowed one packet of seed, it would be a chard—and probably the Swiss kind. Along with the similar (but in my view not quite as tasty) spinach beet, chard has the longest and most prolific cropping potential of any edible plant.

When harvested correctly (see p. 144), chard is cut-and-come-again, with an exceptionally long and steady pattern of production. It will even crop lightly through the winter (more reliably if given a cloche for some protection). Just as important, it is a great supplier in May. In our trials, we've recorded sixty colanders filled from a 1-meter-square patch in one season of harvest. That's incredible. It's a huge producer and reigns supreme in category 1, the big producers (see p. 17). It's also a plant that survives on neglect and an important player in what I call category 2, the "easy edibles" (see p. 21). If you picked occasionally, it slowly carries on producing new leaves, which unravel from the heart week after week.

The huge leaves flop too quickly for most produce stores to sell chard. I have occasionally seen it in a Turkish general store (they know how easy and reliable it is and, in Turkish cooking, it's used daily in filo pies and borek), but those sorts of shops are rare if you don't live in a city. Where I live, chard is in category 4, the "unbuyables" (see p. 25) and it can be pretty handsome too (category 5, p. 25). It's a plant that makes it into four categories: 1, 2, 4 and 5. Don't resist!

In terms of variety, the wide, white-stemmed Swiss chards (such as "Fordhook Giant") are arguably the tastiest with a brighter, less earthy flavor than the super-showy, multicolored rainbow chard. This stands up to winter here too. For summer eating, I'd change that and vote for the more drought-tolerant "Lucullus."

Some people find chard a little bitter and almost too iron-rich. I'd say, blame the chef—not the vegetable. Like spinach, chard is the perfect ingredient for tarts, gratins, soufflés, borek, or the Greek equivalent, spanakopita. I was brought up on chard in a

A basket of Swiss chard.

Bechamel sauce, perfect with roasted meat and potatoes. And it's excellent with pasta when cooked in a ten-minute sauce. All you need is a basket of chard (stems and leaves separated and then sliced finely and steamed), mixed with crème fraiche, nutmeg, black pepper, and plenty of parmesan. All in all, particularly at this time of year when we're still struggling to find fully garden-picked meals, we'd be lost without it. And it's so much easier to grow than spinach.

Spinach is a crop best grown on the shoulders of the main growing season. Sown in March, May is its peak production moment. Sown again in early August, spinach is perfect for September and October harvesting. It doesn't thrive in heat or cold, bolting fast in the sun and sulking in the frost. Now is its ideal time.

Our two favorites are spinach "Rubino," with crimson stems and veins, lovely picked small for salads or wilted at full size. This takes frost without a hiccup. Not quite as hardy but still excellent for spring and autumn is "Medania," a lovely deep emerald-green and super tender.

As we know from Popeye, spinach is a powerhouse of vitamins and minerals. You want as much as possible in your diet. The leaves are dark green because they contain high levels of chlorophyll, as well as the carotenoid lutein, a phytochemical that reportedly has anti-inflammatory and anti-cancer properties. Spinach is also important for healthy eyes, helping to prevent macular degeneration, the leading cause of blindness in older adults. If you want the ultimate take-care-of-your-eyes meal, eat spinach (or chard) and eggs together. You'll then get the maximum amount of fat-soluble pigments—lutein and zeaxanthin (another carotenoid)—from two potent sources, and the fat from the egg yolks will help your body to absorb them.

I think it's worth bearing in mind that spinach is one of the plants that, if conventionally grown, has a high pesticide residue. In fact, even after a good wash, it's been proven to be among the highest. That's another excellent reason to grow it rather than buy it.

With chard as your stalwart and spinach as your slightly trickier diva-vegetable, May meals can be a joy.

Harvesting Chard and Spinach

Chard

Chard needs to be picked in a certain way to last through winter and come into full production in spring. Cut just the outer leaves and leave the heart intact. Leaving the center allows more leaves to grow and fill out the plant again and again. In winter, you must not—as you can now—cut leaves down to almost ground level. If they are cut down in the winter or a cold spring, they will rot from the cold and damp and they struggle or die.

With chard harvested like this you encourage the plant to form what looks like a sort of tree—with a trunk from which a tuft of leaves grows from the tip. This lifts the leaves and heart away from the cold and clammy soil. With this technique, our autumn-sown plants will crop until the summer.

From now in late spring, when growth rates increase, we start to thin out, but, every so often, when the row or clump threatens to run up to flower, we take out the heart as well (see p. 39 and p. 62). If you get in there quick, you can usually stop the bolting. We do leave one or two to bolt, providing great host plants for ladybugs.

Spinach

Spinach does not form a heart in the same way as chard, but you still need to pick only the outer leaves until mid-May. Then you can harvest the whole plant at once, moving down the row, cutting to 5 cm (2 in.) from the ground. When the spinach is cropping at full tilt, we try to harvest it at least three times a week to keep it going. This helps to hold it back from bolting. Even if we don't want to eat it that often, we still pick it and freeze it. We find that, along with soft fruit and tomatoes, which are also hard to keep up with, it's one of the crops we freeze most. Its cropping window is quite narrow (unlike chard), and yet it is lovely to have spinach to eat all year.

When freezing either chard or spinach, I de-stem (not young spinach plants), roughly chop, and then blanch it in boiling water for a couple of minutes and then cool it instantly in a sink of very cold water. Once cool, strain and squeeze it hard to make palm-sized spinach nuggets. I spread these out on a baking tray to go into the freezer overnight. Once frozen, I bag them so they are easy to cook and eat (great for breakfast) straight from the freezer in portions.

Best of the chard

Even if you only have a deep window box or pots on a balcony or doorstep, you should grow some chard (Beta vulgaris subsp. cicla var. flavescens).

1 "Fordhook Giant"
In our trials, all the large white-stemmed, so-called Swiss chards seem pretty indistinguishable, but we go for the huge-leaved "Fordhook Giant." This is my number one chard: delicious, exceptionally long-producing, and handsome with it.

2 "Lucullus"
Bred in Australia, and with a pale green stem, this variety may not look as good as its brothers, but it's all-weather tolerant, including sun and drought. In the summer of 2018, we had week after week of unusually hot weather for the UK. All our chards bolted except this one.

3 Rainbow chard
We grow lots of this colorful type of chard (also look for cultivars "Bright Lights" and "Rainbow Chard") to pick up on the color of polyanthus and tulips in spring. With stems in red, yellow, orange, and white, this chard is one of the most ornamental edibles you can grow. Once its leaves are large, its flavor is not as clean as the Swiss chards, but this is an excellent crop picked as a baby or small leaf for salad.

Best of the spinach

As with arugula, the plants we know, grow, and call spinach encompass different families that are not even closely related.

1 Callaloo
Amaranthus retroflexus
In the amaranth family, along with quinoa, this is harvested not for its seeds but for its leaves. It is excellent for growing in May through to August as it gives you a leafy green when it's hot and dry. It's popular and widely grown in the Caribbean (in the UK, it's often known as Chinese spinach or common amaranth), as well as hot Mediterranean countries such as Turkey and Greece. There, you'll find it in many a back garden and used in kitchens in layered filo pies or pockets. It's served widely in summer as wilted greens or *vlita*.

2 *Chenopodium giganteum*
With a brilliant pink center to every leaf, that looks like it has been dusted with glitter, this plant is splendid when the leaves are young. As a baby leaf, it is a lovely raw addition to salad. Keep picking regularly to keep this fresh leaf flush, or resow little and often. Once fully grown, it looks like its relation fat hen (*Chenopodium album*), but it still tastes okay as a wilted green.

3 Japanese spinach *Brassica rapa* Perviridis Group
Also known as spinach mustard, this one is from the cabbage family and has long stems and large green leaves. The larger, mature leaves of "Hohei" are great for stir-fries, while the smaller leaves can be picked for salads.

4 New Zealand spinach
Tetragonia tetragonoides
A perennial sown in autumn, this is a massive, spreading cropper under cover and invaluable for huge leaf production. It is a good flash-in-the-pan wilted green. Grown outside, it can be harvested from June to late October, or until the first frost. There's something slightly slimy about it raw, but a few leaves added to a mixed salad are a good thing.

5 Spinach beet
Beta vulgaris var. *cicla*
This is a leaf beet, so it more closely resembles chard than soft-leaved spinach. It will grow slowly outside even in winter. You can increase production with a cloche or by planting it under cover. Like chard, this is low-maintenance and keeps on producing leafy greens on minimal TLC.

6 Red mountain spinach
Atriplex hortensis var. *rubra*
With a beautiful, rich purple-crimson leaf, this is as much an ornamental as an edible. It's good when picked young as a wilted green and raw in late spring salads. Once it has formed a flower spike, its leaves dull in color and become a little tough, so keep cropping regularly or resow. It is a prolific self-sower.

7 Spinach *Spinacea oleracea*
I love soft-leaved true spinach and find the elegant, red-stemmed "Rubino" survives frosts in the garden, so that's our main crop for winter. Sown in March for spring picking, we also grow "Medania" (pictured). There are slower-to-bolt varieties such as "Renegade" and "Toscane," which are better for the heat and dry of summer.

May

May is the month for mass planting. Once you are certain the frosts are over, even the half-hardies are safe outside. Every trowel, barrow, and watering can is constantly at the ready at Perch Hill. We move from what I think of as the kitchen garden's cold-weather season (October to April) to the warm season (May to September). See p. 12 for more on this.

What we do when varies a little from year to year according to the weather, but as a benchmark I always think to myself: if we're happy to have lunch but not yet dinner in the garden, our half-hardy edible crops are happy to be out there too.

May is also an important weeding time. Lots of annual weeds are coming up to flower very quickly, and they mustn't be allowed! We choose a morning—ideally after a night of rain (so the roots come up easily)—to start weeding using hands or hoes. If we can see from germination rates that a particular area of the garden is full of annual weed seeds, we also mulch heavily after weeding.

Cut perennial herbs such as chives, lovage, fennel, and oregano now, right to the ground and they'll be up again in a couple of weeks with leaves that look and taste fresh. If left to flower, chives tend to get rust and the flavor goes out of the leaf, so a May shearing is key.

Planning Your Planting

Sometimes, but not always, we have a planting plan to help us organize the barrowloads of seedlings that are coming out from the polytunnel. But even without one, we don't plant willy-nilly.

As we decide what to put with what, and where, we consider four things. The first is crop rotation, the second is color (aiming for some beautiful combinations), the third is the efficient use of space by intercropping where we can, and, finally, and most important for us, is the concept of companion planting. We've spent years experimenting with this. I am a great believer in its effectiveness.

1. Crop rotation

The driving logic behind the traditional system of crop rotation is first pest and disease control and second nutrient and mineral depletion. If you whack the same crop in the same place year after year, you will increase your chances of trouble on both fronts.

Yet we don't follow a classic four-bed crop rotation system. The main reason is that we don't grow similar volumes of the four main rotation groups (potatoes, other roots, legumes, and brassicas), so it's difficult to make this system work for us. Also, the bulk of the plants we grow are salads, herbs, and leafy greens, which are remarkably disease-free. In fact, several are known and grown as good soil-cleansers (such as several of the herbs and the mustards).

We find that mulching deeply with organic matter keeps the soil in excellent heart. By growing a wide range of different cut-and-come-again plants, neither persistent pests nor diseases become an issue.

Previous page **Planting**
bean seedlings with sweet
peas alongside a silver
birch support.

Instead, we keep records of where plants have been and, with certain crops such as potatoes, we don't repeat their position for 4 years. They take so much from the ground and have a tendency to attract pests such as eelworms, so moving them makes sense.

Similarly, if we get a problem with disease (for example, blight on outdoor tomatoes, or onion white rot), that crop won't go in the same spot again for a few years either. With the fungal spores able to survive on decaying plant matter over winter, and so there ready to reinfect the host plant, it would be asking for trouble.

To avoid the danger of club root—and so failure to thrive—our brassicas also need to be planted in a new place every year.

So instead of a pre-set system of rotation, we follow common sense. I've found that so far, for 30 years, this has been successful.

2. Decorative planting

The second strand we have in mind when placing and planting is to always have a colorful, decorative show. Edible flowers and companion flowering plants are planted as an under- and overstorey throughout the vegetables. You'll see that in all the pictures of the kitchen garden.

3. Intercropping

This system is about choosing to interplant a slow-to-crop plant with a fast-to-crop one. The fast one will have been harvested before the slow one needs the extra room. For example:

- As we direct sow very slow-growing parsnips, we mix in very fast-growing radish seed (see p. 125 for more on this).
- As we plant our brassicas, we often scatter viola seedlings below and interplant with lettuces. Lettuces like a bit of cool shade through the summer, which the brassica plants provide. We've picked from the lettuce and then taken the lettuce out (once bolted) by the time the kale or purple sprouting broccoli needs to be netted in a couple of months' time.
- When we plant tomatoes in the greenhouse, we spread carrot tape out in the spaces between them. The tomatoes act as a barrier, and they don't suffer. This gives us pristine carrots without carrot-fly damage.
- Last summer, we had success growing prolific dwarf pole bean "Hestia" up our sweet corn.

4. Companion planting

Most of us love the idea of companion planting. The concept suggests that by combining one plant with another, we can free a plant from the scourge of a particular pest or problem. Important to everyone here at Perch Hill are all type of bees, butterflies, and birds. We grow plant varieties to attract all three. That's partly down to wanting to reverse the persistent declines in their populations and partly because birds, butterflies, and bees are (mostly) helpful in a garden. Companion planting, combined with trying to take good care of our resident garden birds, means we can now produce healthy crops pretty easily *and* without the need for chemicals.

Below Two excellent
companion plants: hyssop
and *Tagetes tenuifolia*
"Red Gem."

Companion Planting

Companion planting has many different strands
that are worth exploring.

Camouflaging scents
Plants with strong scents can camouflage the
smell of precious crops that pests are attracted
to. This works best in a sheltered site, so the wind
doesn't carry the strong aroma away. We've had
good results with the following:

Marigolds combined with tomatoes,
cucumbers, chilies, and peppers This is a
pairing I swear by. In a greenhouse, particularly
where whitefly can rapidly build up, you want
marigolds at ground level and maybe even in
baskets hanging from the roof, so that the top
and bottom of the plants are both protected.
We grow the compact varieties *T. tenuifolia* "Red
Gem," "Tangerine Gem" and *T. patula* "Strawberry
Blonde" in baskets and pots so we can move them
around to best effect. I also love the handsome,
taller *T. p.* "Burning Embers" and *T. p.* "Konstance"
for planting between our edible rows. The flowers
draw in pollinators too.

Basil with fruiting vegetables, tomatoes,
eggplant, and chilies This is based on the
tradition of having bush basil on the table in
almost every Greek taverna. The strong smell of
basil, which is slightly astringent in leaf flavor,
acts like citronella and keeps the bugs at bay. We
have found swathes of basil seem to help to keep
our greenhouse tomatoes clean. We let some
basil plants flower as these draw in pollinators
and so increase pollination and harvest. In
Greece, basil is closely planted with eggplant
and allowed to flower to aid bee, hoverfly, and
butterfly pollination.

Scented-leaf pelargoniums to repel aphids
We've noticed that in the winter greenhouse,
when the pelargonium collection all comes
inside, unscented varieties can suffer terrible
aphid infestations, but the scented-leaf ones

Tagetes tenuifolia
"Tangerine Gem" forming
a companion-planting
carpet to help keep our
tomatoes aphid-free.

seldom do. We are going to try underplanting our tomatoes this year with pelargoniums to see if this successfully repels the aphids.

Summer savory with fava beans The aromatic herb summer savory prevents black bean aphid (blackfly) being drawn in. Planting the very old, traditional bean variety "Martock" (which is having a bit of a renaissance) among the fava beans is effective too. Blackfly prefer this to anything else. Combined with snapping off the tips of the fava bean plants, this has kept us pretty much aphid-free here for many years.

Direct sow summer savory all around your fava beans anytime from late March to May.

Mint to repel ants Mint is very effective if you have an ant infestation. It has been very successful for us placed on benches in the greenhouse. If the ants become a nuisance, just tear up a bunch of mint and scatter it around. Repeat every few days and the ants disappear.

Hyssop with kale We've also had success here with *Nicotiana tabacum*, the true smoker's tobacco, protecting our brassicas from cabbage

Garlic chives: the plant
most visited by bees in
our whole garden.

white caterpillars. The tobacco grows to a good 1 ¹/₂ m (5 ft.) to form a natural brassica cage, masking the cabbages and kales with its strong smell. However, you need a large garden to fit it in. To save space, we now use the very pretty hyssop to do the same job. It's much smaller than tobacco, and you don't need much of it. Only three or four plants in a 1 ¹/₂ m x 5 m (5 ft. x 16 ¹/₂ ft.) brassica bed have a repellent effect. If the brassicas are planted in May, come June and July the cabbage white butterflies coming in to land will get a whiff and move on.

Carrots with onions We've had less success with carrots and onions. The jury is out on growing carrots with any of the onion family. It hasn't worked reliably here. The late gardener Geoff Hamilton did controlled experiments with this duo and found no evidence that the onion gave any protection, backed up by more recent trials by no-dig organic gardener Charles Dowding. It's best to revert to Enviromesh or fleece around the edges of the carrot bed, stretched as a screen 90 cm (3 ft.) high. The carrot fly is a ground flyer and won't make it up and over the screen.

Attracting beneficial insects

Here I'm talking about the type of companion planting that draws in beneficial insects, rather than repelling the destructive ones.

Flowers to attract predators Two strong colors, orange and yellow, appear to draw in hoverflies, lacewings, and ladybugs, which are the best natural predators of aphids. At Perch Hill, we intersow kale with calendula for just this reason. The female lacewing larvae feed on its protein-rich pollen before laying eggs on colonies of aphids. Successional sow calendula or sow them once or twice, then follow up by introducing meadowfoam (*Limnanthes douglasii*) or marigolds.

Flowers to attract pollinators Almost all vegetables are insect-pollinated (with a few exceptions, such as sweet corn, which is pollinated by the wind), so

Perfect companions:
Calendula officinalis
"Indian Prince" and kale.

frequent visits by large pollinator populations ensure a better harvest. There are many examples of this that we've found effective at Perch Hill. Here are a few we make sure to plant:

- Basils Can be planted with eggplant (see p. 153).
- *Phacelia tanacetifolia* Easy to sow direct, quick to germinate, pretty in the garden, good for cutting and, most importantly, hugely busy with butterflies and bees.
- Garlic chives Grow as an edging to vegetable beds. It's a plants favored by honey bees.

- *Dahlia* "Bishop's Children" As well as being an excellent edible flower for our salads, this single dahlia is attractive to pollinators, as are the collarette, anemone-flowered and semi-double dahlias we grow.
- Sweet peas These are traditional attractors of pollinators in a vegetable garden. We plant crimson snow peas such as "Blauwschokker" with matching sweet pea "Lord Nelson" or "Black Knight."
- Salvias Early in the greenhouse and late in the garden, salvias attract the full range of pollinators.

- **Colorful flowery climbers** These are grown up on the same frame as our tomatoes and cucumbers in the greenhouse. Asarinas, thunbergias, and cardiospermums all thrive with the extra protection under glass and flower their socks off from midsummer until winter, drawing pollinators to all our fruiting crops (tomatoes, cucumbers, chilis, eggplant).
- **Verbenas** Those such as the compact *V. rigida* are great for edging edible plant beds. They flower for 4 or 5 months, are perennial and draw in tons of pollinators over their whole flowering season.

Attracting beneficial birds

Garden birds keep on top of the worst aphid attacks and have a great appetite for slugs and snails, so we consciously grow plants that birds use as food. We grow various varieties and species of each of the four below. Garden birds are attracted to all their seeds. The great thing about them is that, unlike a plant like teasel, they are not overprolific self-sowers and look great.

- Sunflowers
- Amaranths
- Grasses (such as panicums)
- *Nicandra physalodes*

Sacrificial plants

These are the plants that are so attractive to pests that they draw them away from your more precious plants.

Lettuce for slugs I've seen lettuces go to flower and seed around vegetable beds at Chatsworth. It is a sacrificial crop for slugs who eat these plants rather than the more precious things in the middle.

Nasturtiums with kale Nasturtiums secrete a mustard oil that insects love. They will seek this out in preference to any brassica. Nasturtiums in the greenhouse protect tomatoes and cucumbers against whitefly, as they will go for the nasturtiums first.

Just good companions

Then there are plants that are just generally friends. Planted together, they give you a better crop than each grown in isolation.

Cucumbers with sunflowers Cucumbers are excellent planted with sunflowers and supported on the same frame. The cucumbers luxuriate in the shade of the sunflowers.

Beans, sweet corn, and squash This is a renowned trio that indigenous Americans called the "three sisters." The corn provides the climbing frame for the beans—though under our typically grey skies in the UK, we've found the dappled shade in the center of a block of corn is not ideal for good bean production.

Parsnips and carrots with kale Grow plants with tap roots next to brassicas as they bring calcium from deep in the soil closer to the surface for better brassica leaf production.

Dwarf beans, beetroot, and potatoes Plant these in alternate rows; they will help each other to stay healthy and give a good yield. This is one we are still trialling.

Pest Control and Disease Prevention

We always bear a couple of things in mind when it comes to pests and diseases. First, healthy plants fight off pests and disease, so good soil and a good situation are key. Second, we always use green manures if no crops are due to go in. White mustard is one of the best, as it is a natural soil fumigant. With the weather warming up, it's also time to order biological controls for use outside and in the greenhouse. Be ready to introduce one at the first sign of whitefly to make sure your tomatoes, cucumbers, eggplant, and chilies remain free from pests for summer cropping.

Slugs and snails

It's time to think about slugs and snails and to make a plan to control mollusk attacks.

If you're only getting minimal damage, enclose slug-prone plants in a good moat of grit or oyster shells when you plant them out. If you have an army of either, go for a spray-on treatment such as the biological Nemaslug and concentrate it at the bases of hedges and around walls and steps, as nooks and crannies are where snails tend to live.

I made our first vegetable garden at Perch Hill after a visit to the beautiful productive parterre garden made by the late gardener Rosemary Verey

at Barnsley House in Gloucestershire. Inspired, I came back and planted lots of box cuttings. Three years later, I took the whole lot out, as not only did the box fill too much of my precious bed space (which I wanted and needed to grow food), but I realized that the dark, moist box was providing perfect day hotels for the mollusks. They'd emerge to a lovely dinner party I'd laid out for them every night. I witnessed it by torchlight again and again.

I think box-edged beds in productive gardens may look good but are a mistake. If you want one, go for an aromatic edging plant such as the annuals *Salvia viridis* blue-flowered or *Tagetes patula* "Burning Embers," or a semi-permanent lavender (such as the compact "Miss Muffet"), or rosemary "Miss Jessopp's Upright." We also use an edible-flower hedge such as dahlia "Bishop's Children."

Black bean aphid (blackfly)

Once the bean pods at the bottom of your fava bean plants are the size of a little finger, pinch off the tips. This helps protect against blackfly infestation and directs the plant's energy into producing a better crop. The tops that have been removed can be cooked and eaten. I love them wilted over a primavera risotto of baby vegetables.

Carrot fly

Carrot fly is the bane of carrot lovers like me. There are few more delicious things than a bunch of freshly pulled small carrots, just washed and steamed or boiled, but carrot fly can ruin all that. The adult carrot fly lay eggs at the base of the foliage. When they hatch, the grubs burrow down

into the root, munching as they go. This results in heavily channelled roots that don't make great eating.

There are many systems used to discourage these pests. We've tried intersowing with spring onions and garlic (not very effective in our trials, see p. 155). Growing carrots only in raised beds works pretty well, but the most fail-safe protection is to use carrot tape for sowing. The well-spaced seeds sit in the tape so there's no need to thin, and it's the smell of the thinning that attracts adult flies. We also enclose the carrot bed with a physical barrier (such as Enviromesh). Because the adults fly quite close to the ground, this prevents an infestation.

Flea beetle

Flea beetle is an important pest to bear in mind if you're planting arugula, mustards, or mizunas, which all are members of the brassica family. Brassica attack by mature beetles starts in April or May. In May/June the eggs are laid and the larvae crawl up the plants and tunnel in the leaves. In July/August, the next generation of adults emerge and it's these that cause the late-summer damage. They will overwinter in garden debris and start the cycle again the following spring.

The strongly aromatic plants of the *Artemisia* genus are good for confusing flea beetle. We grow so many brassica salad leaves we'd need a glade so, sadly, we need to swathe our brassica plants in fleece in May. Flea beetle will otherwise reduce our leafy lines to lace within a month or so. Or we just skip sowing for now.

In the Greenhouse

Planting in Greenhouse Beds

Before we start planting outside, we get the greenhouse planting ready for summer and autumn. Under glass, even with a light frost, plants are planted safely now.

Tomatoes

By the first or second week of May, with night-temperatures no longer plummeting, tomato plants can be planted in the greenhouse.

- First, dig in lots of manure to the planting soil to ensure good water retention and tip-top flavor.
- A tomato plant has superficial feeding roots that grow relatively close to the surface of the soil, as well as deeper water roots that quest farther in search of water. We use ring-culture pots to maximize plant production and flavor. These pots enable you to feed into a central, shallow chamber—where the feeding roots grow—as well as to water into an outer moat, which directs moisture deep into the soil toward the longer roots (see opposite). This way, there's no soil erosion or waste of feed, and the tomato flavor is not watered down.
- If you can't get hold of a ring-culture pot, you can use a recycled plastic bottle such as a water bottle or a detergent bottle. Cut the base off the bottle, leave the lid on, and pierce a few holes in the lid to allow water to drip through. Then bury the bottle, lid-side down into the

ground next to each tomato seedling. Angle it slightly to aim the lid at the tomato roots and then water into the base of the bottle. This will help with efficient watering once the plants really start to take off.
- Space your seedlings 60 cm (2 ft.) apart, so that the leaves of the fully grown plants don't overlap.
- Plant the seedlings quite deep into the ring culture pots (if using). The stem is usually purple to about 2 $1/2$ cm (1 in.) above soil level, so bury it to the level of the green stem to encourage the production of more surface-feeding roots, which will give you stronger, more prolific plants.
- Water in well.
- Water a patch in the greenhouse and then direct sow the companion basil or marigolds near your tomatoes (see p. 153). If you scatter the seed widely, you won't need to thin. Water again every couple of days and you should see germination in about 10 days.
- Our tomato frame is made from chestnut posts holding aloft a large sheet of steel mesh. It reaches about 2 m (6 $1/2$ ft.) high. You can make a similar frame to fit your greenhouse using five posts: make two A-frames and lay the fifth pole between the two to create a tent shape.
- Whatever size of frame you have, tie hop-bine string to hang down from the upper horizontal pole directly above each plant. The string should reach the ground. If you're using ring-culture pots, you can attach the

string to a hole that is usually on the pots. If not, make sure it is securely attached to the ground using a peg.

- As the plants start to grow, everything is in place for their pinching and training (see p. 202). It takes an average of 50 days from flower to fruit production.

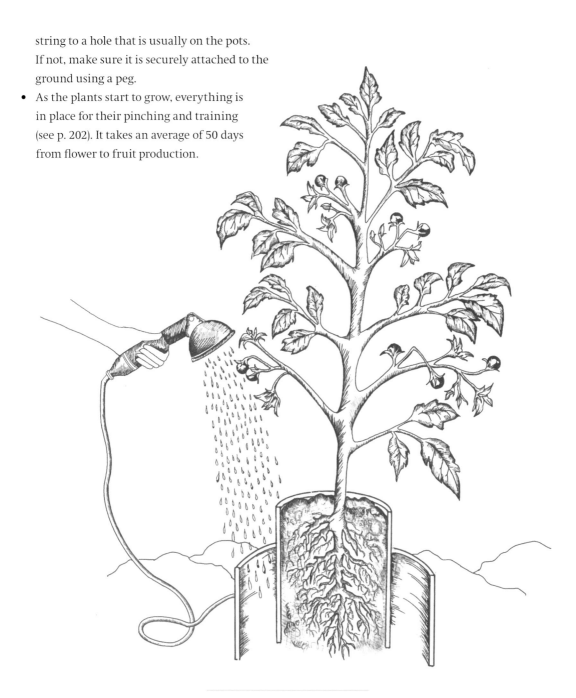

Eggplant

We plant half our eggplant outside toward the end of May, and half in the greenhouse at the same time as the tomatoes. My tried-and-tested two are both excellent for the British climate. The first is "Slim Jim," which is Asian in origin, cooks quickly, and is traditionally used for stir-fries. It is a bit too small for griddling. So for that, I use my second choice, the Mediterranean "Moneymaker No. 2." Space plants about 60 cm (2 ft.) apart.

Chilies and sweet peppers

These are the last crop to go into the ground in the greenhouse or polytunnel. The key to success with these is a good root system, which needs to get established early on. Then, they'll just take off and pretty much look after themselves.

- Select your plants carefully. You want the ones with a decent crown, like a tree.
- They benefit from manure. Ideally, manure has already been added to the planting soil a few weeks before. You can use ring-culture pots (see p. 160), but they don't seem to make as much impact as they do with tomatoes.
- Space the young plants widely. Go for 45 cm (18 in.) between plants and 60 cm (2 ft.) between the rows. Make sure there are good paths between the rows so that you can easily get in to harvest; otherwise, the plants tend to stick to your clothes as you walk through them and you'll tear branches off.
- Peppers (hot and sweet) both like a lot of potash. Douse them in comfrey fertilizer (see p. 206) every couple of weeks, at least initially. Reduce this as the season progresses.
- They also need staking, as whole arms can break off. We fix every plant to its own bamboo or hazel cane with a supporting cage of string. Do this about 45 cm (18 in.) above the ground, where they form their first fruiting branches.
- All peppers tend to succumb to aphids, but with the added tonic of comfrey fertilizer and companion planting (see p. 153) you will hopefully avoid it. The plants will be fine and continue growing and fruiting.
- They are susceptible to mildew and botrytis (hence the wide spacing), so keep an eye on them. We spray prophylactically with a chive remedy (see p. 207) to minimize problems.

Cucumbers

Our glasshouse isn't heated, but it does stay warm once the sun's been out, which makes it an ideal place to plant the cucumber seedlings that were sown in March. We do this in early May, but if you only have outdoor beds, see p. 165 for instructions.

Cucumbers are hungry plants and benefit from a good layer of well-rotted manure before planting. Lay it on about 10 cm (4 in.) deep and dig it in a little. Depending on the variety, cucumbers can climb from 1 $\frac{1}{2}$ m (5 ft.) to nearly 2 m (6 $\frac{1}{2}$ ft.), so we also add a large birch teepee for the plants to climb. Although they are planted in the beds, the ground is mainly compost and manure, so we only give them a seaweed feed once a week when the fruit starts to set. As soon as the fruits are big enough, we harvest them to promote more flowers.

In the Garden

Planting

May is a great month for planting vegetables outside. See pp. 120–22 for more on planting.

Beetroot

Beetroot (sown in gutters in March) is ready to go out. Once the seedlings are about 2 to 3 cm (1 in.) tall, follow the instructions for closely spaced seedlings on p. 121, ensuring they are 2 to 3 cm (1 in.) apart. To ensure crop succession, use the same gutter to sow your next lot of beetroot.

Lettuce

Lettuce sown in gutters in March are also ready for planting. It's key you don't let these get too big or at all rootbound before they go out. If so, they bolt.

Basil

Wait until the end of the month (once the very cold nights have passed) and then plant basil in the greenhouse with tomatoes, as well as outside.

Brassicas

If sown in March/early April, kale, kalettes, and purple sprouting broccoli will be ready to

plant now. Brassicas thrive at a pH 6.5 to 7.5, so some people lime their soil in autumn, as lime takes a while to take effect. Calcified seaweed is an alternative that lasts longer than traditional limestone.

- Brassicas also love a rich soil, so add plenty of well-rotted manure or mushroom compost in the planting hole.
- Allow plenty of room between plants—about 60 cm (2 ft.).
- Firm soil is also essential. Brassicas are tall plants with shallow roots, so they need a compact soil to help them stand upright. Before planting, bash the soil down with the back of a spade and walk over the soil again and again. If your trowel bends when digging the planting hole, then the soil is just about firm enough. After you've got your plants in the ground, do the same again, trampling the ground around their roots with your feet.

Zucchini and squash

Toward the end of the month, you can safely plant summer and winter squash in most areas of the country (earlier with protection).

- Pick the site. Their large leaves make them vulnerable in exposed situations, so they need a position in full sun and shelter from the wind. Zucchini can go in first, and pumpkins and squash a little later.
- In a windy site, it's worth investing in a few bales of straw to place as temporary windbreaks. These will help plants get established a couple of weeks earlier than they would without this shelter.
- They love a rich soil, so plant them out with lots of manure at their roots. Traditionally, squash is planted on top of a compost heap. If you can't do this, dig a large hole—to at least a spade's depth and a good 45 cm (18 in.) across— and add a couple of spadefuls of manure. Then, cover with the soil you've dug out to create a mound. In the middle of the mound, plant your seedling. The manure helps with feed as well as water retention, which is key for good cropping. The mound also helps rain to run away from the seedling leaves during the plant's first vulnerable couple of weeks.
- Before planting, place the pot or pots in a barrel of water to take up water. This ensures that they go into the ground good and moist.
- Spacing depends on what variety you grow, but most need to be about 1m (3 to 4 ft.) apart.
- Climbing zucchini and squash, such as "Tromboncino," need a structure to support them. One plant will spread out in all directions and cover at least 2 m (6 ½ ft.). To contain them, grow them up over arches and frames.

Beans (pole and French)

We plant our beans from the middle to the end of May. These go alongside a frame such as a bean maypole, tuteur, or hazel arch over a path. The advantage of an arched support over a walkway is that you can see all the beans.

With a tuteur or maypole (which looks great), you must remember to harvest the beans hanging in the center of the structure. Left on, they will reduce further bean production.

- All legumes are hungry and thirsty, so dig a good, deep hole. Try to reach 30 cm (1 ft.) for each pair of plants. Do this alongside the posts of the supporting structure.
- Almost fill the hole with peat-free compost or manure. The manure acts like a sponge and releases food and water at the legume roots.
- Cover over the manure with a 15 cm (6 in.) layer of soil to protect the youngest roots from the richness of the manure.
- Water the holes and plant one seedling to each post, spaced at 15 cm (6 in.) around the base of the structure, and around 5 to 7 cm (2 to 3 in.) away from it. If planting in an aisle, alternate your planting either side of the frame.
- Tie each seedling into the base of the post using twine or flexi-ties. From there on, they will climb the support themselves.
- Mulch. Mulching helps to feed the roots, retain moisture in the soil, and protect against slugs by encouraging blackbirds. If you mulch with your own garden compost, you will encourage ground-feeding birds to come and dig around in it for worms, slugs, and beetles.
- If you have a big problem with slugs, surround your plants with slug prevention, particularly at the early growing stages. We use a 30 cm (1 ft.) wide strip of horticultural grit that is about 3 to 4 cm (1 $\frac{1}{2}$ in.) deep.

Eggplant

Eggplant do well growing outside in a warm, sheltered spot. They also thrive in large pots. We sometimes put three plants together in a large pot. They crop well and look marvellous.

- They need to be gradually acclimatized to the more varied conditions outdoors, so harden them off before planting.
- Enclose a block of plants, spaced about 60 cm (2 ft.) apart in each direction, within a box of straw bales. These provide a cheap and effective windbreak, that can be transformed into a makeshift cold frame by adding a glass sheet or old window over the top.
- If a cold night is forecast, drape with fleece weighted with bricks.

Cucumbers

If you don't have beds in your greenhouse for cucumbers (see p. 162), plant seedlings at the end of May, when the risk of frost has passed. Add a good mulch of manure before planting, at least 10 cm (4 in.) deep. We train ours up and over a hazel dome so the cucumbers hang below for easy picking. The shade created by them is then ideal for growing summer salads such as mustards and mizuna, which bolt quickly in the heat.

Outside, plants tend not to need the weekly feed, as they benefit from the nutrients in the soil, but if they are in large pots, feed them with a seaweed feed once a week when the fruit starts to set. As soon as the fruits are big enough, harvest them to promote more flowers.

Earthed-up potatoes.

Sowing Direct

At the same time as planting seedlings, we direct sow a few things too (see p. 96 and pp. 124–5).

French and pole beans
I particularly love the very slim and tender French bean variety "Speedy." Sow a row at about 2 ½ cm (1 in.) deep and spaced at 15 cm (6 in.) in a staggered double row, with six extra seeds sown at the end of the row as insurance for nongermination.

Radishes
As you eat the radishes transplanted from gutter-sown seeds, direct sow another crop.

Carrots
You'll read and be told that if you sow early or late in the year, you miss the main flurry of carrot fly and your carrots then avoid being destroyed by the maggots that burrow down into the roots. We've tried almost every system and still get damage. Growing carrots can be a nightmare, particularly on heavy clay soil like ours. See p. 124 and p. 158 for sowing and protection tips.

Potatoes and earthing up

May is the classic month for planting main-crop potatoes (see p. 176 and pp. 122–4 for advice), and now is also the time for earthing up the early crop, which are starting to sprout. This needs to be done when the plants are about 10 cm (4 in.) high.

Earthing up means piling the soil from around the plant up over the plants to form a ridge along the row. This stops the tubers that are near the surface from going green in the sun. It also encourages more roots and so more tubers. Some people like to use grass clippings or homemade garden compost to earth up their potatoes. This also ensures the soil is extra fertile and will retain more moisture. Earthing up will also protect the potatoes from frost when they first emerge from the ground and later from the sun.

Potatoes do need plenty of water to get a high yield but, if it is taste you are after, do not overwater. They can usually find enough for themselves as they are quite deep-rooted plants.

Container Planting

May is the moment to plant tender things such as lemon verbena and scented-leaf pelargoniums in your summer and autumn edible containers. These plants can put up with a few chilly nights. I recommend waiting until the end of the month before planting basil and tomatoes outside. Edible containers could be a book in itself, so I'm just touching on them here.

- To help with water retention, soil-based compost is the best thing to use, though it is more expensive. You can add water-retaining capsules. We have found these rot roots in wet summers, so I'm wary of them, but they are excellent in hanging baskets.
- Be creative with what you plant to give a good balance in a large pot. I choose an upward-growing variety to plant in the center. I call this the pillar (such as pole bean "Hestia" grown with some support). Then, I add a downward trailer around the edge, which I call the spiller (such as tomato "Texan Wild," which is a micro-cherry. And finally, I use a third plant to fill in between the gaps. This filler can be something like basil "African Blue."
- If you have limited space, plant edibles and ornamentals in the same container. Go for tomatoes combined with a deep, rich and beautiful marigolds such as "Burning Embers," which will help protect the tomato against whitefly and look good.
- In a deep container, pole beans work well with sweet peas. The scent of the sweet peas will attract pollinating insects and help to set bean pods.
- Whatever you choose, add slow-release fertilizer into the top 2 $\frac{1}{2}$ cm (1 in.) of compost.

June

June is a triumphant month in any garden and especially so in the vegetable plot. Without much bother, you can pick an array of produce from just outside the door.

Huge excitement hangs around the first harvest of new potatoes, which are so much more delicious when freshly dug. It's like pulling all the best prizes from a lucky dip. Burrow away with your hands and you'll keep finding treasure. Whether you're six or sixty, it's always a thrill. I think potatoes are the place to start if you want to get children into growing.

We have forced potatoes growing in containers in the greenhouse, which we dig out and eat in the first week of June. By the end of the month, we are harvesting potatoes from the garden. We dig up the early crop up when the flowers have opened.

With the forced ones (if we are feeding several people), we turn out a whole bag at a time, emptying it into a wheelbarrow. But if there are just a couple of us, we try the "milking" technique: we lift the planted compost bag out of its container (in this case, buckets and baskets, which are there to hold the sacks upright and look good), cut off a bottom corner of the bag, and put our hand in from the bottom to harvest only what we need for that meal. This means we can continue to water from above and (if the root system hasn't been disrupted too much) the plant should continue to grow. Even if it doesn't, the potatoes can be stored there very happily and taste better than if lifted and stored. New potatoes turn green super-quick and the flavor rapidly deteriorates, becoming slightly musty. Dig and eat; that's the thing with new potatoes.

While we're on potatoes, let's not forget mint, which is up and growing strongly now. There are many different forms—from Moroccan mint (this is a spearmint, *Mentha spicata* var. *crispa* "Moroccan"), with almost hairless leaves and an intense sharp flavor that is often used for mint tea, to downy *M. villosa* var. *alopecuroides* Bowles's mint, which we usually use when boiling our potatoes. Mint can take over, so we usually grow ours either in pots or quite bleak spots, such as by the polytunnel, where it can happily take off.

At the start of the month, we are harvesting zucchini from plants inside. Within a couple of weeks, they're joined by a crop from the outside plants. The first are somehow always the best. I usually hate bowls of mixed vegetables with one or two exceptions. I think the sweetness of a baby zucchini, sliced lengthwise and sautéed for just a minute or two before adding a handful of sugar snaps and then fava beans, gives you one of the best June kitchen treats. The smoky, slight bitterness of the fava beans contrasts well with the sweetness of the zucchini and sugar snap peas, all at their tender best. And if sown under a cloche or in the greenhouse between our tomatoes, we have baby carrots to add too. Served as a simple bowl of vegetables, or in a primavera risotto, this June combination is hard to beat.

For great crunchy bowls of summer salad, we've also got lettuces aplenty. Our favorite for summer is spring-sown "Reine des Glaces." This is like an "Iceberg" in texture, sweet and easy to grow, but unlike an "Iceberg," you can harvest it leaf by leaf if you want to. We mix "Reine des Glaces" in lines with the bronze "Merveille des Quatre Saisons," a stalwart for any month of the year.

As the weather becomes mild, it's oddly trickier to find flavorful varieties of salad leaves to mix with lettuce, compared to the depths of winter. Many of the more interesting-tasting leaves bolt quickly in hot and dry conditions and are peppered with flea-beetle holes. The ones to go for now are wild arugula (which fares better than the fleshier salad arugula), plus maybe saltwort (*Salsola soda*, often known as monk's beard), some sea beans and summer purslane. I'd add in a slow-to-bolt mustard such as "Wasabina" for guaranteed punch, just a few torn up leaves to a bowl. These five plants are all happy in summer warmth.

For a perfect salad, you also need soft green herbs. There is nothing lovelier than French tarragon, which is growing at full tilt now. This is my desert-island herb. It transforms fish, chicken, and egg-mayonnaise salad, and is ten times better than cress in my view.

Finally, for June, we have a sparkly array of edible flowers. They won't keep the wolf from the door, but they do make food—and particularly salads—look prettier. We plan to have two or three different varieties and colors to pick every month of the year, but in June that rises to twenty or thirty. There is a mass of options. As well as zucchini, there are baskets of roses, sweet Williams, anchusas, cornflowers, salvias, borage, marigolds, and all the garden pinks. By the end of the month, we add nasturtiums along with pole bean flowers, which both have fantastic flavor. We also start to pick tons of dahlias for our salads, such as the single dahlia "Bishop's Children," which lines the main grass path running alongside the greenhouse.

Potatoes

We love new potatoes in our family—so much so, we have done five trials over the last 25 years to keep up to date with launches of tasty new varieties. We force them inside in March so that we can start harvesting in June, and give plenty of space to them in the garden too.

I remember seeing Monty Don on *Gardeners' World* once, digging up his first new potatoes in June and almost running with them into the house where he already had a pan of minty, salted water ready and boiling. That may sound excessive, but it's true the sugars in these varieties of potato change quite rapidly to starch, so it's best to eat them as fresh as you can. With the right varieties, you then truly have vegetable-garden caviar.

I love them just dug along with other June vegetables: some just-pulled baby carrots, fava beans harvested as small as possible, and maybe a pile of sugar snap peas. I serve them without meat or fish, but with hollandaise sauce or a family favorite called Angelica sauce, which is basically a salsa verde (anchovies, capers, green olives, lots of green herbs, extra-virgin olive oil, and red wine vinegar) with the addition of three or four hard-boiled, coarsely chopped eggs. It's filling and utterly delicious, and the freshness of all the produce is the key.

Potato groups

Depending on when they are planted and ready to harvest, potatoes are divided into three groups: first early crop, second early crop, and maincrop varieties. If you plant one or two from each group, you ensure a good succession.

We get going with the first early crop in the first or second week of April; they take 9 to 16 weeks to harvest. Second early crop is planted by the middle of April; they take 16 to 17 weeks to harvest. Main crops are planted toward the end of April and into May, with a longer maturing time of 18 to 20 weeks.

Potatoes for forcing in a trial.

Best of the potatoes

Having done several potato (Solanum tuberosum) trials here over the years, we have found that many widely available varieties are quite unexceptional in taste and texture. We couldn't really tell the difference between bought or homegrown. The ones I've selected offer something a little unusual. Of course, one handsome potato looks much like another, so we have not included a picture of every variety listed here.

First early crop

These are for harvesting from June to July.

"Arugula"
As its name implies, this is quick to grow and early, with a very white skin and neat, round shape. We find they go green quickly, so they should be eaten as soon as you harvest.

1 "Sharpe's Express"
This is one of our new favorites with delicious waxy yellow flesh and nutty flavor. The skin tends to come away on cooking, so they are possibly best par-boiled and then steamed, and it's lovely baked or peeled and roasted.

2 "Winston"
This is great for delicious, creamy mash or large, quick-growing bakers with good flavor.

Second early crop

These are for harvesting from July to August. It's this group that gives us most of our favorites for forcing in bags early in the greenhouse.

3 "Anya"
Bred from "Pink Fir Apple," this was our number one in our forcing potato trial. It has smoother tubers, so it is easier to use and yet features the same wonderful nutty texture and taste. It's also highly resistant to scab. Its seed potatoes are expensive, but they are worth it.

4 "Charlotte"
The standard multipurpose potato. If picked small and young, it's quite waxy with yellow flesh and good flavor. If left in the ground to grow on, it becomes a good size that you can use for roasting and mash. That's why it's so widely grown.

5 "International Kidney"
This makes long, white-skinned potatoes with a waxy, cream flesh. It can also be grown as a main crop. This came joint second in our forcing trial.

6 "Kestrel"
This is long and white-skinned with distinctive purple eyes. It is good for roasting and frying. We like this one because it is a good all-rounder, midway between waxy and floury.

"Linzer Delikatess"
The favorite potato of my cooking heroine Rose Gray of the River Café. It is reminiscent of "Charlotte"
but with smoother, longer, thinner tubers, that are waxy, pale yellow, and have a really delicious taste. They also give a good yield and store well.

Main crops
These are for harvesting from August to September.

"Axona"
This newly bred variety with pink skin and creamy white flesh is resistant to blight, or certainly more than most. It gives a heavy yield of large spuds that are good for baking and mashing.

7 "Pink Fir Apple"
This is our long-standing favorite potato with nutty texture and excellent flavor even months after lifting. It is late and so is thought to succumb to blight, but this is only because it tends to still be outside in late summer and autumn when blight is rife. Forced early inside, this makes fabulous summer eating. It's also a great storer.

"Ratte"
Another early main crop, this classic French salad potato produces numerous small, nutty tubers. We steam these in their skins and eat them hot or cold.

Zucchini

If I was sent off to a desert island and had to grow my own food, I would try to smuggle some zucchini seeds with me. As long as I was able to find a fresh water supply (they like plenty of water), I would be guaranteed delicious meals for a good 3- or 4-month stretch.

With bright sun, all you then need is some decent soil. The whole squash family—zucchini included—love good, rich growing conditions and are often plonked right on top of a compost heap to grow happily there. The slowly decomposing compost gives off a gentle heat, that evens out the day and nighttime temperatures, keeping the seedlings cozy as they grow, as well as giving the roots a plentiful supply of nutrients.

The fruits first appear now, in June, and that's when they feel the most luxurious—particularly when eaten *really* small. On size, I was educated by the great teacher and chef, Rose Gray of River Café. I remember the day she came to do a cookery demo at Perch Hill. She rejected any zucchini bigger than a thumb, from the wrist to the tip, as the measure. This seemed like infanticide to me at the time, but she's right. Zucchini picked at this size are seedless, nutty, thin-skinned, and a little reminiscent of artichoke hearts in flavor. Left to their own devices, zucchini grow abundantly. The more you pick, the more new ones will grow, so it's baby zucchini all the way for us now—particularly as you can almost never buy them at this size.

I recommend going for one plant of all three zucchini colors if you have the space: a dark green, pale green, and a golden yellow. The best dark green zucchini is "Romanesco," with its characteristic ribs from tip to stalk. For a pale, eau-de-nil, I like the early-cropping "Bianca di Trieste," and for yellow the French "Soleil." Just harvested, all three have a dense and nutty texture, especially when picked small. It's rare that you'll find all three to buy in the shops, so when they arrive on the plate, their message is loud and clear: we are homegrown! Whether you serve them raw, sliced finely in lemon juice and olive oil, straight from the

Zucchinis "Bianca di Trieste," "Soleil," and "Defender." It's key to harvest the yellow zucchini when they're still young and small.

griddle dressed in a little mirin and garlic, or in a typical green filo pie. The flecks and splashes of the colors will make your dish seem all the more delicious.

With the climbers and sprawlers, such as the weird and wonderful summer squashes "Tromboncino," and "Sunbeam" (a yellow patty pan), you should harvest and eat the growing tips as well as the fruit. These two are like giants, growing outward or upward at half a meter a week to a span of 5 m (16 $\frac{1}{2}$ ft.) or more in the right growing conditions. You can leave these ones to carpet a whole bank with their undulating edged leaves, or do as I do and train them up over arches, tying the new growth in every 10 days to encourage them to reach the apex of the arch so that the fruits hang from the frame over your head. They thrive in the same growing conditions as dahlias, which form an excellent lush backdrop to their vertical lines. Either way, flat or vertical, do occasionally pinch off the growing tips. You can harvest them when about 10 cm (4 in.) in length. They make a delicious addition to an omelette with mascarpone or cream cheese.

For all zucchini, keep the soil moist in a dry spell to avoid problems with mildew and harvest very regularly. If you go away for a week or two and the fruit swells, on your return you must harvest everything from the plant to spur it on to produce more zucchini through the rest of the season.

And, of course, with all zucchini varieties, the flowers are delicious. It's worth having a few plants for the flowers alone. In this case, pack them much more closely together than usual, at half the usual spacing—so about 45 cm (18 in.) apart. This stresses the plants and spurs more flower production. From mid-June, we harvest flowers by the basket-load. People tend to feel that harvesting the flowers will disrupt the crop, but not if you pick mostly male flowers and leave the female flowers to grow on. The male flower opens straight off a stem, whereas the female flower will have a baby zucchini at its base (you can pick this too). So as not to bruise them, harvest the flowers one by one and lay them out carefully in a basket. When you want to cook them, open the flower and remove the stigma, which is the short, stout yellow pillar at its base.

To replicate one of my favorite summer recipes, stuff zucchini flowers with a heaped teaspoon of cream cheese mixed with pine nuts and thyme, then twist each one at its tip so that the petals seal each other. Dip them in a fluffy batter and deep fry.

Whether on a desert island, allotment, or in an urban high-rise, zucchini should be at the top of any home-grower's vegetable list.

Best of the zucchini

Zucchini (Cucurbita pepo) are half-hardy annuals that we sow in March for forcing inside, and in April for planting in the garden. They divide into two groups: bush, which need spacing at 80 cm (2 ½ ft.) and form clumps; and sprawling, which are best planted 1 ¼ m (4 ft.) apart, or even better with a climbing frame. This latter group need snapping once their triffid-like tips reach 2m (6 ½ft).

Bush

1 "Bianca di Trieste"
This is a pale, eau-de-nil variety with short, stumpy fruit that is ideal for stuffing. It's also noticeably early. We often like to force it in the greenhouse for cropping from May.

2 "Boldenice"
Of the round types, this has a dense, tight, nutty, and tasty flesh that avoids being watery. They're made for stuffing. Cut in two, remove the seeds and a little flesh, and add the latter into a pork mince or veggie mix to stuff back in.

3 "Defender"
This is a standard, dark green zucchini. It's available to buy in the shops but rarely small enough to be at its best. It has some natural protection against mildew (which the leaves of all zucchini tend to suffer from toward the end of the season), but mildew doesn't usually curtail production in zucchini anyway.

4 "Romanesco"
My favorite variety with the nuttiest texture and taste. It has a mid-green color, immediately recognizable by the prominent ribs down the length of each fruit. This has an RHS Award of Garden Merit, and rightly so in my view.

5 "Soleil"
A heavy cropper with golden yellow skin, this is the one to pick as small as you dare, as the skins of all the yellows tend to get tougher at an earlier stage than the greens.

6 "Zephyr"
A so-called "crookneck" variety, this is much more widely grown in the United States than in the UK, which is a shame as the fruit is dense and tasty in texture and flavor, and good for succession as the plant is later-cropping than most. We can go on picking it well into October.

1

Sprawling / Climbing

Strictly speaking, these are squash, but like many gardeners we treat them like zucchini.

1 Patty pans *Cucurbita pepo*
These come in greeny-white and yellow shades and are shaped like flying saucers. We harvest them young and soft-skinned to use like zucchini in salads and stir-fries. Some plants we allow to expand and ripen (see p. 327).

2 "Serpente di Sicilia"
Lagenaria siceraria
Not only do these gourds look good, they make a tasty soup and stir-fry. More people ask about their large, white flowers at our summer and early-autumn garden openings than anything in the flower gardens. We now pretty much always grow this to trail over our fences and hedges, but you need room. It's not one for small gardens.

3 "Tromboncino" *Cucurbita moschata*
This is a bizarrely shaped variety that often ends up looking like a trombone at full size. It is technically a summer squash, but can be treated like a squash. Unlike any other squash, it is a vigorous climber that produces lots of tendrils by which it attaches itself to a frame—we grow it to make use of vertical (rather than ground) space. The other great thing about it is that the fruits, when eaten young, have good flavor and texture, but if you leave them to grow on, they are still delicious. The skin hardens and ripens to a coral-tinged yellow, transforming into a winter-storing squash with a waxy texture and good flavor.

Edible Flowers

One of my favorite summer sights is a bowl of salad scattered with petals, brilliant splotches of color contrasting with the greens. We love edible flowers here, and it's rare that I walk into the school kitchen when there's not a just-harvested tray of flowers or petals sitting on damp kitchen paper waiting to be used in one way or another. It's now, in June, that the range really balloons.

As a grower of cut flowers, I experiment with edible varieties. At Perch Hill, we've tried as many roles for edible flowers as we can think of. We've had a go at crystallizing primrose and rose petals to add to cakes (a bit fussy for me), making ice-bowls (pretty, but a lot of effort), studding ice bowls with flowers, and adding borage petals to cubes of frozen olive oil for cold soups. We've also created clear fruit jellies scattered inside and out with petals, which are truly splendid. Beyond the edible, we've also used marigold petals to make calendula cream, the most effective homegrown remedy for kitchen burns and insect bites I know.

These are all good ways of using edible flowers straight off the plant, but we cook with them too. We all know about stuffed zucchini flowers (good, if you're cooking for just a few people), but we also harvest lots of calendula buds and dip their whole growing tips into a light tempura batter. I've made the same dish using foraged wild calendulas (common marigold) from the foothills of the Dolomites, in the Veneto in Italy, served with an aperitif. I love recreating it here in early summer when the plants are at their youngest and most tender. Marigold, zucchini and borage flowers all have enough nooks and crannies to hold plenty of crispy batter. Served with a segment of lemon, it's one of my favorite June-garden dishes.

Some edible flowers have a distinctive flavor. Pole bean flowers taste very beany, while nasturtium flowers are peppery and sharp. Nasturtiums don't usually flower until late June. In addition to using them in salads, we add them to mashed potato (great for fish cakes) in place of black pepper. Many salvia flowers taste

A joyful June harvest of baby zucchini, nasturtium, and pole bean flowers.

good and sort of pineapple-like, which makes them particularly suited to cocktails and drinks. I love to add herb flowers to salads and soups to enhance flavor. Dill flowers look and taste good, as do arugula, fennel, and chive flowers.

All this is enough to make me want to grow edible flowers and, along with herbs, they are one of the easiest crops to concentrate on if space is limited. The more I learn about eating flowers, the more I think there may be other, less fanciful reasons to justify giving them space. In Charles Flower's excellent and useful book on restoring wildflowers to the fields and meadows (*Where Have All the Flowers Gone?*), he tells of how farmers used to hugely value the presence of wildflowers in their pastures as a source of supplementary minerals for grazing livestock. The reason for this was that many of the more common wildflowers—bird's foot trefoil, common (or lesser) knapweed, field scabious, common sorrel, and yarrow—have deep tap roots that grow into lower layers of the soil profile than grasses, thus making different minerals available through their flowers and leaves. He has dairymen's records that describe animals entering a new field of perennial rye grass and heading straight for the edges of the field to pick at the wildflowers in the hedges. We've seen this happen ourselves with the cattle on our farm. We open a gate into a new field and they almost always gallop to the hedge and browse there first, often devouring flowering nettles before anything else and completely ignoring the lush grass.

Of course, our human diet is incredibly varied these days. We are not faced with monochrome grass day after day, but even as a visual signal of diversity, there's nothing more enhancing for a salad or a bowl of rice than a sprinkle of edible flowers.

Calendar of edible flowers

Select one plant (at least) to grow from each of these seasonal blocks to make sure you've got flowers to pick all year.

January & February
Viola, polyanthus

March Viola, polyanthus, fava bean 'Crimson-flowered', Chinese violet cress

April Viola, polyanthus, fava bean 'Crimson-flowered', Chinese violet cress, sweet cicely

May Viola, polyanthus, Chinese violet cress, sweet cicely, borage, calendula, sweet William, elderflower, rose, chive, wild garlic

June Viola, borage, calendula, cornflower, sweet William and all dianthus, rose, chive, pelargonium, salvia, hyssop, lavender, zucchini, nasturtium

July Viola, borage, calendula, cornflower, sweet William and all dianthus, rose, chive and garlic chive, pelargonium, salvia, hyssop, lavender, zucchini, nasturtium, monarda, evening primrose, marigolds, pole bean, dahlia

August Viola, rose, chive and garlic chive, pelargonium, salvia, hyssop, lavender, zucchini, nasturtium, monarda, marigolds, pole bean, dahlia, basil, sunflower, evening evening primrose

September Viola, rose, garlic chive, pelargonium, salvia, lavender, zucchini, nasturtium, monarda, marigolds, pole bean, dahlia, basil, sunflower, evening primrose, chrysanthemum

October Viola, rose, garlic chive, pelargonium, salvia, zucchini, nasturtium, marigolds, pole bean, dahlia, basil, sunflower, chrysanthemum

November & December
Viola, rose, pelargonium, salvia, nasturtium, dahlia, chrysanthemum

Clockwise from top left
Edible flowers in spring (polyanthus); summer (marigolds, borage, nasturtiums and violas); winter (*Viola tricolor*); autumn (dahlia petals).

Best of the edible flowers

1 Borage *Borago officinalis*
This is the classic late-spring/early-summer flower, and we grow both its blue- and white-flowered forms. Its starry flowers are pretty, often to be seen decorating drinks in advertisements. They are said to have a mildly cucumber-like taste, but I'm not convinced. Many plants in the borage family are edible, including garden anchusa (*Anchusa azurea*) and the flowers of that rather pernicious and invasive weed, alkanet (*A. officinalis*). All these are true royal-blue flowers in the top spot for adding prettiness to desserts and ice cubes.

2 Chinese violet cress
Orychophragmus violaceus
This is not well known, but one of my favorite edible flowers for early in the year because you can eat all parts of the plant. The flowers are mauve, deepening in color as the weather warms, and the leaves and seedheads are good too, with a mustardlike taste. We grow this inside to ensure late winter/early spring picking, and plant it outside in March for an April and May.

3 Chive *Allium schoenoprasum* and *A. tuberosum*
We grow ordinary chives for purple flowers (*A. schoenoprasum*) and garlic chives (*A. tuberosum*) for starry white pompoms. Both are favored by butterflies and bees. The flowers of both taste like a mild version of the leaves: in the case of ordinary purple chives, mildly oniony; and in the case of white garlic chives, a little more reminiscent of garlic. (For more on chives, see herbs on p. 82.)

4 Common marigold
Calendula officinalis
This cheerful, classic cottage-garden plant offers a range of yellows and oranges in early summer. My favorite is "Indian Prince" with orange petals and a rich crimson back. Pulled apart, the flowers give you orange petal strands, which look good over a bright lettuce salad, or added to pilaf and risotto. We also now grow "Neon" especially for these purposes (as well as for making a topical calendula cream). It has twice the number of petals of any other variety we've trialled. Calendulas tend to suffer from mildew in dry weather, which you can prevent by dousing them fortnightly with chive spray (see p. 207).

5 Cornflower *Centaurea cyanus*
For edible flowers, we grow a mix of colors from crimson-black and white to pink and blue—some a single color and some with frosted tips to their petals, like "Classic Magic" (pictured).

6 Zucchini flowers
All varieties provide plenty of flowers, but "Defender" and "Nero di Milano" are the most prolific flower producers in my experience. Pack the plants tightly at about half their usual spacing, so at 40 cm (16 in.) or so, as under stress the plants flower more prolifically.

7 Nasturtium *Tropaeolum minus* **and** *T. majus*
From now until late autumn, nasturtiums are the thing. They taste the strongest of all edible flowers, and all parts of the plant are delicious. If protected against the cabbage white butterfly with fleece or netting, the young leaves can be added to salads, and then the buds and flowers can be used as the plants. We use the buds in the same way you'd use capers. The current general favorite seems to be the dark-flowered and dark-leaved "Empress of India," but I prefer "Tip Top Mahogany" for the wonderful contrast between its deep red-brown flower and bright green leaves. It looks good in the garden and mixed in food. The one thing to say about nasturtiums is that they can spread like wildfire, so take care where you plant them. They love poor soil too.

8 Primrose and polyanthus *Primula*
You can pick any of the primulas—any primrose, polyanthus, or cowslip—from very early in the year. The modern varieties flower here on and off throughout winter into spring. If we have a few very cold or wet days, they falter, but they perk up again with a bit of sun. They really come into their own in March and April and become prolific flower producers. We find some of the newly bred polyanthus varieties, such as "Stella Champagne" (pictured) and "Stella Neon Violet," are incredibly long producers, starting to flower in November and still good for picking now. I also love the old-fashioned *Primula* "Gold-laced Group" and the similar, newly bred, massive flower producer, "Victoriana Lilac Lace." As woodland-edge plants, these are happy growing in sun or dappled shade, and they like moisture at their roots.

9 Rose *Rosa*
Every rose petal is edible, so pick your favorite color and perhaps a variety with good scent. Use them to decorate cakes and desserts, crystallized or not.

10 Pole bean flowers
These are beautiful flowers with a bean flavor (see p. 224).

11 Sage *Salvia*
We grow a great range of salvias here, with at least one flowering every month from May until December. Most have the typical sagelike taste, but a few are fruity, such as *S. elegans* "Scarlet Pineapple." Others taste of black currant and are great for adding to desserts. There are hardy annual varieties (such as *S. viridis*) and a huge range of tender perennials and subshrubs. All are favored by our pollinators. The buzz of bees around a good clump can be loud on a sunny day.

12 Sweet William and pinks *Dianthus*
All dianthus have that famous clove fragrance, which is particularly strong in certain varieties of garden pinks and pretty much all the carnations. They're all good to eat. We use them from May to December, starting with sweet Williams (we grow "Electron Mix" as a brilliant cut flower with large stems, and a side crop of individual edible flowers over a long season); garden pinks, like the highly scented "Mrs Sinkins"; and then later in the year, carnations grown from seed, such as *D. caryophyllus* "Chabaud Benigna."

13 Viola *Viola*
These are classic edible flowers to sow and grow all year, including winter. The more you pick, the more they flower. They're easy to grow from seed and can be in bloom in 8 weeks from sowing—almost whenever you sow them. The small-flowered violas are better as an edible flower than the large-flowered pansies, which feel like you're eating a wad of felt when you hit one in a salad. I love the stalwart British native, *V. tricolor* (or heart's ease). This and *V.* "Phantom" Sorbet Series both make fantastic winter-into-spring croppers. For spring into summer, add "Antique Shades" and "Tiger Eye Red." I sow them inside, widely spaced into seed trays and transplant into the garden straight from there. You can also sow direct from April to September, and they then self-sow. These are happy growing in very poor soil or even in the cracks of a terrace.

June

With most of our planting completed, June starts to feel a bit calmer in the kitchen garden. There are always odds and ends still to get planted, but we try to clear the polytunnel before thinking about sowing for the autumn, winter, and year to come.

June is about creating cages, supports, and frames for plants that have gone out in the last week or two. That's the main June job and I love it. The garden already has vertical structures in the form of tuteurs and arches. These were made in April from willow, hazel, and silver birch before the climbers were planted in May.

It's now that we move on to making brassica cages and staking all the taller perennials such as French artichokes and dahlias, as well as purple sprouting broccoli and kale.

Because we grow an organic garden, we love plant teas. These homegrown fertilizers and tonics help to keep our plants vigorous and free from pests and diseases. June is the main month for concocting them with everything growing at full tilt.

Previous page, from left to right Tying in tomatoes; homemade brassica domes protect purple spouting broccoli; cucumber tied into a cane.

Tomato Care

My favorite early-morning job for June, whatever the weather (as this is almost always in the greenhouse), is pinching off, training, and sometimes feeding our tomatoes.

Pinching side shoots and defoliating

We keep on top of pinching off the side shoots of indeterminate (cordon) tomatoes. Toward the end of June, particularly if there's any hint of aphids or whitefly, we will start defoliating. This means removing the leaves up to the first truss (flowering/fruiting stem). As the weeks go on through July and August, we remove more and more leaves to help with good air circulation and better fruit ripening.

Determinate (bush) tomatoes don't need pinching or defoliating, but do check which form you're growing before you settle on how to train (or not train) it. See p. 258 for definitions.

Training

You can train tomatoes in various ways. You can support indeterminate varieties with a cane at their side (pictured on p. 200), regularly tying them in. Alternatively—and this is what we now do at Perch Hill—you can secure a length of twine (we use hop-bine string because it is thick and strong) at the base of the plant and also on to a pole above it. We use ring-culture pots so we secure the bottom end of the string to a small hole in the pot and top end to a pole of rebar,

supported within a frame. For more on setting up a frame and ring-culture pots, see p. 160.

The tomatoes are planted close to the string, and as they grow, two to three times a week, we pinch off the axillary buds and twist the leader (the top shoot) around the string, so the vine is strongly supported as it grows. You can spot the axillary buds and shoots, even when they've grown quite long, as they are usually a brighter, fresher green.

Once a tomato vine reaches the top (usually in late June or even July), we pinch off the tip to encourage fruit development and ripening.

Cherry tomato training

We also train our cherry tomatoes, particularly "Sungold," in a specific way. This variety is such a long cropper, still lovely to eat right into winter, that we don't follow the usual technique of pinching out the tip. Instead, we leave our plants to reach the eaves of the greenhouse and then (where we would usually pinch off) we allow the leader and then two side shoots to develop at eaves' level, and we don't pinch those either.

The main stem continues to grow straight up and over the tomato support frame, but will need pinching soon, before it gets too tall and out of picking range. The side shoots we train by turning both at right angles to the main stem, in opposite directions to each other. By mid-autumn, we'll have harvested all the fruit from the vines at the lower level, but with these three continuing shoots still cropping, we're often picking "Sungold" from up in the air until the middle of November.

Below Pinching off an
axillary shoot; training a
tomato vine using string.

Pinching out a tomato
plant's axillary shoots.

Watering

For tomatoes in the greenhouse, we drip water
from our irrigation system into the inner
circle of the ring-culture pots for 2 hours every
morning for a week to get the new tomato plants
growing. Then, we move the drip waterer to the
outside ring where it's on for 3 hours through
the rest of June and July. From August, we cut
down the drip watering to hour a day so that the
ripening fruit has more flavor. If you don't have
an irrigation system, use a drench system, such
as a rubber pipe with lots of tiny holes in it (or, in
our case, a pipe with regularly spread water jets)

left on for several hours just once a week. Then,
you can almost forget the plants until you see the
first fruits in July, when you will need to decrease
the watering.

Feeding

All these fruiting plants need a regular potash-
rich feed. Feed when they start flowering and
every 10 days or so. We have experimented with
other methods. One year, we didn't feed the
tomatoes at all, but instead spread 4-year-old
manure at a depth of about 10 cm (4 in.) around
the plants. The results were fantastic, with no
yellowing leaves on the plants.

Blight

Blight is a disease that affects the fruit of tomato
plants, resulting in rot. Keeping tomatoes free
from blight depends on a few things. The first
is the variety you are growing. Certain varieties
seem to have better natural resistance to blight,
such as "Stupicke Polni Rane." The second factor
is under-cover protection. We have not had
blight on our tomatoes here for 20 years because
we grow them inside. And, finally, good air
circulation is crucial, which is why defoliating
the bottom of the plant is a good idea. It helps
prevent fungal spores proliferating by reducing
the risk of a humid, moist environment.

In the Greenhouse

Seeds to Sow Now

There are only a few groups of plants to sow now.

Polyanthus and primroses If sown in early summer, these flower 5 to 6 months later for winter and spring. As perennials, they are also very easy to divide once you've got established clumps. If you already have plants, dig up a clump and tease different root sections apart. Next, replant the sections in pots until they've rooted through the holes in the bottom, and then plant.

Sweet Williams These are biennials we use as edible flowers. Sow into a seed tray (see p. 54) in June and plant in August/September.

Florence fennel Many of us tend to sow bulb fennel too early in the spring. It will be trying to bulb up at the hottest, driest time of the year in July and August, which encourages it to bolt, not bulb. It's safer sown now into modular trays or guttering (see p. 57) before planting. (You can also sow direct, see p. 96 and pp. 124–5). If sown now, bulbing will happen as we enter the cooler months of autumn, which should give you delicious, meaty bulbs that won't be stringy either raw or cooked.

Sow two seeds to each cell or every 15 cm (6 in.) along the gutter. If both germinate, thin to one, leaving the seedlings to grow spaced well apart. Transplant to the garden (or greenhouse)

4 weeks after they have germinated. When planting, earth them up a bit (gather the soil in a mound around the stem) as the root bulbs start to swell at about 8 to 10 weeks.

In the Garden

Using and Making Plant Fertilizers

We have made comfrey and nettle fertilizers at Perch Hill for a while. The first is rich in potash, the second in nitrogen. Potash is necessary for good root, flower, and fruit formation, while nitrogen is the major component of chlorophyll needed for photosynthesis and plant growth. It's what you want for creating lots of new leaves. You can use them separately or mix them together for a more broad-spectrum feed. We have recently added chive spray to our preparations. This contains sulphur (a natural fungicide) in its mineral make-up, which helps to keep plants fungus-free.

Comfrey fertilizer
This is good for root, fruit and flower formation.

Tomatoes We use it to feed tomatoes every 10 days from the start of June, which is usually when they have started to flower well.

Beans and peas Along with sweet peas, these thrive with a high-potash feed, which encourages flowering and podding and reduces the chance of mildew at the same time.

Compost Use it to reactivate a compost heap. Water the heap well and then sprinkle on some comfrey juice in its concentrated, not diluted, form. Alternatively, you can spread the comfrey leaves straight on to the compost in layers.

Nettle fertilizer
This is great for overall plant growth.

Pots We use it as a foliar feed for our plants in pots, particularly for hungry plants such as brassicas. We add it once a fortnight starting about 4 to 6 weeks after planting, essentially once the compost's own nutrients start to become depleted.

How to make comfrey or nettle fertilizer
- Cut the comfrey or nettle plant back to the ground. It will grow back quickly for a later harvest. Gather up all the stems and leaves in a garden basket or wheelbarrow.
- Chop everything up (you can include the flowers) and pile it into a box, bucket, or water barrel. Ideally, your container will have a tap in the base, so you can extract the liquid. A lid is useful as the mixture starts to smell as it breaks down, but any watertight container is fine. Odd as it may sound, one of those wine or beer boxes with a tap at the base works well. Cut the cardboard top off and make a small hole in the bag, which you can then stuff with leaves. Whichever container you are using, cover the leaves with water (filling up the container) and add a lid (or secure with a peg, in the case of the wine box). Then, leave somewhere outside.
- Leave the mixture to steep for 3 to 4 weeks.
- Strain off the liquid and store in bottles somewhere cool and dark. Alternatively, just take the liquid from the mixture as and when

you need it, always topping up your container with water and plant material.

- To use the concentrated fertilizer, dilute with water to a ratio of about 1 part tea to 10 parts water, then apply to the plants. We do this in a watering can and pour it liberally over the roots of the plant every week or so.

Chive spray

This is a great natural fungicide.

Sweet peas This is useful for keeping mildew at bay. Spray on once the plants start flowering properly—usually, in early June.

Calendula These tend to get mildew in a hot, dry spell. We've found this chive remedy, used liberally, will delay this but not prevent it.

Zucchini It's too late once the plants have mildew, but a fortnightly dousing is effective as prevention. Pour on the chive liquid from the end of June for plants inside and end of July for those outside.

How to make chive spray

Unlike the comfrey and nettle fertilizers, this does not need to be fermented. Chop up the chive leaves, cover them in boiling water, and allow the mixture to steep. When the liquid is cool, strain the liquid and use it straight away, at that strength, sloshing or spraying it liberally over the foliage and stem of the plant being treated, covering as much of its surface area as possible.

Creating Crop Cages

It's in June that you need to make sure your brassicas are protected from cabbage white butterflies, as they start to increase in numbers now. Instead of an off-the-shelf brassica cage, we make ours from homegrown black bamboo and silver birch, and always use black netting rather than white. It's much less visible and the frame looks beautiful and architectural.

We have a couple of huge clumps of bamboo in the Oast Garden that need thinning each year. The thinnings are perfect for making these arched frames, but you can use any pliable branches from your garden. Don't worry if the branches have leaves; you can just strip them off.

How to make a crop cage
You'll need about eight lengths of bamboo or pliable branches (uprights) that are roughly 1 1/2 m (5 ft.) long. You might need more or less depending on the size of your frame, but you will always need an even number of uprights. You'll also need tightly meshed soft netting (enough to cover the structure) and U-shaped metal pegs.

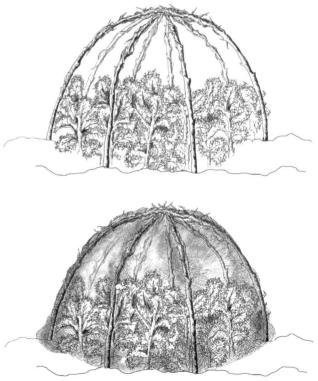

- Create the outline of your cage by pushing the uprights in a circle and at least 30 cm (1 ft.) deep, so that they don't spring out when you start to bend them.
- If you want straight, tall cages for tall brassicas such as kale "Redbor" or kalettes, secure just four uprights at four corners and then attach additional uprights to create arches from the four corners. This square formation will require more netting but will allow extra headroom for your plants as they grow.
- For compact kales, you can use just the uprights, aiming at about 1 $\frac{1}{4}$ m (4 ft.) apical height.
- To form an arch at the apical section, join two opposing uprights at the top by pulling together and aligning them as they meet, side by side. Secure tightly with flexi-tie.
- Add in further lengths of branch on each side by the same method to form arches across the width and length of your cage, making sure that they are all tied at the same height.
- This will give you an arched frame over which to stretch your netting. Use pegs to secure the netting to the ground. Be careful not to leave any gaps as determined cabbage white butterflies will find their way, and you'll have created a perfect, safe habitat (with no birds) for the caterpillars. Also make sure the leaves don't touch the netting, as the butterflies will lay their eggs from the outside.

Staking

Heavy-stemmed plants such as single dahlias grown for pollinators and edible flowers, kale, kalettes, purple sprouting broccoli, and French artichokes, will now all have grown so much that they will need staking as early in the month as you can manage. Tomatoes, which are happy outside now, also need staking and training (see p. 202). On a smaller scale, dwarf beans often crop best with a short stake.

We use flexi-tie for most of our staking, as it is gentler on the plants and has a bit of elasticity and give, which prevents breakages. It's also easy to undo and reuse. I have a bag of previously cut lengths in the potting shed that I take out with me around the garden.

Staking advice
- It's best to stake each plant individually with a stake and flexi-tie or twine. We use willow or hazel sticks knocked firmly into the ground. Place them 5 cm (2 in.) away from the bottom of the main stem. Check the final height of the plant you're growing and support them with a loop at both one-third and two-thirds of its final height.
- You can also support a group of plants together by pushing stakes around the outside of the plants and then using twine or flexi-tie to zigzag in and out from the center to create an enclosing cage.

Opposite Hazel uprights to support fava beans, with willow woven between them and flexi-tie threaded from one side to another.

- If you want to loosely attach the plant to the stake, use a clove hitch. This knot is ideal for staking as, once attached, it stays in place and never slips, unlike a normal granny knot. A clove hitch is a knot worth learning. Start with a forward loop of twine or flexi-tie, right over left, followed by another forward loop next door, which then looks like two rabbit ears. You then tuck ear two behind ear one. (Just tuck, do not rotate them.) That double loop then goes over your stake and you twist the longer end of twine onto the plant with a figure of eight, looping it back on to the stake.
- Don't pull the stem tight up to the stake or it will snap in even a light breeze. The figure of eight means that there's a layer of twine to act as a cushion between the stem and stake; it also gives more support than a straight loop.

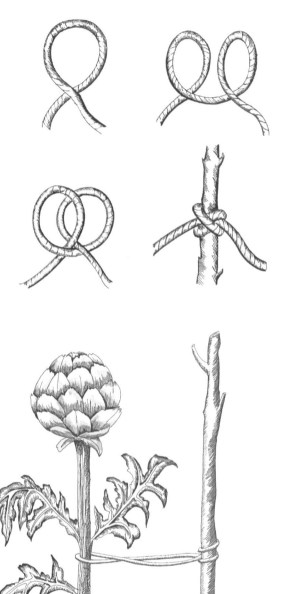

July

When I think of an ideal July in the garden, I picture an avenue of sweet peas lining our garden paths with a basket of just-picked vegetables sitting underneath. This includes baby zucchini with their flowers still on, a few beetroots, the first early tomatoes (my favorite, "Sungold," is usually ready now), and some yet-to-become stringy baby pole beans. Add in a French artichoke or two, some lettuce, fava beans, carrots, and bunched herbs for tea (not just for cooking), and you've got my perfect vision of July's garden produce.

July is a big month for teas (or rather tisanes) here, most often made with the leaves of plants like lemon verbena, pelargoniums, mint, and chamomile—mainly on their own, but increasingly combined in a blend. We serve them in a clear glass teapot—a so-called tisanière—and they look as good as they taste, with a few leaves of this and a flower of that.

I also love French artichokes at this moment, dismembered with the base of each scale dipped into lemon butter, or even better into a salsa verde made from a garden harvest, with a coarsely chopped hard-boiled egg added in. When I was a child, we used to holiday in the medieval hill town Asolo, an hour or so from Venice. My love of artichokes stems from my time there. Several times a week, we'd go to one of those splendid markets which moved through the towns nearby—Castelfranco Veneto, Bassano del Grappa or Montebelluna—and buy a bag of three different varieties, all of which I now grow.

The first to crop at Perch Hill is the delicate "Violetto di Chioggia." If you pick it as a baby and strip away some of the spiny outer scales, slice what's left thinly (downward through the pared-down stalk), and marinade this in olive oil, lemon juice, and plenty of salt for half an hour. This process makes the artichoke tender enough to eat raw. Then there's my personal favorite: the big, fat, green one called "Green Globe"—the classic for eating boiled, as it comes, with a dressing. And finally, the late-cropping French variety "Gros Vert de Lâon," is grown for its huge hearts alone.

I'd always thought French artichokes weren't hardy enough to grow reliably here, but that's rubbish. We've got large French artichoke beds. Here in the south of England, the plants are usually evergreen, looking fantastic, bright, and silvery even through the winter. In fact, they look so good for so long that way they make ideal plants to integrate into a mixed border. Even if you don't have a large vegetable patch or allotment, you could still grow a few. In terms of productivity, it's true to say that, measured per square meter, the yield is paltry, but these plants are drought-resistant and very low maintenance. If you cut them back at the end of July (just as they start to look ragged), their huge silver leaves romp up almost instantly. This not only gives you new leaves but also induces a second crop for eating through the autumn.

It's usually in early July that we pick, braid and store garlic, shallots, and onions. These aren't cut-and-come-again, but I love

Previous page An uplifting July harvest of zucchini, beans (the start of the pole beans and end of fava beans), spinach, lettuce, carrots, and tomato "Sungold."
Opposite French bean "Blue Lake" making its way up its birch frame.
Below Carrots, beetroots, and beans getting into their stride with cosmos and dahlias lining the paths for the pollinators.
Next page The vegetable garden in July with pole beans and sweet peas aplenty. In the background, the hay has been cut in the fields.

the neat vertical spires they add to the free-flow form of the kitchen garden. They give a bit of structure, like punctuation marks, which is aesthetically needed. In my view, there's no point growing ordinary old white onions. You can buy them anywhere. We grow the super-sweet varieties such as "Rossa Lunga di Firenze," which is fantastic in tarts, easy to grow, yet difficult to buy. We also grow shallots: "Jermor," for its mild, sweet flavor; "Griselle," which has a strong spicy sweetness; and the robust "Longor." They all store well into winter. And I love the spring onion "North Holland Blood Red." You can eat this as a red-skinned spring onion. Any you don't pull at the pencil stage go on to form mild, sweet, bulbing onions that also store quite well. It's versatile, tasty, and very easy to grow from seed. In terms of garlic, elephant garlic is a personal favorite. Its flavor is mild enough to be grated raw over a salad to give it bite without the classic garlic aftertaste.

Finally, we have an avenue of different pole beans, a handful of each, grown here in the summer and early autumn more for their flowers than the beans.

Beans

Climbing beans—pole beans, French beans, and drying beans such as cranberry beans—have three main assets in a vegetable garden.

First, they provide Jack-and-the-Beanstalk verticals. You'll probably have lines of carrots, beetroot, lettuces, and radishes at this abundant time of year, but you need some vertical growers to break that up. Like trees and shrubs in a garden, beans make the place feel balanced and beautiful. Last year, we made teepees for three varieties of pole bean ("Polestar," "White Lady," and "Painted Lady"), which stood well over twice my height. We did them as a sort of joke, thinking we'd lop the tops off at some stage, but the beans rapidly romped right to the top of their climbing frames and looked superb. Standing as high as the hedge around them, they gave almost instant structure and architecture, which is so often lacking in a productive garden.

Their second asset is that they give you huge square-meter productivity, so even if you are only able to grow in pots or on a balcony, these should be included. Pole beans, in particular, but also French climbing varieties such as "Blue Lake" or "Blauhilde," are prolific. That's why when you're driving through the countryside in summer, its pole beans (and zucchini) you'll see most often next to the honesty box at the end of the drive.

When we trial vegetables at Perch Hill, we measure their productivity relative to how much space they take up and for how long, including the time it takes for them to get to cropping size. With pole beans, they're right up there jostling for the highest position with other massive producers such as chard, kale "Red Russian," and the cut-and-come-again salads. They'll give you countless meals and yet require almost no TLC. Plant them with generous amounts of organic matter in their planting holes and they'll grow 30 cm (1 ft.) a week. Farmyard manure or rich kitchen compost is ideal as they need plenty of nitrogen to enable their rapid growth curve. In fact, gardeners have been known to dig trenches in April and throw in raw kitchen waste. Covered with soil, this then rots down gently and supplies nutrients and minerals just where and when the bean roots want them.

Towering pole bean
"Painted Lady."

There's one last asset that I can't miss: you can eat the flowers as well as the beans. I'm obsessed with edible flowers in the garden, rarely serving a salad at any time of year without a topping of colorful flowers. So if you're sick of pole beans, don't be. Just pick the flowers from the plants instead. They taste deliciously beany. If you grow four different colors as we do—"Sunset" (coral pink), "White Lady" (white), "Painted Lady" (red and white), and "Polestar" (scarlet)—you've got color as well as flavor.

One last important thing to remember with pole and French beans: if you're finding it difficult to keep on top of the harvest and some are getting away and growing huge and tough and stringy, pick the lot. Bring them in and shell them. Then, cook up the swelling beans (rather than the whole pods). Cooked gently in lots of good olive oil in a dish like a ratatouille, you'll find them so delicious that you'll want to grow beans for this harvest alone. Cropping all but the smallest babies on the plants will also spur on a whole new flush of flowers, which you can eat or leave to develop into a new generation of tiny and tender beans. Eat your late-season pole beans at the size of your middle finger and it's like enjoying a whole different vegetable.

Opposite Pole bean "Polestar."
Below From left to right, the pole bean flowers of "White Lady," "Polestar," and "Sunset."

Best of the beans

Beans (Phaseolus) are renowned as hugely prolific producers, and it's true. We find that even if we harvest the flowers quite hard, we still get plenty. These all look great growing in the kitchen garden and are delicious in the kitchen.

Pole bean *Phaseolus coccineus*

1 "Hestia"
This is my semi-dwarf pole bean of choice. It is excellent for deep pots and containers. We grow it in large water troughs that stand outside the cookery school. With bicolor flowers in red and white, it is also very pretty.

2 "Painted Lady"
We have found this climber to be the most prolific flower producer, going on to produce huge quantities of slow-to-become-stringy pole beans.

3 "Polestar"
A classic allotment climbing runner, with scarlet flowers and stringless, tender beans, it is well known and much loved for its quick crop and reliable production.

4 "Sunset"
This soft salmon-pink climbing runner is new and is lovely growing in an aisle with other colored beans. We use whole vines (with flowers) as trailers in our cut-flower vases. The beans are great picked young and tender and are slow to toughen. "Aurora" is another coral-pink variety, almost indistinguishable in all its characteristics.

5 "White Lady"
This climber has pure white flowers with good flavor and the runners are tasty and prolific. It has an RHS Award of Garden Merit.

French *Phaseolus vulgaris*

1 "Blauhilde"
This climber is popular in northern Europe as it is known to be hardy. It has purple pods that smother its quick-growing vines. It also has great flavor.

2 "Blue Lake"
This is my favorite climbing bean, with exceptionally heavy cropping and tender, round beans that have great flavor. The one downside is that it can be sporadic in germination, so make sure you store the seed carefully and use it in good time. It has an RHS Award of Garden Merit.

3 "Borlotto Lingua di Fuoco"
This climber has been the most reliable cranberry bean in our trials. It is earlier to crop than most and with beautiful crimson flecked pods and a long

cropping pattern. You can eat the pods like pole beans, but we usually leave the beans on the plant and harvest them in August/September.

4 "Cobra"
This is a stringless, tasty round climbing bean that we often sow in succession with an early cropper like dwarf French bean "Speedy." As a climber, "Cobra" is later to crop, whereas we can start harvesting "Speedy" in early July.

5 "Limka"
Halfway between a French and a pole bean, this climber has large, flat pods. It is a heavy producer with white flowers and crops all summer. It is also quick to crop, so it is ideal for an early harvest inside or out. It has good disease resistance, which is ideal for organic growing.

6 "Rocquencourt"
This is a tender and very early French dwarf bean with good weather resistance, which makes it good for sowing early and late. Pick it while it's still primrose in color (not golden) for a tender texture and the best flavor.

Herbs for Tea

We all know countless cups of strong coffee and even a lot of black tea is not good for us, but since I'm more a fan of the carrot than the stick, we did a trial here a couple of years ago with the aim of expanding our range of herbs and garden plants that can be infused in boiling water. Tisanes have long been served here at all our courses and garden openings, and I was keen to find year-round, homegrown options that could be picked fresh during our main growing season, and then dried and stored for use in later seasons.

Chamomile, mint, and lemon verbena are popular and well known, but I wanted to dig deeper and discover the very best mints, the most delicious scented-leaf pelargoniums and the herbs that perform best when steeped. For our trial, we planted twenty different herbal varieties and tasted the lot. We had six mints, eight varieties of scented-leaf pelargonium, three basils, lemon verbena, lemon balm, and lemongrass. There were some clear front-runners, delicious day or night, boiling hot or chilled with a lump of ice. And what's doubly good about these edible plants is that you don't even need a garden to grow them. They all grow happily in the confines of a pot or window box.

True Moroccan mint (*Mentha spicata* var. *crispa* "Moroccan") famously has the best and most intense flavor for tea. It rated highly in our trial but did not come top among the mint brigade. The number one spot was taken by black peppermint (*M.* × *piperita* "Black Mitcham"), which is intensely minty with a strong and delicious aftertaste. It is also prolific and easy to grow, which allows for a continual late-spring and summer harvest.

If buying plants from garden centers you need to take care you're getting the right forms of these precious mints. True Moroccan mint has a bright green, smooth leaf that's pointed at the tip. Its surface is quite strongly indented by veins so it looks almost frilly. It has green stems that are purple at their base. Black peppermint (I get mine from herb specialist Jekka's) has bigger leaves than the Moroccan form. They are smoother and less indented with dark crimson stems. They are both upright growers.

A window box planted with *Pelargonium* "Lemon Fancy" and *Salvia greggii* "Stormy Pink." These two look good all summer and autumn, are drought tolerant, and provide a harvest for tisanes and edible flowers.

We grow the mints in pots and troughs, as well as in out-of-the-way corners, which means that it's a joy (not a problem) when they take off. They are famously invasive but, whatever people tell you, you can't just leave mint in the same pot—however big—for years on end. The soil minerals that are required for the synthesis of the essential oils that give them their flavor will, in time, be depleted, so you end up with almost tasteless leaves. If grown containerized, they'll need to be replanted in new soil every year to maximize their taste. And don't forget, you must keep harvesting so that the plant keeps producing fresh and strong-tasting leaves.

Along with the mints, lemon verbena was another top-ranker, easily outdoing lemon balm and just beating lemongrass in our taste trial. Lemon verbena's flavor is brighter, stronger, cleaner containerized, and even more lemony. It's a tender deciduous shrub, but planted with very good drainage in a sheltered spot in a south-west-facing corner, it has overwintered fine for 10 years, even on our heavy clay. It's also very happy growing in a pot, which can be brought into a shed during the cold winter months and put outside again in the spring (as it's deciduous, it doesn't need light while it is dormant). Close behind lemon verbena was lemon basil in our trial. The flavor is exactly as described in the name: a warm basil, nicer in tea for its hint of citrus. In a tisane, we preferred this to ordinary basil or cinnamon basil.

Then there's *Backhousia citriodora*, known commonly as the sweet verbena tree. It's reputed to have the highest concentration of citrus oil in its leaves of all the plants mentioned here. This is a less prolific leaf producer and not hardy, but it is evergreen, so we grow it in the greenhouse for winter tea leaves. It's also resilient, needing minimal TLC, so it is ideal as a houseplant and for picking from a windowsill.

To extend the season, it's to pelargoniums that we turn, which can be harvested from July through to December. The scented-leaf pelargonium "Attar of Roses" has been my favorite for years. It's easy to grow, prolific, quick to strike from cuttings, and nice-looking, with its downy, bright green leaves and pale pink flowers. It makes a lovely rose-flavored tea, reminiscent of Turkish delight with a hint of lemon. For cordial, we pick the leaves regularly, boil them briefly in water, and then steep them overnight to turn into a syrup. As well as sugar, I also add citric acid (to preserve it) and fresh lemon juice. We picked so much of this last year that the plants were almost bald, so we've made a tea bed in the greenhouse and have discovered some outstanding new performers.

Our favorite is "Mabel Grey," which is the pelargonium the twentieth-century cook Elizabeth David raved about (she used it in her blackberry and apple pie) and it has long been popular for flavoring Victoria sponge. It also makes a lovely tisane. Next in the pelargonium ranks is *P. longifolium*, a variety used widely in Greece to flavor jams and drinks, and rightly so. It is bright and fragrant in tea, followed closely in flavor by *P.* "Sweet Mimosa," which is similar but slightly spicy and warm. Since the trial, we've also gained three new favorites, the citrus-tasting *P. crispum* "Cy's Sunburst" (and similar *P.* "Queen of the Lemons") and *P.* "Orange Fizz." The first two taste of lemon, the second, as you'd expect from the name, is distinctly orangey.

We plant a mixed hedge of these specifically for tea harvest, propagated from cuttings taken in August or September. They all seem to keep going well here until we hit −3°C (26°F) or less, which is usually not until January. If we wait until April to tidy the frosted tops, we find most have survived and become perennial. And even if our plants die, we always have plenty of cuttings to ensure our tea hedge can be planted again in spring. All of these are healthy *and* delicious, and can be harvested year-round. They are also cut-and-come-again to a degree. If you cut above a pair of leaves, just like with cut flowers, axillary buds will form below the cut and those quickly develop into new stems with fresh leaves.

We mainly serve our herb teas as single flavors, in a glass teapot so you can see the (usually) vivid green color. But a friend of mine in the United States has started growing her own herb-tea plants and then drying and mixing them in a blend. Her favorite mix for dry herbs is two teaspoons chamomile, two of lemon balm, one teaspoon peppermint, and one of lemon verbena. She then adds a little of whatever else is freshly available, like lemon thyme, lavender, basil flower, or fennel seeds to move it in another direction. Place a couple of good spoonfuls in a teapot, steep in boiling water for 5 minutes and pour. This makes enough for two to three cups. That's the next step for us here: combining our herbs in blends. There are more experiments, trials, and blend tastings to be had.

A year of tea

January, February & March
Garden: Sweet cicely leaf
Greenhouse: Lemongrass, pelargonium, sweet verbena tree
Dried: Chamomile, lemon verbena, mint

April
Garden: Sweet cicely seedpod, mint, lemon balm

May
Garden: Sweet cicely seedpod, mint, lemon balm, lemon verbena

June
Garden: Mint, lemon balm, lemon verbena, pelargonium

July
Garden: Mint, lemon balm, lemon verbena, pelargonium, basil, chamomile, fennel seed

August
Garden: Mint, lemon verbena, pelargonium, basil, chamomile
Greenhouse: Lemongrass
Garden or dried: Fennel seed

September
Garden: Lemon verbena, pelargonium, basil
Greenhouse: Lemongrass
Dried: Fennel seed, chamomile

October
Garden: Lemon verbena, pelargonium
Greenhouse: Lemongrass, mint
Dried: Fennel seed, chamomile

November & December
Garden: Lemon verbena, pelargonium
Greenhouse: Lemongrass, lemon verbena (we have a plant in the greenhouse for harvesting late in the year after the outside plants have shed their leaves), sweet verbena tree
Dried: Fennel seed, chamomile and mint (in November, we can pick fresh leaves from potted clumps, but in December we move to dried)

Clockwise from top left
A harvest for teas in spring (sweet cicely seedpods); summer (Moroccan mint); winter (dried chamomile); autumn (pelargoniums "Attar of Roses," "Cy's Sunburst," and "Orange Fizz").

Best of the herbs for tea

All the plants here have distinctive flavors and are easy to grow. This list does not include rose petals, calendula, and cornflowers—all lovely edible flowers that can be added to teas for prettiness but not for flavor. The ones below all carry some punch.

1 Basil *Ocimum*
It's not basil variety "Sweet Genovese" (see p. 271) that's best for homegrown tea, but one of the more aromatic varieties, including the delicious lemon basil, pictured, also see p. 270). Tulsi, (*O. tenuiflorum*), known as holy basil, also gives a warm, aromatic flavor.

2 Chamomile
Chamaemelum nobile
A self-sowing perennial, chamomile makes one of the best tisanes, especially as a nightcap. It's also easy to grow in the garden, prolific, and strong-tasting, so you won't need many flowerheads for your evening mug of tea. Pick the flowers, hang them upside down and, once dry, store them in an airtight jar.

3 Fennel *Foeniculum vulgare*
Fennel seed has a well-known aniseed flavor and is often brought to the table in traditional Indian restaurants, either dry-roasted or fresh, as a digestive. I don't much like it on its own it's (a bit too medicinal), but a small pinch of seed in a tea blend adds something special. We harvest it fresh in the summer months and dry any surplus to use throughout winter.

4 Lemongrass
Cymbopogon citratus
Well known for its use in curries, this grass tastes of ginger mixed with lemon, and it makes an excellent tea. You can use the most intensely flavored, swollen leaf bases (as you would in cooking), but we tend to use those in the kitchen and reserve the grassy tops for drinks. We grow it in the greenhouse for a supply through autumn and winter.

5 Lemon verbena
Aloysia citrodora
There's nothing quite like this for almost gingery sharpness and brightness with a strong citrus punch. We grow this outside in a sheltered spot in our herb garden and one large plant in the greenhouse, just in case. The latter loses its leaves a good month or two later than those outside.

6 Mint *Mentha*

Almost any mint will give you delicious tea that aids digestion. We've found that black peppermint (*M.* × *piperita* "Black Mitcham," pictured) is the most intense-flavored mint, and has some of the biggest leaves. Moroccan mint (*M. spicata* var. *crispa* "Moroccan") is the classic, fresh, clean-tasting mint used in Morocco for tea. The key is to use enough. Really pack a good

handful of leaves into a pot or a mug for a decent cup of tea.

7 Pelargonium *Pelargonium* "Attar of Roses" is my favorite for drinks, hot or cold. It's the classic scented-leaf pelargonium (pictured). "Mabel Grey" is now quite difficult to find, but do try as it has a distinctive, sharp lemon-sherbet flavor and is strong, so you don't need many leaves. *P.*

crispum "Cy's Sunburst" is the next best thing—an upright grower with small, crinkly leaves that are strongly and deliciously lemony in flavor. Unlike "Mabel Grey," this is compact, so it is ideal for those with little space. There are several citrusy scented-leaf pelargoniums. I love "Queen of the Lemons," but also "Orange Fizz," with its pretty, quite showy flowers. It's a

pink variety with a prominent purple-crimson splotch at the heart of each flower. It is worthy of growing as an ornamental pelargonium as well as having tasty, orange-scented leaves. "Prince of Orange" is another favorite, that we harvest for flavoring jams, cordials, and teas. This is a bushy grower with small, pale mauve flowers.

8 Sweet cicely *Myrrhis odorata* Sweet cicely is one of the first things that can be picked from the garden in spring—first, the leaves and then the powerful licorice-flavored seedpods. Taste a pod straight off the plant and you won't believe the intensity of flavor.

9 Sweet verbena tree *Backhousia citriodora* Reminiscent of a miniature citrus tree but in fact not related (it's a member of the myrtle family, and also known as lemon myrtle), this plant is a great addition to the greenhouse. It's evergreen, so you can pick it when there's little else to harvest. The taste is strong. Often, I'll make a mug of tea with just one coarsely chopped leaf (use two leaves to a 1-liter pot).

9

July

With so many crops close to being ready, the big thing for July (and August and September) is harvesting. Aside from that, July in the kitchen garden is about lots of small jobs rather than one overarching task.

If your purple sprouting broccoli and kale aren't netted, look out for cabbage-white-butterfly eggs on the undersides of brassica leaves. Squash these whenever you find them or apply a biological control. If you walk around your brassica patch twice a week squashing as you go, you can keep caterpillar damage under control. If not, enclose the crop in Enviromesh or a brassica cage (see p. 208).

For tomatoes, you need to check that you're getting good pollination and that the flowers are forming fruit, not just dropping off. Underplanting with plants that attract pollinators will help, or you can walk through the plants tapping the top of each vine quite vigorously to help dislodge pollen onto the flowers below. In June, we start to feed with an organic tomato food, or potash-rich comfrey tea—ideally, every week, but particularly in the early stages. By the middle of July, once the plants have taken off, we can reduce the feeding.

As vegetables including fava beans and shelling peas finish cropping, remember to harvest some seed before you pull up the plants. Select individual plants that have done particularly well and have thrived in your microclimate. If you go on doing this year after year, you'll develop your own mini-clone that's suited to the conditions in your garden. Store seed in a paper bag, adding a date and label.

To pull the finished plants up, twist them off at ground level and take them to the compost heap. Leave the roots in the ground as they have nodules containing nitrogen, which releases into the soil as they decay.

There are also lots of plants that need pinching to stop them from growing and instead to start producing. Carry on pinching tomatoes at least a couple of times a week and pinch off the tips (if you've not already done so in June) when the plants reach the top of their frames. Toward the end of the month, eggplant must be pinched to encourage them to form flowers and fruit, rather than prioritizing vegetative growth. When pole beans reach the top of their supports, pinch off the tops. This will promote side branching and a larger harvest. Water them well when they're in flower to get good pod formation. Pinching off growing tips is also key with climbing zucchini and squash. Do this as they reach the top of their frames to encourage more and earlier fruit formation.

Overall, things are a little quiet in midsummer, and with a little spare time on our hands our attention turns to garden infrastructure. One of the key things for us is compost, and it's now that we tend to make improvements to our composting system.

In the Greenhouse

Storing onions, garlic, and shallots

When their leaves have yellowed, onions, shallots, and garlic are ready to harvest—and that's usually now. They are best stored in a way that allows for plenty of air circulation, hence why the French are famous for their braids. This technique works equally well, if not better, for storing hardneck garlic as they have more pliable stems.

Our garlic always seem to be of differing sizes—never quite as standard as commercial growers. We start with the larger bulbs at the bottom, moving up to the small ones. It looks better hanging, and it also means that you save the lovely large bulbs to use until last.

Shallots tend to have shorter stems that die back when ready to harvest, so they're not easy to braid. Instead, after harvest, we leave them to dry for a week in the greenhouse. Once dry, we rub off the dirty outer skins. This reveals a beautiful, clean, coppery-pink skin, which looks lovely laid out in a bowl or garden basket.

Braiding onions

- When you harvest your onions, try to keep the stem as long as possible.
- Dig them up gently and lay them out in a warm, dry place for a few days.
- When the stems have dried but are still a little pliable, start your braid. Clean off any dried soil and loose skins.
- Grade your onions by size, with the stems facing toward you.
- Pick the three largest and tie them loosely together at the top of the bulbs with a piece of string. Start your braid by bringing the right stem over the central stem, then the left stem over what is now the central stem, then the right stem over what is now the central stem.
- At this point, add in two or three more onions so that you have six stems and repeat the above, but with one original and one new stem held together each time, so that the onions are captured in the braid.
- At the end of the braid, tie around with string and make a loop with the excess string so you can hang the braid somewhere cool and dry. Cut off any excess stems to leave a neat end. When you need an onion, simply cut one off the braid, leaving the rest intact.

In the Garden

Understanding Compost

A question I'm often asked is how to get hold of lots of cheap organic matter. The answer is: make your own if you possibly can.

Compost is what forms when organic matter decays under controlled conditions. When added to your soil, it will continue to decay. When organic matter reaches a stable state and is no longer breaking down, it has become humus. There are three main stages.

Stage 1

Mesophilic bacteria starts the process of decomposition, breaking down organic compounds and producing heat. They thrive between 20°C and 40°C (68°F and 104°F). There is some activity below 20°C (68°F) by psychrophilic bacteria, but this is slow compared to the next stages. As the heat rises, thermophilic bacteria — which thrives between 40°C and 70°C (104°F and 158°F), starts to take over and decomposition is more rapid as cellulose, protein, and fats are broken down.

Use an iron bar as a heat probe (touch it to feel the heat being conducted by the metal) or a thermometer to find out the temperature of your compost heap about once a week. If the temperature is dropping, it shows that bacterial activity is slowing down and that the heap needs turning (mix the edges into the middle) in order to heat up again. Turning can also be used to cool a pile that is overheating, as excessively high temperatures will kill off the beneficial bacteria and decomposition will stop.

Stage 2

The pile begins to cool as most bacterial activity drops off due to lack of nutrients, at which point different decomposers get to work. Fungi and actinomycetes (a type of bacteria) work efficiently at temperatures around 20 to 25°C (68 to 77°F). The compost is now best left unturned.

Stage 3

As the compost matures and cools further, macro-organisms like ants, beetles, woodlice, centipedes, and worms can get to work. As opposed to the chemical breakdown performed by the bacteria and fungi, their contribution to the composting process is by physically breaking the matter into smaller pieces. The compost will be ready for use when it is dark brown with a not-unpleasant smell.

Making Compost

The key to making good, quick compost is to keep the whole decomposition process aerobic — with lots of oxygen available to allow microbes to thrive. To achieve this, you need to do two essential things: turn it regularly and keep the carbon/nitrogen balance equal. This will keep the oxygen-loving bacteria alive. With a lack of oxygen, the anaerobic bacteria move in. It's the aerobes we want to encourage to guarantee garden-ready compost as soon as possible.

Top left **Material for the compost heap: straw, grass, and salad leaves.**
Top right **Material to avoid: citrus, egg shells, wood shavings, thick roots,** bark, and cooked food.
Bottom left **Compost activators: comfrey and nettles.**
Bottom right **Homemade compost.**

To create enough of the lovely stuff, you ideally need to make some wooden structures, but any sort of bin is better than nothing. Even an open loose pile (enclosed perhaps in a chicken wire frame secured around four round or square posts) will produce compost.

- The classic set up is a three-bay system—with each bay of equal size and as big as you have room for. Place twiggy material in the bottom of the bay you are filling to help with air flow.
- Fill bay one completely. This will sink quite quickly so keep adding material until it is very full. When full, the contents can be turned into bay two. Bay one can be filled up again. Keep the third bay empty.
- When filling the first two bays, add garden and kitchen waste. Straw needs to be added in equal quantities in layers between the green waste. Straw is rich in carbon, while green waste is rich in nitrogen. Layering the two allows you to keep the carbon and nitrogen in balance. You can get straw from agricultural-feed suppliers or pet shops. You can also substitute it with shredded paper, cardboard, or chopped-up twiggy material.

- When it's time to turn your heap, the contents of bay two can be turned into the empty bay three, which means that the contents of bay one can be turned into bay two, and so on. You will be able to rotate the material from one bay to the next as and when you need.
- Turn the compost when the temperature of the heap starts to drop. Depending on the size of your bays, this can be quite a feat if you're doing it by hand with a shovel (less so if you have a front-end loader on a tractor as we do).
- If the compost is dry, spray a hose over the whole bay for a good 5 minutes.
- You can add activators such as chicken manure, comfrey leaves, or nettles every 4 weeks to speed up the composting process.
- When adding to the heap, ideally ensure layers of equal depth of both nitrogenous green material and carbon-rich material.

Add
- All grass clippings, but not in thick layers; mix with chopped-up twiggy material
- Cut flowers
- Kitchen waste, fava bean pods, discarded tough or damaged outer lettuce leaves
- Weeds that are not going to seed
- Weeds that are not persistent perennials
- All cardboard and paper, if not very heavily inked or glossy (make sure it is shredded)
- Cotton or other natural-fiber clothes (shredded)

- Seaweed (chopped up)
- Leaves (shredded; we run over ours with a lawnmower)

Do not add
- Cooked food (it encourages rats and flies)
- Citrus peel (excessive quantities can make the compost too acidic; instead, bake skins on a low heat in the oven and then use as firelighters; the wax in the citrus skins helps them burn)
- Egg shells (too slow to break down)
- Coarse bark (too slow to break down)
- Wood shavings (most are treated with preservatives, and they also take a long time to rot down and therefore use available nitrogen in the heap)
- Roots from perennial weeds such as bindweed (they will start to grow and invade the whole heap)
- Plants that have gone to seed (they will shed their seed, which will germinate when you scatter the compost)
- Anything diseased such as wood infected with honey fungus or zucchini with mildew (this will encourage the spread of fungal diseases)
- Manmade fabric (this will not decompose)

August

August is my favorite month in the kitchen garden and greenhouse, with much of the food we grow at its peak. Everywhere you look there's something exciting to pick and eat, and no two days are the same. It can be hard to keep up with the produce, but that's a good feeling—particularly, if you have a freezer to stash away the surplus.

Unparalleled in their August marvellousness are, of course, tomatoes. The smell of the stems and leaves that lingers after pinching is almost as good as the taste of the fruit. We grow groves of tomatoes in the greenhouse here, and these are sometimes supplemented with the hardier and more reliable ones growing in a sunny spot in the garden. And we plant lots of basil in our tomato jungle.

I love the volume of color from all the nasturtiums, dahlias, salvias, and other edible flowers reaching their late-summer peak, along with the wild bird food provided by the sunflowers, amaranths, and grasses (see p. 317 for more on these). Together, they create carpets of general froth and floweriness.

August is also the month that our birch and hazel frames, covered top to toe with climbing squash and beans, erupt through these carpets of color. It's now that the potatoes are emerging from the ground like presents and we're harvesting our main crops. We may leave "Axona" and "Pink Fir Apple" until later, but the early main crops, "Ratte" and "Belle de Fontenay," are lifted now and stored in paper or burlap sacks somewhere cool and dry so they can be eaten through autumn and winter. Unlike the early crops, they don't lose flavor or texture in storage.

There are baskets of cucumbers, which once they start coming, do so thick and fast. I like the look of their big lily-pad leaves studding the hazel frames over which they grow. We often end up making cucumber pickle to cope with the oversupply. The mini varieties (like "La Diva" or "Petita") are easy to get through—perfect just-picked when they're still warm and at their sweetest, and then dipped into hummus or baba ghanoush.

We're eating sweet corn a few times a week. You can usually tell when it's ripe by the beards, which should be turning brown. To double-check, indent a kernel with your thumbnail. If it weeps white liquid, it's ready. Twist each cob off the stem and aim to boil it in salted water within a few minutes of harvesting. This prevents the sugars converting to starch and will ensure the best possible flavor.

It's hard to keep up with zucchini production, and we need to make sure we harvest regularly. Toward the end of the month, we often give up on our zucchini plants, particularly those that have been growing inside. The huge leaves tend to succumb to downy mildew no matter how much we water and douse them with our chive remedy. And besides, we've been eating zucchini since June. By the last week of August, we're happy to move on to our September produce of eggplant, peppers, chilis, early squash, beetroot, and Florence fennel. I love to change the fresh vegetables we eat pretty much every week, and that's exactly what you end up doing if you have your own kitchen garden.

August—and on into September—is the moment you could face potential oversupply, but remember, don't get bogged down. Ask your family to come and pick what they want. Take boxes of homegrown produce with you whenever you meet friends. It's at this time of year that the old saying, "The generous gardener has the most "flowers," is most apt, and it applies equally to the edible garden. August truly is about harvest, harvest, and then more harvest! I can't bear to be away.

Tomatoes

It's indisputable: a homegrown tomato—of the right variety—always tastes best. It has that strange tobacco fragrance in its flavor that shop-bought ones rarely retain. This is incentive enough to grow them in my view, but there are also few nicer tasks than going into the greenhouse (or at Perch Hill, also along the sunny, south-facing bank where we grow easy-ripening cherry tomatoes) and filling a bowl with a load of tomatoes, enjoying that extraordinary, acrid scent that fills the air as you pick. It's one of life's good experiences: pick, plop, pick, plop, working down the line.

Another great thing is that you don't have to have a garden to grow them. A sunny, sheltered doorstep or, with the right tumbling, bush varieties, a good window box are both fine places to grow these fruits. When I lived in London, I grew tomatoes in a deep window box every year. Even if I lived on the fiftieth floor of a high-rise building, I'd still grow tomatoes.

With tomatoes, almost more than any vegetable we grow, I think it's key to be super selective in your varieties. In my experience, even with homegrown, there's a big difference in the volume of harvest and intensity of flavor among different tomatoes. We've found over the years that there are tasty tomatoes, super-tasty tomatoes, and tomatoes with almost no flavor at all. That's why a tomato taste trial was one of the first edible trials we did here over 20 years ago. We've repeated it four or five times since. I want us to keep up to date, growing new varieties as they come on the market and comparing them with our stalwarts.

It's also important to grow several varieties. Any decent cook will tell you it's best to have a mix of tomatoes in any dish, raw or cooked. Each one has a different level of sweetness and acidity, and together this gives a greater depth of flavor, as well as looking more interesting on the plate.

I remember visiting the National Trust garden Knightshayes in Devon where the gardeners were growing ordinary red cherry tomatoes, as well as orange ones. Both of these were served in the

Tomatoes in the greenhouse, including "Noire de Crimée," and "Country Taste." Most of the lower leaves have been removed by August to encourage good air circulation and to decrease the chance of blight.

self-service café, though separately, on the same salad. The plates with the orange outsold the ones with the red tomatoes by more than double. When the customers who'd bought the orange ones were asked why, almost all said it was because they assumed the red had been bought in, whereas the more unusual orange variety had been grown right there in the garden. In fact, both were grown there.

Growing different-colored varieties is an easy thing to do, and with it comes the message "I'm homegrown, and fresher, tastier, and healthier than the others." It's true you can get mixed colors and shapes at fancy produce stores in bougie little cardboard baskets, but, in my experience they often don't taste as good as they look.

My favorite all-round variety is good old "Sungold." It's hard to beat with its intense sweetness, pretty orange-yellow skin, and huge productivity from the end of June. I'd still recommend the large cherry variety, "Gardener's Delight," which has good flavor and a handily long, light cropping pattern. You can go on eating from your "Gardener's Delight" plants for at least 3 months if they are grown inside. The variety has another advantage: its fruits ripen on one vine at much the same time. The first fruit nearest the

Opposite Tomato "Red Alert" and basil "Sweet Genovese."
Below Tomatoes growing outside in a line alongside the south face of the greenhouse. It's very sheltered here.

Clockwise from top left
A mix of tomatoes (including
"Green Zebra") ready for roasting;
tomatoes "Noire de Crimée" and
"Indigo Rose"; a harvest of our
outdoor tomatoes, including "Noire
de Crimée," "Stupice," "Sungold,"
and "Gardener's Delight."

plant turns red and sweet only a couple of days before the one
at the tip, so you can harvest the whole vine and roast all the
tomatoes together, which looks good on the plate and tastes great.

I always add the strange-looking, but utterly delicious "Noire de
Crimée" (or similar "Black Russian," which can be easier to find)
to my growing list every year. It is outstanding eaten raw with a
sprinkle of flaky salt in a salad. In fact, I'd say this was my favorite-
ever salad tomato.

Classification

Tomato varieties divide into so-called "determinate" or "bush"
types and "indeterminate" or "cordon" types.

Indeterminate tomato plants (also known as cordon) are the
vine varieties. They grow tall and will keep going until you tell
them to stop by pinching off the growing tip. They will need
training and their side shoots need pinching off (see p. 202). Bear in
mind there is no point in having them so tall that you can't reach
the fruit, so be practical when deciding when to take off the tip.

Determinate tomato plants (also known as bush) are the bushy,
often more compact varieties. They get to a certain size and
then stop climbing/growing, instead bushing out and starting
to flower and crop heavily—usually, for a shorter season than
indeterminate varieties. The advantage of the determinates is that
you don't need to train them or pinch off the lateral shoots. I love
the pinching part, but it can be a bit of a chore and puts beginner
growers off tomatoes. These are ideal for pots, window boxes, and
edible hanging baskets, though bear in mind they may still need
to be supported with a stake. Do note that the determinate group
divides into bush and trailing types according to their natural
habit. Bush forms need a cane to support them and are very bushy
in their growth habit, while the trailers are shorter and have a
tendency to trail.

Best of the tomatoes

These are our stalwart tomatoes (Solanum lycopersicum), *but any tomato grower will have their own favorites. I'd advise to trial, trial, trial. To build up your own list of favorites, select two or three this year, stick with one or two of those next year, and trial a new one every year. Select three or four from any on the following pages and you will never want to buy a supermarket tomato again.*

Indeterminate

1 "Chocolate Cherry"
A new, trendy, brownish-skinned tomatoes, this one is prolific and an eat-in-one-go size. It did well in our trial outdoors and cropped heavily, almost as well as in the greenhouse. The downside is its flavor, which is nice but not outstanding.

2 "Costoluto Fiorentino"
This is the handsomest tomato—a cartoon-looking, Mediterranean market tomato. Its name means "pleated of Florence," and that's just what it is. It has good flavor, if not quite as good as "Noire de Crimée." It has a tendency to lose its leader and go blind as it grows, so sometimes you need to train a lower axillary shoot (not pinched, obviously) to become the leader. Despite that, we grow it every year.

3 "Country Taste"
This is of the heaviest cropping beefsteak tomatoes we've trialled, with succulent, intensely flavored fruit. It's excellent sliced or chunked for salad. It is a recent addition to our must-grow list.

4 "Gardener's Delight"
A classic that produces fruit that's somewhere between a cherry and a medium-sized tomato, it is reliable, sweet, tasty, prolific, and grows happily outside.

5 "Green Zebra"
This one has good flavor, but we mainly grow it because it makes a tomato salad look fantastic when it's combined with red, orange, and dark varieties, plus it is juicy and not too sweet.

6 "Indigo Rose"
Tomatoes are the richest source of a powerful and important antioxidant called lycopene.This blue-black tomato contains good levels of anthocyanin too (famously good for our brains and the pigment that gives blueberries their color), so it is an extra-healthy option. The flavor is good but not exceptional, but these tomatoes are among the latest to ripen, which helps to lengthen the tomato harvesting season.

7 "Noire de Crimée"
This is a beefsteak-sized tomato that's worth growing for its exceptional flavor, texture, and reliability. It comes from Russia and is tolerant of the northern hemisphere's light levels and temperatures. It has delicious flavor and juicy firm flesh. My number one.

8 "Orange Banana"
This is a tall indeterminate type that grows to 2 m (6 ½ ft.) or more if you let it, with very little leaf compared to stem. It makes it look oddly gappy as it grows, but it's a huge producer even in quite bad light levels. We tend to grow this one right up to the eaves of the greenhouse and then train it sideways. The fruit is medium to large (150 to 200g/ 5 to 7oz per tomato), with excellent flavor and texture, and a great shape. It starts to crop early and continues to the first frost.

9 "San Marzano"
Year after year, we try plum tomatoes. The trouble with most plum types is that they are bred for cooking, canning, and bottling, and tend to be quite dry with a grainy texture and are not so good eaten raw. That's certainly true of this one, the foodies' favorite "San Marzano," which I don't think can compete with the others here in terms of flavor. However, if you love regularly making tomato sauce, this is your tomato.

10 "Santonio"
This is a cherry plum we tried in 2020: delicious, juicy, and sweet but with a good sharpness. This is among our top three tomatoes to grow at Perch Hill.

11 "Stupice"

A prolific, so-called potato-leaved cordon type from the Czech Republic. The fruit is small to medium-sized (about 125g per tomato), with very thin-skinned, it does not crack and has a sweet but gentle flavor. We grow lots here. "Stupice" (or "Stupicke Polni Rane" as it's also known) is very early to fruit (from mid-June in the greenhouse), prolific until September (one plant will produce about 10 kilos of fruit), and is the last to succumb to blight, so it can also be grown reliably outside too.

12 "Sugar Plum"

A cherry plum, sweet, thin-skinned and very prolific (you'll also find it sold under "Red Grape Sugar Plum"), this is our head gardener Josie's favorite. It was in the top three of our recent taste test. Everyone liked it for its strong tomato flavor that's sweet but not overly so, and for its firm, not mushy, texture. It has a slight acidity running through it, which all sweet tomatoes need. It ripens quite late compared to "Sungold" and produces for a long period of time. It's lovely in a mixed salad with the larger varieties.

13 "Sungold"

A small cherry form with thin, yellow-orange skin and an exceptionally sweet flavor, it is the longest and biggest cropper in our greenhouse every year and wins almost every taste trial. It also grows happily outside. As with produce that crops early, having a tomato that crops into autumn (when those you can buy from the shops have become tasteless) feels like a luxury. "Honeycomb" is a more recent, similar variety that seemed to be even sweeter in our last taste trial.

14 "Tigerella"

There are a couple of medium-sized tomatoes that I particularly like—"Tigerella" being one of them. Its skin has a greenish tinge, even when fully ripe, and pretty flecks and stripes in dark red. For a crunchy, firm salad tomato, or for slicing into sandwiches, this is the best. My twin sister has grown this in her greenhouse in Edinburgh for 2 years squidgy so I know it does well in the north of the UK too. Here in the south, it's happy inside or out.

14

Determinate

1 "Red Alert"
If you don't have a greenhouse and have limited space or maybe just a window box, "Red Alert" is a good choice. It's happy growing outside, is a tumbler and needs no training. It will produce vast amounts of relatively tasty fruit. It outshines all other tumblers, I've tried in terms of flavor, including "Tumbling Tom."

2 "Texas Wild Cherry"
Producing masses of tiny, so-called "currant" tomatoes, this quick-growing tumbling variety is ideal if you're a cook who loves scattering tomatoes through things like risottos and tabbouleh. The downside is you really need to pick these almost daily. We also like picking whole branches for vases in the style of a Dutch still life. We also grow the plants in terra-cotta pots as table centers for our events and garden openings. To do this, we grow them sort of bonsaied, reducing their bulk by removing some of their leaves so they look delicate and elegant.

3 "Tumbling Tom"
The first tomato I grew was in a window box in my London garden. I was training to be a doctor at Charing Cross Hospital and short of time. I failed to pick my heavy-cropping "Tumbling Tom" regularly enough. Overripe fruit dropped on the pavement below, which stained it red right through to the following spring. It tastes good, but I grow it mostly for nostalgia.

Basil

If you're growing tomatoes, you've got to grow basil too. There's nothing like torn basil scattered over a tomato salad. They make perfect companions in the garden too, not only because the basil helps to keep tomatoes aphid-free, but also—if left to flower— it draws in pollinators that can top up your tomato harvest. We go for drifts all around the bases of our tomato vines.

August is basil's month. The plants are big and bushy now, thriving on the long days. Nights can be too cold for basil in September, making it prone to botrytis (the growth tips start to rot with mold), so August is the month to pick and enjoy all things basil.

We grow four or five different varieties. There are many different flavors, from lemon (I like) and lime (it's okay) to cinnamon (too medicinal for eating, although I love it for flower arranging). If you only have time and space for one, you must choose "Sweet Genovese." This is the variety you can buy at the supermarket, which can have a wishy-washy flavor. Homegrown, it has a warming, highly aromatic, and sweet taste.

There are a few things to bear in mind to have success with basil through late summer. If you're growing basil outside—and that's a good place for it, as there's less risk of whitefly—don't plant it out until you are happy to have supper in the garden. If it's warm enough for you, it's warm enough for basil to be out there too. This applies as much at the beginning of summer as it does at the end. If you try to put your plants out earlier, or leave them out later, the foliage and stems turn black and stop growing. In the early autumn, dig up any young plants with good-sized root balls and pot them to bring inside. They should then keep going for a few more weeks.

Basil likes its nights mild and its roots moist, but as I was told by an organic basil grower with six glasshouses full of the herb: "Never send basil to bed wet." If you want to keep your plants growing, water them in the morning not the evening. If the basil leaves are damp, slugs and snails have a great feast overnight.

Basil "Horapha Nanum," which we grow to make Thai green curry paste.

Basil "Sweet Genovese" and bush basil; *Dahlia* "Josie" with basil "African Blue" (we harvest both for edible flowers); dark-leaved perilla (a popular flavoring and salad leaf in Japan) with basil "Sweet Genovese" lining a path through the vegetable garden.

Dry foliage also helps to discourage the tendency to succumb to mold. We've experimented with direct sowing, rather than planting plugs, and certainly the basil seedlings outside are too vulnerable to slug attack as they emerge tiny and tender from the ground. We do successfully direct sow in the greenhouse once our tomatoes are planted in early May, but we must keep our eyes peeled for any slug or snail slime, or they can have the lot in one night.

Basil doesn't need space, so window boxes and doorstep pots are also ideal. Again, remember to water several times a week, ideally from below and in the morning. I take the whole pot (if manageable) and leave it soaking in a bowl or barrel of water for 15 minutes while I get on with something else. I then let it drain before returning it.

One of the joys of the high-summer vegetable garden is enjoying at least one basil and a couple of different tomato varieties, both in the garden and on the plate.

Harvesting Basil

It's worth knowing how to pick your leaves. Don't just grab a handful as you would with the more prolific and resilient mint or parsley; instead, harvest with scissors, cutting out whole sections of a plant down to a pair of leaves lower down the stem. This will promote the growth of axillary buds. These become the next generation of leaves, ready to eat in a week or two. If you just snip off the tips, you're left with an ugly stump and mold is more likely to strike. This can then move down into the rest of the plant and kill it. A careful, layered haircut is what is needed rather than a straight swipe.

Best of the basil

If you're only going for one basil (Ocimum) to cook with and add to salads it must be "Sweet Genovese," but we grow various others for different reasons and roles. You can propagate most from seed and all of them from cuttings (these are best struck in water, see p. 275). Here are my favorites.

1 "African Blue"
A tender perennial basil best grown from cuttings rather than seed, it has a correspondingly long season and still looks good into October outside and even until Christmas if brought into the greenhouse. The flavor is sharp, not sweet, so we tend to grow this as an ornamental pot filler rather than for the kitchen. Sprigs picked to add here and there to drinks and as a garnish are fine, but it's not a good choice as your main basil supply.

2 Bush basil *Ocimum minimum*
Also known as Greek bush or Greek basil, this small-leaved form can be carefully pruned like a mini box ball once or twice a week. It grows happily inside or out in a bright, cool place. My husband Adam is godfather to a girl who is half Greek and at her christening on the Greek island of Hydra, all the godparents were given one of these plants potted into a beautiful, patterned, and empty can of olive oil. The globe looked fantastic in the rectangular tin. We picked from it hard from our kitchen windowsill in Greece for 2 months or more. I now recreate this idea with a line of three or five down the middle of our outdoor dining table and find that bush basil has the longest picking season than any other I've tried.

This form is said to be a good mosquito repellent, acting like citronella—hence its appearance on taverna tables.

3 Lemon basil *Ocimum × africanum* (syn. *O. × citriodorum*)
This makes the most delicious tea (see p. 236) if you soak a handful of leaves in boiling water for 5 minutes. In the summer, I can drink this for most of the day without ever tiring of the flavor. There used to be a variety called "Mrs Burns' Lemon" that seemed particularly lemony, but is now it is now difficult to find.

4 "Lettuce-Leaved" (syn. *Ocimum basilicum* lettuce leaf)
Its flavor is not quite as sweet strong as "Sweet Genovese," and the texture not quite as soft, but this is the most prolific variety I've grown and has vast leaves. I love basil-leaf tempura, and its large, crinkly leaves can hold on to a lot of crunchy batter, which is ideal. As a huge producer, it's good mixed with "Sweet Genovese" to make pesto.

5 "Red Boza"
We had a trial a few years ago of a few dark-leaved basils and only one or two did really well ("Red Boza" and "Purple Ruffles" won the day). Most of the crimson-black forms grew slowly and had repeated moldy patches that killed off whole sections of a plant. Some of them recovered, but they were left with distorted shapes. I think you need a hotter, drier climate for them, but this dark-leaved form is one that thrives.

6 "Sweet Genovese"
This is undoubtedly the basil with the most intense, sweet aromatic flavor. One of my favorite summer things is just-picked tomatoes with buffalo mozzarella topped with plenty of raw basil. This variety reigns supreme in that role.

7 Thai basil
This type has a unique basil flavor overlaid with aniseed. It's an essential ingredient in green or red Thai curries. Once cooked, the nearest approximation to flavor would be an equal combination of chervil, dill, and sweet basil. It's a three-in-one. We grow "Horapha Nanum."

August

As with July, this summer month involves lots of smaller tasks in the vegetable garden that need regular attention, rather than one big job.

We are quite busy taking care of tomatoes and pinching the tips of our eggplant, pepper, and chili plants (for those that didn't get pinched in July, see p. 241). All these fruiting crops need a regular potash-rich feed (see p. 206), and our pumpkins and squash (hugely hungry feeders) also benefit from a regular (every 10 to 14 days) liquid feed. We use a fertilizer based on seaweed for these, which contains a good balance of nitrogen, phosphorus, and potassium, or we mix our nettle and comfrey fertilizers together before watering the mix on (see p. 206).

With trailing varieties of squash, such as "Early Butternut," it's also key to repeatedly pinch off the tips in August and through September, as they will be growing like mad. Without this, the plants put energy into vegetative growth at the expense of fruit development. You'll see nascent tiny fruit just drop from the vine.

Make sure all of your potatoes are lifted soon—hopefully, before blight strikes. For main-crop varieties, you can lift any time after the foliage starts to die down. Dig over the potato area carefully to make sure you pick up every potato, however small. This will avoid too many "volunteers" returning next year to mess up your rotation and spread disease. We dig and dry them (but not wash, as they store for longer unwashed) before storing in burlap sacks; making sure to keep them completely dark, dry, cool, and frost-free.

We have plenty of space at Perch Hill, so in summer and autumn, we tend to grow our edible crops in the ground rather than in pots. With the heat and drought that goes with summer, containers need lots of maintenance, but if that's all the growing space you've got, pots it's got to be. I've included some tips here on the TLC they need.

In August, we also start propagating our tender perennials from cuttings. Relevant to the kitchen garden are all our scented-leaf pelargoniums, as well as edible flowers such as salvias. And we often take rosemary and sage cuttings in the same way.

In the Greenhouse

Taking Cuttings

People are often surprised when they walk into our polytunnel in August to see it is full with pots of cuttings. Many gardeners take their cuttings in spring, but we find it's now that our cuttings root the fastest, when many of the herbs and tender perennials (like our scented-leaf pelargoniums) are growing at full tilt. The edible plants we take cuttings from in August include:

- Pelargoniums
- Rosemary
- Lavender
- Thyme
- Salvias (edible-flower and leaf-sage varieties)

How to take cuttings
- Cut a short piece of stem from the main plant, ensuring it is from the current year's growth. Ideally, choose a nonflowering stem that has a soft tip but has hardened at the bottom.
- Trim to just below a leaf node (joint), so the cutting is 5 to 6 cm (2 in.) long. (Lavender cuttings will be even shorter.) Short cuttings root better than long ones. Just below a leaf node is where there is the highest concentration of natural rooting hormone. We don't use rooting hormone powder as we find a high percentage of our cuttings root consistently and quickly without it.
- Strip off all leaves except the top pair.

- Remove the stem tip. It's at the top that the growth hormone concentrates, so by pinching it off, apical dominance is removed to encourage root formation.
- Fill a series of small pots with a mix of one part fine grit to two parts compost.
- Insert the cuttings round the edge of the pot, spaced about 4 to 5 cm (2 in.) apart so their leaves don't touch. By placing them around the edge, not in the center, you encourage quicker root formation, as the new roots quickly hit the side of the pot, break, and branch into more lateral rootlets.
- Water the compost well.
- Place the pot under cover in light shade. Put the pots on a bed of grit (or capillary matting) for the next couple of months and only water lightly when the top of the compost is dry.
- Cuttings often root in 3 or 4 weeks. Check for roots showing in the drainage holes and, once formed, pot each cutting individually.
- If any of the cuttings show the slightest signs of botrytis (browning of the cutting or visible mold), take them out, as this will quickly spread to the others.
- Store them under cover through the winter for planting next spring.

Previous page, left
Cucumber "La Diva"
with *Eccremocarpus
scaber*, a long-flowering
climber that helps draw in
pollinators.

Below Basil (of all types)
roots quickly in water. We
germinate mother plants
from seed and then take
cuttings a couple of times a
year, which keeps us in basil
for months.

Taking basil cuttings

Whether it's a seed-grown form, such as "Sweet Genovese," or one of the tender perennial forms, we've found that the easiest way to encourage young plants to keep going into autumn is to take cuttings to root in water.

- Cut the mother plant back by one third, cutting above a pair of leaves. It will then grow back quite quickly.
- Strip the lower leaves from the stems you have cut.
- Put the stem (with leaf tips) into a jam jar filled with water. In a short time, roots will appear.
- Leave to grow on, with the stem base always submerged in water for 2 to 3 weeks. After this time, new basil leaves will have grown on top, ready to harvest.
- If it's still August or early September when the roots appear, you can pot the cuttings and put them on a sunny windowsill. You should be able to keep harvesting for another month or so.

Seeds to Sow Now

There is very little sowing to do this month. We do our main sowing for our winter and early spring crops in September, but there are a few key things that tend to be slow developers, so they need a few extra weeks to reach a decent size for autumn planting. If you leave them any later, they don't put on sufficient growth to make it through the winter. We sow all of these in lengths of guttering (see p. 57) and keep them under cover, but if you're short on space, they can be sown directly outside now.

Leafy greens

It's time to sow spinach for greens and salad through late autumn and winter. I also do a further sowing of Swiss and rainbow chards. We sow once in spring and again in late summer or early autumn.

Parsley

Sow parsley now to pick right through the winter. It's slow to germinate and won't be harvestable for about 10 weeks. I leave some outside for picking regularly in a mild winter, and plant some in the greenhouse to make sure we've got a reliable winter-long supply.

Florence fennel

Do a repeat sowing of bulb fennel early in the month, and then transplant to beds in the greenhouse in 4 to 6 weeks (see p. 205).

In the Garden

Taking Care of Pots

Here are my tips for keeping containers looking good and producing food for as long as possible.

Watering

Small table and windowsill pots dry out quickly when it's hot. To avoid this, sit them in saucers so they can continue to absorb the water that's initially drained away. If it's dry, plunge the bottoms of the pots into a bucket of water until bubbles stop rising from the compost.

With our larger pots, Josie, our head gardener, uses this triple-watering technique, which must be done three or four times a week, or daily if it's very hot and dry. Otherwise, on duller or cooler days, we stick a finger in the compost to see if it's damp and water according to what we find.

- Use a hose pipe, not a watering can, as it's more efficient for the volume of water required. Be aware, if you leave your hose unwound, particularly if it's black, the first water that comes out at the end of a hot day can be so hot it will damage the plants. Let the water run away for a minute or two (saving it in a bucket) before you start watering.
- Step one in the three-stage system is to water every pot in the group thoroughly for a minute or so, giving them a real drenching. If the container compost has dried out, water quickly runs out of the drainage holes. It's easy to think this means the container has

had enough, but that's usually not the case. When dehydrated, the compost can't hold on to moisture. If it's rained in the last day or two, this first stage may not be necessary.
- The second stage is to water the group of pots again, but not for quite so long this time. Water them for about 30 seconds.
- And then, finally, water them a third time for another 30 seconds, so everything gets three solid waterings. By then, the whole plant root system will be fully hydrated.

Feeding

- Compost usually contains enough nutrients to feed the plants well for 4 to 6 weeks, so you don't need to start feeding May-planted pots until July. By August and September, every pot here is fed once a week. We use liquid seaweed feed or our comfrey fertilizer (see p. 206).
- For the first 6 weeks or so, we do so at the strength recommended on the bottle. By September, we move to a double concentration.
- If it's very dry weather, we spray with our sulphur-rich chive remedy (see p. 207). This helps to protect against mildew, which can become an increasing problem with plants such as container-grown zucchini and beans—particularly in a dry year.

September

August and September are like twins in the vegetable garden. Both months feature similar crops, but each has its own personality. Whereas August is about juicy ripe tomatoes, September is when the slower-growing fruiting vegetables—eggplant, chilies, and sweet peppers—come into their own.

Toward the end of the month, with our tomato vines picked almost bare, it's a real boon to have these early-autumn croppers. I can't claim they are massive producers, but they are life enhancers with a touch of the exotic that makes them especially fun to grow.

All three of these September crops love a warm, sheltered spot, so if you have a greenhouse, polytunnel, sunny porch, or deep window ledges, you've got the ideal location for growing them. This extra, under-cover protection will extend their flowering (and therefore fruiting) season into late autumn, giving you up to a month of cropping time. But even without any under-cover space, there are varieties to suit you, particularly if you live in an area with a favorable climate.

We've trialled eggplant and peppers, both hot and sweet, under cover in the greenhouse, two or three times over the last 30 years. And we've done a trial of both of these outside with some success. For chilies, I'd recommend "Hungarian Hot Wax" and "Cayenne Red" as the most reliable varieties outdoors. For sweet peppers, I can vouch for "Marconi Rosso," and, for eggplant, "Slim Jim." All have done well on the south side of the greenhouse at Perch Hill, helped along (at least initially) by straw bales for protection on the windward side. We give them this extra buffer for a month or so after planting in the middle of May until they're established.

If a cold or very windy night is forecast, we drape the straw bale frame with fleece that's weighted with bricks.

It's important that these warm-climate plants are ready to harvest before the weather turns properly cold. September is a month much like March, where light levels and temperatures can drop drastically between the first few days and the last. Because many varieties of fruiting plants are bred in the United States or the Mediterranean, not all work for us here in the UK. We need forms that crop rapidly to give us a decent harvest before cold nighttime temperatures cause them to struggle. As well as excellent flavor and good rates of productivity, our trials explicitly look for cultivars that crop reliably in our temperate climate.

The other important thing with these three crops is that you must keep picking as the fruit ripens. Don't leave it languishing on the plant. In the past, I've been wary of harvesting these apparently less prolific crops, not absolutely sure when the fruit is ripe and ready, but picking regularly really does encourage more. This is true almost as much of chilies, peppers, and eggplant as it is of famously prolific pole beans, cucumbers, and zucchini.

If growing outside, as the temperatures drop toward the end of this month, we either harvest all the fruit and make batches of things like chili jam, or we dig the plants up, shake the soil off the roots, and hang them in a warm place (such as against the greenhouse wall) and the green fruit will continue to ripen giving us a harvest for a few more weeks. Depending on the weather and season, the plants may still be covered with a lot of unripe fruit. In that case (and particularly with chilis), we dig up the whole plant, pot it, and move it into the greenhouse to give us several more weeks of cropping. Chilies cope pretty well with a bit of root disturbance.

There are plenty of delicious culinary uses for eggplant and peppers—both so central to Middle Eastern recipes—many of which have been made accessible and fashionable in the last decade or so by great chefs such as Yotam Ottolenghi and the team behind the restaurant Honey & Co. You'll almost certainly have a plethora of recipes up your sleeve for cooking with these ingredients, but maybe fewer options for using up a continual supply of fresh chilis. To keep up with them, we pick at least once a week in September and October. I use them mainly to make preserves, and sometimes I combine them with the last of the tomatoes in chili jam or with apples in flavored jellies.

Opposite top Rosemary, hyssop, oregano, and thyme in our herb beds in autumn.
Opposite bottom A homemade brassica cage (see p. 208 for how to make one).

These key September players are joined by many of our year-round stalwarts. We still have the heat-tolerant, late-summer salads—lettuce, wild arugula and bok choy—along with the start of autumn leaves such as salad arugula and spinach. These begin to thrive again as temperatures fall. And there are masses of annual, perennial, and evergreen herbs to be picked too. Add to that plenty of chard and usually an early kale harvest, and there's plenty to bring into the kitchen.

September is also a high point for edible flowers. Unless we've done an early summer sowing, our hardy annuals such as calendula and borage are usually fading, but we have a confetti of salvia and dahlia petals to replace them, as well as French marigolds (*Tagetes patula*) in abundance. And I mustn't forget pole bean flowers and nasturtiums—both there not just for a splash of color but because they truly taste delicious.

Nasturtiums are currently fashionable as a cut flower and an edible one, and they are invaluable companion plants for protecting crops (see p. 157). As a result, there's been a great burst of breeding. It seems hardly a year goes by that we don't have three or four new ones to trial here—the latest batch offering slightly softer, more muted colors, such as "Ladybird Rose" and "Purple Emperor," and several soft yellow cultivars such as "Bloody Mary" and the peachy "Salmon Gleam." We find "Bloody Mary" stands out better than any other in a salad bowl, and we seem to pick it by the basket load.

By this point in the year, if any bean pods (pole or French climbing) have escaped our beady eyes and become too big, we pick them so that the plants can continue to crop. They are usually a little tough and stringy by this stage, but I bring them in, shell them, and, like the French and Italians do with cannellini or flageolet, cook and eat the inner beans. They're delicious and so much creamier than canned or dried. They can be eaten with the last tomatoes and maybe a sweet pepper in a ratatouille, which is one of my favorite September meals from the garden.

Peppers (chili and sweet)

Peppers divide into hot and sweet: chilies and bell or sweet peppers. They're brothers, and you can grow them in just the same way. In general, sweet peppers will not crop as hard as hot, so if space is limited, concentrate on chilies. Having said that, once tasted, you'll never want to go back to a watery, not-very-sweet, shop-bought sweet pepper. Try to find room for at least a couple of varieties of these as well.

Chili peppers

Growing chilies is so popular in part because they can be cultivated on a windowsill as a houseplant, and you can harvest a crop whether you have a garden or not. I know many people who have found growing them quite addictive. I wonder if this is because eating chilis is slightly addictive in itself. The hotter they are, the more they make compulsive eating.

Chilies contain an oil-like compound, capsaicin, which sends a burning sensation from the nerve endings in the mouth to the brain. The body defends itself against this "pain" by secreting endorphins, natural pain killers, which cause a physical rush in a similar way to the opium-derived drug morphine. As a result, you feel good and the high keeps you coming back for more.

The highest concentration of capsaicin is in the seeds and the "ribs" that attach the seeds to the fruit walls. If you've got mild chilies like "Hungarian Hot Wax" in their unripe, green stage and want to maximize their heat, chop them whole and leave the seeds in. If you have a hot variety such as the pretty, tangerine-colored "Habanero," you may want to cut them open and scrape out and discard the seeds for a less fiery experience. This makes all chilies hugely versatile in the kitchen.

A chili's heat is ranked on the Scoville scale, which is named after the chemist Wilbur Scoville. Nowadays, heat analysis is carried out by high-performance liquid chromatography, but traditionally a "Scoville heat unit" was assigned to each chili based on how much it needed to be diluted before it lost all heat.

Brilliant-colored peppers in a basket, including chilies "Bulgarian Carrot," "Aji Delight," and "Scotch Bonnet," and sweet pepper "Shishito."

"Hungarian Hot Wax" is ranked 5,000—10,000 on the Scoville scale, while the popular "Jalapeño" comes in at 2,500 to 8,000. "Scotch Bonnet," meanwhile, is considerably hotter, ranking at 100,000 to 325,000, as is "Habanero" (100,000 to 350,000). That's hotter than I want to go in my cooking, but there are varieties with an even higher grade.

As well as being down to variety, a chili's heat varies according to how and where it is grown, which explains the wide range of the Scoville scale. Grown harder, outside in the garden, chilies tend to be noticeably hotter.

You can buy chilies at the supermarket, but most of the interesting varieties are not widely available (they are very much in categories 1 and 3, see p. 17 and p. 22). So for a more exciting crop to cook with, you're best off growing them yourself—ideally, from seed sown under cover from the middle of February or from seedlings. They're very easy to grow. Oddly, we find that some of the early fruit succumbs to rot, but if we leave the plants to get going they're soon cropping well and are unstoppable. They will set tons of fruit, which given a bit of sun, will normally go on ripening until at least the end of October.

The plants look fantastic too. From the middle of summer right up until Christmas, they make the perfect houseplant or greenhouse plant. They also genuinely thrive in containers, so if you don't have a garden but do have a sunny yard or even a porch, these are the autumn crops for you. As houseplants, the small-fruiting varieties such as "Numex Twilight" and "Pearls" fare better than the bigger, fleshy plants. They will need some light pruning and preening in the winter (remove the odd yellow leaf), but overall they're handsome, and low maintenance, and a boon in the kitchen.

Sweet peppers

I love growing at least one or two varieties of sweet peppers, even though they don't earn their space in the same way as tomatoes and chilies, as they have a less abundant harvest. I love the red horned types, such as "Marconi Rosso"—this variety came out on top as the most prolific in our trials here, both in the greenhouse and outside. In East Sussex, it's hard to find peppers you can fry for tapas (such as "Friggitello," and "Padron") in the shops, so I love having these to pick—they're great thrown into a hot frying pan with olive oil until blistered, then dusted with salt for a quick and delicious side plate in late summer and autumn.

Best of the chili peppers

It's easy to think that one variety of chili pepper (Capsicum) will do, but that's a bit like saying "Let's stick with 'Iceberg' lettuce for every salad." There's a huge range of different flavors, intensity of heat, and good looks among this group of plants, so why not grow a few? In this selection, SHU stands for "Scoville heat units"—the higher the score, the hotter the heat.

1 "Bulgarian Carrot"
This is a lovely orange variety that's good in meat dishes. It has a gentle flavor but a bit more zing than a pepper such as "Padron" (see p. 294). You can also cut this up and add it raw to a salad. It mixes great with tomatoes. (12,000 to 30,000 SHU)

2 *Capsicum baccatum*
There are several varieties of *C. baccatum*, which is commonly referred to as aji. All are easy to go and prolific. We grow "Aji Delight" (also known as Peruvian aji, pictured), which is a fruity and sweet chili with all the flavor but none of the heat (0 SHU). We also grow, "Aji Limon," which produces short, pointed chilies in a variety of colors from yellow, orange, and red to white and purple. When cooked, it has a citrus flavor and a healthy kick of heat (30,000 to 50,000 SHU). Tearing away as seedlings, aji types produce large, rangy bushes carrying tons of fruit. They have the longest picking season of all the forms we've grown and are very cold-weather tolerant. You can even overwinter these in a polytunnel on a regime of total neglect.

3 "Cayenne Red"
This chili is really fruity, with some depth to it. You know you've eaten it, but it does not take your head off. The flesh has substance and the seeds are good for spicing up food. It's interesting to eat raw, sliced over a salad. It's also very handsome as a plant, and the yellow variety is just as good. (30,000 to 50,000 SHU)

4 "Cherry Bomb"
An excellent variety with fruits that look like tiny red apples, they are medium-hot. Together with "Hungarian Hot Wax," they are the first to ripen, harvestable as early as late June. They are another easy-to-grow and vigorous variety and prolific producers of fruit. The flesh is quite thick, which makes them ideal for salsas. It's also easy to scoop out the middle and stuff them. Both "Cherry Bomb" and "Hungarian Hot Wax" are lovely stuffed with cream cheese and barbecued. (2,500 to 8,000 SHU)

5 "Hot Shakira"
This chili was outstanding in our trials. Sort of half pepper, half chili, its large, long, horned fruit can have a mild kick. It's also prolific. The seed is expensive, but I think worth it. (5,000 to 30,000 SHU)

6 "Hungarian Hot Wax"
This is one of my favorites for general all-round use. The fruit has a pointy, horned shape and sweet taste. It's hugely prolific (weighing in with the largest harvest in our trial) and not too hot if picked when yellow or orange. Once red, it's really hot! (5,000 to 10,000 SHU)

7 "Jalapeño"
Another winner, this is a medium-hot, general-purpose chili with chunky, fleshy fruits and fantastic productivity. Most commonly harvested when green, it actually has a sweeter taste when left to become red. The fruit has characteristic vertical striations on the skin, which make it look like it's cracking, but in fact mean it's in its prime. This lack of perfection rules out "Jalapeno" for supermarkets, so it's a good one to grow. (2,500 to 8,000 SHU)

8 "Nepalese Bell"
This is very similar to "Christmas Bell" and technically an aji type (see *Capsicum baccatum*, p. 290), which is easier to source in the UK. It is very late to ripen, it is so a real asset when you want fruits late in the year. In September, you'll get your first chilies, but it will keep going often into November. This is hot, but with a more subdued heat than "Christmas Bell," which lingers longer on the tongue. (5,000 to 15,000 SHU)

9 "Numex Twilight"
This is another searingly hot and beautiful-looking chili with multicolored cream, green, red, and purple fruits covering the plant at the same time. It is small and compact—ideal for growing on a window ledge. The chilies are good culinary all-rounders, excellent both dried and fresh. (30,000 to 50,000 SHU)

10 "Pearls"
A fabulous looking and hugely prolific variety that is one of our most recent discoveries (also known as "Biquinho"), its fruits have a medium heat. It is an easy plant to look after and makes an ideal autumn houseplant, producing perfect, tiny, teardrop fruits that start off pale green before ripening through peach to orange and then to red. I've been pickling these in sherry, which then makes them an excellent addition to sauces, soups, and gravies. (500 to 1,000 SHU)

11 "Scotch Bonnet"
In brilliant hues of yellow, orange, and red, these balloon-shaped chilies are the ones you'll see in many African and Arabic grocery stores. It is super-hot. To be honest, we grow this more because it looks so lovely as a houseplant (or greenhouse plant) and less because we want to pick and eat it. But even so, you must still harvest continually. (100,000 to 350,000 SHU)

Best of the sweet peppers

There are a few varieties of Capsicum that would usually be classified as hot peppers. They are prolific, like hot peppers, but they score low (or zero, with no heat at all) on the Scoville scale, so I've included them here. You grow all these peppers in just the same way as chilis.

1 "Etiuda"
There are many orange and yellow peppers available and, to be honest, they seem to be pretty similar in taste and cropping pattern, but we particularly like this orange one, which has done well in our trials. It's sweet and, if you keep picking it, produces fruits for a long time. (0 SHU)

2 "Friggitello"
This is a newly bred F1 hybrid that we recently trialled and liked very much. It's an Italian pepper that gave us a plentiful harvest of sweet, small- to medium-sized fruits from August until October. It is delicious eaten like a "Padron," still green. (0 SHU)

3 "Jimmy Nardello"
This looks very handsome, like "Cayenne Red," (see p. 290), but the fruits have a more gentle flavor that's very sweet with almost no heat. It's a hugely popular variety in the United States and is prolific and easy to grow. (0 to 100 SHU)

4 "Marconi Rosso"
This is a red pepper and one we grow here more than any other. In our trials, it is the most prolific, often with more than ten fruits ripening on the plant at any one time. The fruit is sweet, thin-walled, and shaped like a horn. (0 SHU)

5 "Padron"
Originally from Galicia, widely available and very prolific, this variety produces green fruits that are delicious when blistered in a frying pan with olive oil, sprinkled with salt, and served as a tapa. As the season goes on, a few get hot, so eating "Padron" peppers is famously like playing Russian roulette. You don't know exactly how hot each one is going to be (500 to 5,000 SHU). There is a similar Italian form called "Lombardo" from Genoa. Its fruits are particularly good with seafood, such as squid or cuttlefish. (0 to 500 SHU)

6 "Shishito"
This is the Japanese equivalent to the "Padron," but on the whole less hot, so this gets my top vote. It's good raw, sliced over a salad, but even better cooked. (100 to 1,000 SHU)

Eggplant

I love the look of eggplant as they grow, with their large, crinkled purple flowers above slightly felted grey-green leaves. Once harvested, they're one of the best things for a vegetable still life, sitting on a flat plate in the center of the table—and they last well out of the fridge.

In the kitchen, they have a certain meatiness to them, which adds substance to any dish, and they're super high in fiber so they really fill you up. That makes them invaluable as one of the main ingredients for a vegetarian stew.

We always grow the big, glossy "Moneymaker No. 2" and the long, svelte "Slim Jim," which although bred in Italy is used commonly in the Far East in curries and stir-fries. "Slim Jim" is not only quick to cook but speedy to ripen, which makes it ideal for a temperate climate. We have even had success growing it outside in a sheltered spot.

Then, there are the stripy, Italian forms like "Listada de Gandia," which is among the earliest of these more hardy and earlier-ripening forms, so they are a feasible option for growing outside in the UK, but better in a greenhouse. And I like the large, egg-shaped, white "Clara," which is a heavy cropper, under cover.

In terms of growing, I'd say there are several keys to success. The first is to sow early. We aim to get our eggplant sown in February. The plants are short-lived perennials and slower growing than annuals, so they need a good, long growing season before they fruit. Make sure you pot them regularly as they grow to avoid holding the roots back at any stage. It's tempting to push them straight from the seed tray to their final position, but they then just sit and sulk. So like raising a child, it's best to coax this tender fruiting vegetable from one stage to the next. Start them off in nursery-school-sized tiny pots, pot them into medium-sized pots, and then to 1-liter pots before they're ready to graduate to the garden or into soil beds in the greenhouse.

Once you've got a good-sized seedling that's ready for its final position, think about where to plant it. In our experience,

Eggplant from a trial, including "Slim Jim" and "Clara," which we still grow.

eggplant are best grown under cover in the UK. If they're being planted outside, wait until the end of May or early June, and even then give them protection. Space plants about 60 cm (2 ft.) apart in each direction and enclose them with bales of straw to protect them from cold winds.

To aid pollination, you can mist the plants with a fine spray of water from a mister or spray bottle, but an easier way is to plant them alongside pollinator-friendly flowers such as marigolds or lemon or cinnamon basil. The purple in the leaves of cinnamon basil goes well with the eggplant's starry flowers and the scent of the herb draws in the pollinators. They will busy about making sure each flower is fertilized.

Eggplant are hungry plants, so integrate plenty of manure in any planting spot. That will also help the soil to retain water. Once the fruit has started to set, feed with an organic seaweed fertilizer or comfrey fertilizer every 2 weeks.

They'll need staking once they get to about 30 cm (1 ft.), and you will also need to pinch off each main growing tip once they reach 45 to 60 cm (18 in to 2 ft.), but check the instructions for the variety you're growing. Then, remove the tips of lateral shoots and remove any remaining flowers when five or six fruit have set. You can leave more on smaller-fruiting varieties as they produce lots of flowers and therefore fruit. Eggplant plants generally reach about 60 cm (2 ft.), although "Little Fingers" and "Fairy Tale" are shorter at about 45 cm (18 in.).

One final thing we notice regularly enough to make it worth a mention is that for every ten plants we grow and that reach a well-established fruiting size, one or two collapse with verticillium wilt, a fungal disease. Maybe just one branch gets it, with yellowing leaves that drop off or the whole plant keels over. Being organic, we've found there's nothing we can do but whip out the affected plant and hope the rest don't become cross-infected. Note that its key not to plant eggplant in that spot again, ideally for 5 years. This soil fungus is long-lived.

Best of the eggplant

None of the eggplant (Solanum melongena) listed here need salting before cooking to prevent bitterness. The risk of bitterness was an old trait that has been bred out of these more modern varieties.

1 "Clara"
This is a beautiful, ivory-white variety, which along with the similarly white "Snowy," has a delicate, sweet favor. The fruit is small (like a large egg) and matures early, making "Clara" ideal for the UK's short summers. It's prolific too.

2 "Fairy Tale"
The stripy, white and lavender-purple, drop-shaped fruit grows to about 10 to 12 cm (4 to 5 in.) on compact plants that reach 60 cm (2 ft.). The eggplant are sweet and delicious with no hint of bitterness. Another compact, small-fruited variety with similar taste is "Little Fingers," with fruit that grows green at the top and deep purple below.

3 "Listada de Gandia"
This variety from Italy is an early cropper, with medium-sized fruit that is often ripe from August, particularly if grown in the greenhouse. Its oval, white fruit is are striped with purple.

4 "Moneymaker No. 2"
This reliable, relatively heavy cropper does better in the UK's colder, greyer climate than many others we've tried. If fed well, it can grow enormous fruits, which are amazingly dark and glossy when ripe.

5 "Slim Jim"
One of the so-called "finger eggplant," this plant produces a clutch of flowers, followed by fruits that hang together like fingers or sausages off the plant. They don't ripen to the deep black-purple of many other eggplant, rather they remain slightly lighter in tone.

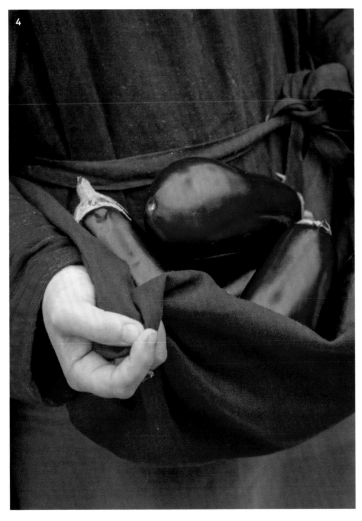

September

This month takes us back to full-on sowing. Most of our food production for October through until next March or April is dependent on getting seeds sown pretty fast. The brassicas, kale, kalettes, and purple sprouting broccoli are sown in spring, and the chard in late summer. Early autumn is the moment for lettuce, salad leaves, annual herbs such as parsley and coriander, and a few things to scatter over dishes such as spring onions and radishes.

As well as preparing for the winter and next spring in terms of sowing, we are also busy lifting, tending, and cropping the last of this year's plants. Now is the time to lift main-crop potatoes (if this hasn't happened already in August) before the slugs get the best of them and well before the frosts can burn the tubers.

Outdoors, tomatoes are in danger of blackening overnight without protection, but you can experiment with cutting the plants down from their supports and lying them on the ground (ideally, on top of hay), and covering them with a polythene tunnel so the fruit can continue to grow and ripen for a few more weeks. We have had success with that method here, and it gave us at least three more weeks from our outdoor vines.

If you have chard or hardy winter lettuces already out in the garden, change your harvesting method now. Instead of chopping the heart of the plant all at once, pick leaves round one by one, leaving the heart intact (see p. 39 and p. 62). As temperatures fall, this technique lifts the crown away from the cold, clammy soil and ensures you can go on picking over the winter.

Days are becoming shorter and light levels are dropping, so this is a good time to remove any shade netting from greenhouses or wash off shade paint. Cucumbers will keep cropping into autumn, so make sure vents and doors are closed overnight to keep in the warmth. Water plants sparingly. It's worth damping down the greenhouse by watering the floor each morning. Higher humidity will lower the plant's demand for water and also deter red spider mite.

In the Greenhouse

Seeds to Sow Now

September is much like March in the edible garden, and the jobs that need doing are similar. We line up our gutters and get sowing early in the month. Hopefully by the start of October, before soil temperatures and light levels fall too much, the seedlings will have reached a decent size of about 2 to 3 x 2 to 3cm (1 in. x 1 in.), and be ready for planting.

Sow hardy salads and herbs as soon as possible. Our vegetable patch is usually still full, so we leave the seedlings growing in gutters in the greenhouse and transplant them outside in about a month's time when there should be more room. Plant in a sheltered spot in the garden and they will give you crops through autumn, winter, and into early spring.

Lettuce Sow winter-cropping lettuce. In the south of the UK, "Salad Bowl," "Merveille des Quatre Saison," and "Solix" will all grow well once planted, even if we get snow, but in colder areas, these are safest grown with the protection of a glass cloche or polytunnel.

Salad leaves Sow the hardy cut-and-come-agains such as mizuna, mustard "Red Frills," and salad arugula. As soon as mizunas, bok choys, and mustards germinate and have grown on to at least the first true-leaf stage (true leaves are those that look like the mother plant), get them out into the garden.

Herbs Hardy annual/biennial herbs such as parsley, coriander, and chervil are best sown now. Chervil is an invaluable winter herb that has a delicious aniseedy flavor. It will only germinate as the weather cools, but it is hardy and will happily grow outside through rain, snow, and hail. Coriander does well from an early autumn sowing, thriving in the cooler weather and decreasing hours of daylight. Sow it now and you may well be harvesting right until next April or May. Space the seed at least 2 to 3 cm (1 in.) apart, so once germinated you can slide your hand in between each plant and push the seedlings out, one by one, into their final garden positions.

Leafy greens Spinach does not like it too hot and dry, or too cold and wet, so it always does best sown on the shoulders of the year in spring and autumn. You'll be picking baby leaves in about a month and, if thinned out (removing only the outer leaves, not the heart of the plant), it will keep going for a couple of months after that.

Edible flowers It's a good idea to start some edible flowers under cover in early autumn.

- *Viola tricolor* (heart's ease) will flower about 8 weeks from sowing and right the way through winter. Small posies are lovely to have beside your bed, and you can pick the flowers to scatter over salad.
- Cornflowers are also truly hardy annuals. Sow now and plant after 4 to 6 weeks. Here in Sussex, they are pretty much guaranteed

to survive the winter outside, however harsh it might be, and will be in flower by mid-May.

- Other half-hardy annuals such as borage, calendula, Chinese violet cress, and *Salvia viridis* can all be sown now and may survive winter outside, but we also keep some seedlings protected in a cold frame and plant them out during a mild spell in March. These will be in flower by the middle of April and will carry on flowering until midsummer.

Pea tips Sow some pea plants, such as "Serge" or snow peas or sugar snap, for their pea tips.

These add delicious crunch to salads or as a last-minute addition to pastas and risottos.

Sow the seeds into a length of a guttering, large pot, or an empty polystyrene or shallow wooden crate. You don't need much depth of compost for these quick crops. Scatter the seed across the length and width of the compost, cover, and put them somewhere cool and light (ideally, in a greenhouse or under a cloche). You'll get at least three crops from the same roots if you pick just the tips. Also see p. 91 for station sowing and p. 336 for sowing in a crate.

In the Garden

Sowing and Planting Direct

Now is the time to tackle the hardiest of hardy salads.

Radishes Do a last sowing of radish. With the soil still warm and moist with dew, you should be eating these within 4 to 5 weeks. Pull one or two regularly to check when they're ready so you don't miss the perfect moment when they are swollen but not woody. Serve them dipped into anchovy mayonnaise.

Arugula Sow a line of arugula. There's no flea beetle in the garden now so it won't need any protection. Salad arugula in particular thrives in the cool, grey autumn weather.

Winter purslane This is a slightly fleshy, succulent, cut-and-come-again salad plant that's very rich in vitamin C and also completely hardy. It is in fact a British native that will happily self-sow in a sunny or partially shaded corner of your garden, germinating in the autumn or early spring. It is an invaluable addition to salads in the leaner months. To get started, direct sow in a block or line. Once it's in your garden, you'll get to recognize self-sown seedlings, which you can then dig up and transplant if you want them elsewhere.

Spring onions Sown early in the month, these will be ready to eat before the frosts hit in most parts of the UK and, even if frosts are forecast, they are fine under a glass or plastic cloche. They can be harvested through autumn and into late winter. My favorite is the quick and easy "North Holland Blood Red," which has a red outer skin and goes on to form a full-sized and tasty onion if you fail to harvest it at the spring onion stage. "White Lisbon" is a good one to sow now too. Rake over the soil to achieve a fine tilth, water the line, and sow as finely as you can.

Onion and shallot sets Prepare a bed for an autumn planting about 4 weeks before planting them. Incorporate well-rotted compost to improve fertility. If your ground becomes pretty wet through the winter (ours does, as we have heavy clay soil), then a raised bed may be a better option. Plant the sets from the end of the month or in November (traditionally, the shortest day of the year). We also do a second planting in spring (see p. 121). Ensure the tip of each bulb is just protruding from the soil (see p. 342 for instructions). Cover with a cloche temporarily if you find birds keep pulling the sets out. On our heavy soil, we often start our sets off in modular trays so they already have roots when planted. We've had better success with this system.

Dividing and Mulching Rhubarb

Rhubarb is one of the lowest-maintenance edible plants you can grow, but in September there are a couple of things that you need to do as they go into their dormant season.

Cut off any flowering spikes and then mulch the crowns generously with a good, soil-covering moat of farmyard manure around each plant. Rhubarb plants are heavy feeders and love the feast that manure provides, as well as its ability to support a more moisture-retentive soil.

September (or at the latest October) is the month to lift and divide any large clumps. You can divide individual plants in rotation, tackling a few each year. Like any perennial, rhubarb needs dividing regularly to prevent the heart of the crown becoming too congested. Take the new plants from around the edge of the old clump or crown and plant in a well-drained soil that has not had rhubarb growing in it over the last few years. Dig in plenty of well-rotted organic material and plant the crowns 5 cm (2 in.) below the soil surface. Don't harvest in the next season. Just mulch your new plants—not too close to the crown—and let them grow and establish.

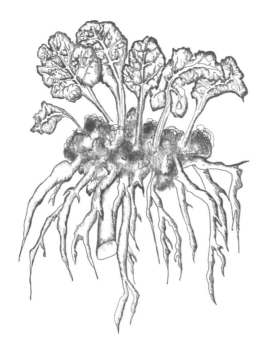

Protecting Squash

Pumpkins and squash may rot if they are constantly sitting on wet soil, so put a tile, brick, or piece of wood underneath each one. Pinch off the tips of the plants to stop them trying to form more fruit and help existing fruit to ripen. Also remove any leaves that are casting shade — shade prevents the full development of the fruits' color, and, with that their taste.

Encouraging Garden Birds

Nesting boxes
Now is a good time to thoroughly disinfect any nesting boxes you have in the garden. The best way of doing this is by scrubbing them with boiling water. It's tempting to use a cleaning fluid, but these tend to have a strong smell that can put off birds from roosting in the boxes until the scent has gone. Allow the boxes to fully dry and then position them in a new site so that local breeding pairs of birds, such as blue tits, are aware of their presence and wrens can use them as overwintering roosts. Now is a good moment to put up new boxes too. See p. 64 for more on nesting boxes.

Hedges
Late September is the moment for planting hedges. The earth is still warm and there's usually plenty of rain. It's traditional to plant a mixed native hedge in spring, but we've also had success with planting them in autumn. Evergreen hedging can be planted now, but don't leave it any later than October as the plants may be damaged by frost. See p. 97 for more on hedges.

October

Purple, orange, and crimson are my three favorite colors, and with squash and beetroot being the two most prolific plants at this time of year, those colors are what this month is all about.

In the vegetable garden here, these two groups of vegetables are set among a mass of late-season companion plants and edible flowers. There are dahlias and salvias aplenty, the handsome and velvety *Tagetes patula* "Burning Embers" in swathes, and nasturtiums flowering away as ground cover in almost every bed. When you add in a backdrop of leaves turning autumnal and russet shades in the woods that surround Perch Hill, October is a month that's full of color.

Sometimes, we get one of those perfect, clear days when the garden looks glamorous, which I love. At the other extreme, it's also beautiful here when the weather is foggy, and the chard, kale, and purple sprouting broccoli glow grandly in the gloom.

Pumpkins and squash have a huge presence in October, pushing out over the paths and covering the ground with orange and golden balloons. Most are trailers and they can be real giants—each plant spreading to cover many meters of ground at full tilt. We grow the forms with small fruits up and over frames to save space and provide vertical color. Recently, we had a perfect trio of supports and plants: a willow tuteur clad with the flame-red squash "Red Kuri"; a silver birch teepee with its broomstick-style twigs swagged in the bright tangerine pumpkin "Munchkin"; and a simple dome in the center of the vegetable garden studded with the cream and green squash "Delicata." As well as these, we have an avenue of the climbing "Tromboncino," which keeps going for at least a month longer than any other summer squash—healthy and productive without a hint of mildew on its leaves.

We bring in a mass of squash into the greenhouse too. We dry them on a big table or over a slatted drying rack, or we make string hammocks for each one and hang these along the back wall of the greenhouse alongside the grapes. This ensures good air circulation over their whole surface area and helps to cure the skins ready for storing through the winter.

Out in the garden, growing between the squash, we have blocks of beetroot in three colors—crimson-purple, orange, and bright pink—their globes swollen so full by this stage of the year that they sometimes push themselves out of the ground. The leaves of most varieties are deep emerald-green, but the bright stems and leaf veins reveal the color of the roots beneath.

Gutter-sown salads that were planted in August are looking good. We plant them so that the colors create stripes or checkerboard patterns, and they've filled out fully into a solid, patterned carpet by now. As well as giving us a daily crop, they provide boldness and color to the cool, east-facing slope of the vegetable garden.

Previous page We have dahlias aplenty at this time of year, planted side by side with purple sprouting broccoli—huge and newly released from its caterpillar cage.
Opposite Our pumpkin, squash, and ornamental corn harvest ripening before being stored.
Below We lift our beetroot to store when a hard frost is forecast (or we cover the plants with a cloche).
Next page We remove the nets from our brassica cages by mid-October but leave the frames in place to give architectural presence through the winter. They may become too brittle to use again next year, so they will need replacing.

For good contrast in leaf shape, I love to intersperse these with the feathery foliage of late-sown carrots and fennel. October is also a high point for spinach. Sown in August or early September, it grows quickly and we find we can pick baskets of spinach every week right through autumn.

And I mustn't forget our avenues of scented-leaf pelargoniums, which are planted in alternating blocks with culinary sage. Both of these are at their bushy best in October. We grow silvery culinary sage (*Salvia officinalis*) rather than the purple-leaved variety, as it has more tender leaves and a more intense flavor. It looks fantastic together with lots and lots of *Pelargonium* "Attar of Roses," which I grow to make one of my favorite herb teas.

There's an abundance of produce, but that's not the only story here at this time of year. Perch Hill's autumn edible garden would not be the same without drifts of plants that double as bird food. We cultivate curtains of both crimson and green amaranth, which are looking handsome and standing more than a meter tall now, for their seed. We also grow quinoa (which is similarly in the amaranth family), which is a grain that's popular with nutritionists and unusual among seeds in that it's high in protein as well as

Panicum miliaceum "Violaceum";
sunflower heads are left in place
for the birds; *Panicum* "Frosted
Explosion"; mountain spinach
(*Atriplex*) and *Ipomoea lobata* look
good and help to feed the birds.

carbohydrate, and packed with manganese, copper and other vitamins and minerals. It's as good for the birds as it is for us.

Alongside the amaranths, we have a couple of ornamental millets: violet millet (*Panicum miliaceum* "Violaceum") and *P.* "Frosted Explosion," which the goldfinches flock to. Then, there are sunflowers, the ornamental *Chenopodium giganteum*, and red mountain spinach (*Atriplex hortensis* var. *rubra*), which we allow to repeatedly self-sow through the year, hoeing off the seedlings if they get too much. In spring, as tender seedlings, these look and taste good in salad, but we leave them now for their seed. A final garden-bird favorite in October is the shoo-fly plant (*Nicandra physalodes*). It's very handsome at this time of year. Its seedheads are crowded with blue tits as they pierce the apex of each seedpod to access the small, applelike fruit beneath, which is full of seeds.

With all these plants allowed their place in our garden, we get a flurry of birds. I'm sure there may be some who think, *Why give up precious space to grow bird food?* But I love the extra life and color they bring, and I love that they help keep troublesome pests under control. You'll hear thrushes breaking open snail shells on the brick paths and, between them, the birds seem to devour the smaller slugs and pick plants clean of aphids and caterpillars. That's a great favor for any organic gardener.

It makes sense that if you encourage more birds to overwinter with you, they'll be there—and hungry—come spring. At that time, they will be busy feeding their young, and caterpillars, slugs, and snails are just the protein-rich stuff they want. With each clutch fledged, you get into a virtuous breeding circle. I can't say we have done a proper trial on their contribution to pest control but, without a doubt, they have made a huge difference since we started consciously nurturing the garden birds several years ago.

Squash

I can't claim squash compete with their close relations zucchini when it comes to productivity per square meter (see category 1 on p. 17), but they're ideal if you have an allotment or large garden and a lack of time to attend to it. These plants take off without much care or attention, and they look impressive for a good long time. I include pumpkins in this group, which are essentially winter squash.

Though we sow and grow all squash in the same way, they divide into summer and winter varieties. Summer squash are cut-and-come-again plants and very prolific too. However, the fruits won't store for long and are best eaten fresh. It is also possible to force them into cropping early. Winter squash, meanwhile, give you a fraction of the overall harvest of summer squash, but they make up for this with a thicker skin, which means you can store them for weeks if not months. In fact, winter squash often need to be stored (and the skin cured) for better flavor.

There are varieties that sit somewhere between summer and winter squash in terms of their characteristics and they are, to a degree, cut-and-come-again. For example, we've found that "Delicata," "Spaghetti," and "Rolet" may not be as prolific as zucchini, but they are still very abundant. If you keep harvesting, more will come. These ones don't have the density or richness of flesh of the winter varieties, and I used to consider them to be watery when compared with the classic winter squash such as "Early Butternut," but with three or four times the volume of harvest, I've stopped making comparisons. I now think of them as a whole different vegetable with a taste and texture all of their own. I love to eat any one of them with a good slosh of olive oil (or butter), salt, and plenty of black pepper.

From mini "Munchkin" to vast "Atlantic Giant," the varieties of squash we trial covers a huge range. We stick with the old stalwarts but experiment with new ones every year.

There are three things that help production of all trailing squash, be it a summer or winter variety. The first is moisture. They thrive with a regular dousing of water, so we try to leave a hose on to gently flood the roots occasionally. The second is mulch. We mulch the soil around them to help with water retention.

And the third crucial element is to pinch off the growing tips once each arm has grown to over 1 m (3 to 4 ft.). This is usually by the middle of August, but you must keep on doing it. Rather than concentrating on leafy growth, pinching off the tips makes the plant conserve its energy for flower and fruit production. Without that, the quick-growing varieties in particular (such as "Early Butternut" and "Delicata") tend to drop their flowers or their fruit fails to develop and rots on the vine.

As well as making delicious homegrown meals, squash is good for us. One of the interesting things about the winter varieties is that their nutrient content goes up after storing. They're one of the rare foods that aren't better for us when eaten fresh. They're rich in vitamins B and C, high in fiber, and have a high beta-carotene content, which makes them excel in terms of nutrition. Beta-carotene helps protect us against cancer and is very good for our eyes. You can tell by the color of the flesh that they're a good source. The richer the color, the more of it there is.

To maximize the nutrient content, it's best to roast these types of thick-skinned squash whole (skin on) for 30 to 40 minutes, depending on size. Only then, attempt to peel them, cut them in half, and scrape out the strings and seeds. Trying to cut these varieties raw is hard anyway, and the carotenoid pigment is at its highest concentration just below the skin. Roasting it first makes peeling much easier, which means you only end up removing the minimum of this packed-with-goodness outer flesh.

Best of the squash

With all squash (Cucurbita), we sow seed in April and plant in May. I've split the list into winter and summer squash. The winter varieties produce less fruit that's finite in quantity but that has thicker skin, which means they can be stored for months. Much like zucchini, summer squash are cut-and come-again, but they usually only store for 2 to 6 weeks. I've added the approximate weight of the fruit to give an idea of scale.

Winter squash

1 "Crown Prince"
A famously tasty variety and one of my favorites, it is medium-sized but often gets too big to eat in one meal. It has beautiful blue-green, verdigris skin and is a relatively good producer. It is very happy to be stored. Its orange flesh is dense and holds together well, making it ideal for roasting. It has a waxy texture and great flavor. With any squash, it's good to save some seeds (for drying and eating) when you scrape them out, but the seeds of this variety are oddly horrid. 3 to 6 kg (6 ½ to 13 lbs.)

2 "Early Butternut"
This has a typically bright orange flesh and sweet, dense taste. It is quick to ripen, and so it is ideal for the shorter growing season we have in the UK. This is the most popular year-round squash and readily available to buy in the shops, which is maybe a reason not to grow it, but it is also the perfect size for two or three people to eat for lunch or dinner. It will store for about 4 to 6 weeks. 1 ½ kg (3 lbs.)

3 "Kabocha"
A relatively new hybrid variety with a deep green or orange skin and a bountiful harvest, it has rich, flame-orange, dense flesh without a hint of wateriness and a bold taste to go with it. It is a little sweet, but not too sugary, with a slightly nutty, sweet potato flavor. It is also the perfect size for about four to six diners to polish off as a side dish. It also makes just the right amount of soup for four. 1 to 2 kg (2 to 4 ½ lbs.)

4 "Marina di Chioggia"
The knobbly-skinned "Marina di Chioggia" produces only three or four fruits if you're lucky, but each one is enormous (the same can be said of the "Pink Banana Jumbo"). Unless you're going to make a huge batch of soup for the freezer or have tons of friends round, they're tricky to use up in one go, but they look and taste great. They are a classic choice for planting to trail over a compost heap, as they are large plants with huge fruits and are very hungry feeders. In Italian markets, they get around the size issue by having one huge and handsome fruit on the stall from which people purchase slices. 4 ½ to 5 ½ kg (10 to 12 lbs.)

5 "Munchkin"

This is the smallest pumpkin of any we've grown and is also known as "Jill Be Little." I roast these whole on a bed of rosemary or sage—all pumpkins and squash go well with both herbs—and then I cut the top off, scoop out the seeds, add salt and pepper, and a drizzle of olive oil, and eat the flesh with a teaspoon. 100 to 200g (4 to 8 oz.)

6 "Red Kuri"

Shaped like an onion, this has a deep orange flesh and sweet flavor reminiscent of chestnuts. You'll also find it under the name "Uchiki Kuri" and "Japanese Onion Squash" (it is very popular in Japan). It's a fantastic squash and one we grow lots of, as it's the ideal size for about four people to eat as a side dish or as soup. The plants are small enough to train as climbers. 500g to 2 kg (1 to 4 ½ lbs.)

Summer squash

1 "Delicata"
Sometimes referred to as "Cornell's Bush Delicata," this looks more like an ornamental gourd than a pumpkin or squash, but it has surprisingly sweet, orange flesh. The great thing is you can pick almost twice as many from each plant compared to others in this list. The squash can be picked and eaten as soon as it is mature (from August or September), and more will form. From our trials at Perch Hill, this has emerged as a new favorite. "Sweet Dumpling" is similar in appearance, taste, and productivity. 500g to 1kg (1 to 2 lbs.)

2 "Little Gem"
You can store this squash for about 2 months if kept cool, though strictly speaking, it is a summer, not winter, squash. It is cut-and-come-again and very prolific. We tend to grow "Rolet," which is very handy in the kitchen. I roast or boil it whole until it's soft to the tip of a knife (about 40 minutes at 180°C/350°F, or 30 minutes at a gentle rolling boil), and then slice off the top, sprinkle in salt and pepper, and eat it like a boiled egg with a spoon. I also love them stuffed with a bit of pork mince and pine nuts,

there are lots to choose from ("Spaghetti Stripetti" is pictured). If kept cool, it will keep for 2 to 3 months. Diners divide on this one: once cooked, the flesh can be split up with a fork so it ends up looking a bit like spaghetti. Its texture and flavor are much less rich and dense than others in this list, but it is delicious all the same. Boil for 30 minutes, slice in half, remove the seeds, and douse liberally with fruity olive oil or butter and salt and pepper, then mix these into the flesh. 1 ½ to 3 ½ kg (3 to 8 lbs.)

flavored with chili, rosemary, and sesame oil and roasted until soft. 200 to 300g (7 to 10 ½ oz.)

3 Patty pan
We alternate between a yellow patty pan such as *Cucurbita pepo* "Sunburst" and an ivory-colored flying saucer like *C. moschata* "Custard White." These can be picked and eaten while they are small and tender, just like zucchini. At that stage, they are perfect in a stir-fry (see p. 187). Or you can allow them to grow on and become larger, picking them to make soup or a squash mash. Patty pans are cut-and-come-again and prolific. 500g to 1 kg (1 to 2 lbs.)

4 "Spaghetti"
This is another squash that stores relatively well, and

Beetroot

I'm crazy about beetroot, though I know not everyone likes its earthy taste (see p. 332 for an exception to that flavor rule). Beetroot plants are not cut-and-come-again, but many have an excellent characteristic of being cluster-seeded (so-called multi-germ): the seeds look like nuggets of cork with each apparent seed in fact made up of a little cluster. That means if the beetroot has been well-spaced when planted (or sown), you can carefully harvest down the line, picking the biggest roots. Then, you can go back again 2 or 3 weeks later to harvest a second lot. As long as you firm in well whatever is left behind and water the plants, you can go back a third and even a fourth time. It's uniquely a root that goes on giving, and it is perfect for both gardeners with a large vegetable garden or just a few containers.

Beetroot is also such an easy plant to grow. Even if you've never grown a single thing in your life, you will succeed. They germinate quickly and easily and can be left to get on with it in the garden for weeks without any attention. That's the main reason they are an allotment classic. There's no fuss and bother: no feeding, watering (in all but an extreme dry spell), thinning, pest protecting, or basically anything. Whatever your site or soil, beetroot is far easier to grow than carrots.

We always grow three different colors, usually a standard purple called "Boltardy," an orange called "Burpee's Golden," and the pink-and-white striped "Chioggia" (or candystripe beetroot). They taste much the same and are equally good for you, but with this mix of colors, they look glamorous on the plate. If boiling all three, do so in three separate pans to keep the colors clear.

Beetroot is also very good for us, packed with vitamins and minerals. They're a good source of calcium, magnesium, iron, phosphorous, potassium, manganese, folic acid, and vitamin C. But it is the natural dietary nitrate content found in beetroot juice that has really excited the scientific world. Nitrate helps us

A tricolor harvest of beetroot.

create nitric oxide, which dilates our blood vessels. This can both reduce blood pressure and increase blood flow to muscles and the brain. That's why sports people are so keen on beetroot. The increased blood supply to muscles increases the oxygen supply to those muscles. This oxygen can be used in addition to the stuff you breathe to generate more energy when pushing your body to its limits. Crudely, this is essentially what "blood doping" in sports is all about—but with beetroot juice, it's legitimate. The nitrates in beetroot juice are also undergoing clinical trials for the treatment of high blood pressure (hypertension). Most drugs that are currently available work in just this way—dilating blood vessels and so decreasing the pressure within them.

In terms of nutrition, as with most root vegetables, you want to avoid peeling them if you can. It makes sense that the highest concentration of antioxidants is nearest the skin where it is more vulnerable to pests and diseases. The skin is only nice to eat if you've harvested baby roots, but always leave the skin on when you roast your beetroot and then simply flake off the outer layer before you eat it. As with squash, this is easier than peeling it while it's raw and removes less of the valuable skin (see p. 323).

Opposite Beetroot seedlings in rows, each row a different color: white, purple, pink, and orange. Below Late harvests of tomatoes, carrots, and beetroot "Burpee's Golden," with the foliage of beetroot "Boltardy" in the foreground.

Best of the beetroot

You can grow beetroot (Beta vulgaris) to harvest early in the year or in autumn. Sow seed in a gutter under cover in March for a harvest in June to August, or sow directly outside in May for beetroot that reaches perfection in both size and flavor in September and October.

1 "Albina Ice"
I find white beetroot a little less sweet than the other colors, so I don't grow it every year, but it does look good with other beetroot on a plate.

2 "Alto"
A cylindrical, purple beetroot that is prolific and easy to grow, it's the perfect choice if you want big roots.

3 "Badger Flame"
If you don't like beetroot's earthy flavor (which comes from a compound called geosmin), this is the one for you. A relatively new series developed in the United States, it retains nutritional value while decreasing levels of geosmin. The beetroot is sweet and crunchy.

4 "Chioggia"
The most handsome of the lot,

this beetroot has pink-and-white striped flesh, though it merges to pink when cooked.

5 "Boltardy"
This is a standard, round, crimson beetroot with good flavor and rich coloring. It stands well for ages, almost whatever the weather, hence its name, presumably a portmanteau of 'bolt' and 'hardy'.

6 "Bull's Blood"
We sometimes grow this for its crimson leaves, using it as an ornamental plant in containers and bedding. We pick it as a tender baby leaf and add it to salads. The beetroot is fine to eat, but it's the leaves that are lovely. The seeds can also be sown in a shallow tray for microgreens.

7 "Burpee's Golden"
A long-standing favorite

here at Perch Hill, this golden variety is currently being trumped by "Golden," which did better in our most recent trials, germinating well. I still love "Burpee's Golden," but germination has been a little sporadic in recent times.

8 "Pronto"
An old variety we have long grown and harvested as baby beetroot, it is quick-growing, sweet, and delicious.

October

With the year winding down, October is the month for lifting, storing, and preserving as much of this year's produce as we can to eat through the approaching winter and spring. We do a final sowing of things like salads and beetroot for greenhouse planting.

A warm autumnal day is also the perfect time to add manure to next year's potato patch. We used to double-dig, adding plenty of manure into the base of a trench before turning the soil of the next trench over that manure. Becase our heavy clay has been much improved over the years, we have now moved to a no-dig system and just spread the manure out, teasing it into the soil lightly with a fork.

It's also the month for making leaf mold to enhance the compost we add to pots and integrate into our sowing compost. It's an easy and rewarding job, but we try not to get over-zealous when collecting the leaves. Allowing some leaves to remain where they fall is good for biodiversity as it provides food for invertebrates and, later, the microorganisms and mycorrhizae in the soil benefit from this added organic matter.

With crops such as chard and winter-hardy lettuce already out in the garden, we change our harvesting pattern now, moving from periodically chopping the heart of the plant all at once, to only picking round (see p. 39 and p. 62). For chard in particular, as temperatures and light levels fall, thinning out lifts the crown away from the cold, clammy soil and helps ensure we can go on picking over the winter.

In the Greenhouse

Seeds to Sow Now

It's at this time of year we sow a few winter
herbs and salads in containers for easy picking
from a windowsill or the back door.

- Go to a friendly fishmonger, produce store,
  or wine merchant and ask if they have any
  wooden or polystyrene boxes or crates. These
  need to be about 20 cm (8 in.) deep.
- Knock several drainage holes in the bottom.
- Fill the crate with compost and sow the seeds.
- Cover the boxes with plastic wrap to enclose
  the moisture and put them somewhere warm
  to germinate. This could be in the greenhouse
  or cold frame on a heated base. An airing
  cupboard is also fine, but if you're leaving
  them somewhere dark, you'll need to check
  every day for signs of germination.
- Move the seedlings into the light as soon as
  there are any signs of green. Once the
  seedlings are up, take the plastic wrap off.
- Allow the plants to reach about 7 to 8 cm (3
  in.) and then start cutting. You should get two
  or three cuts from the same seedlings before
  they collapse exhausted.

Storing Greenhouse Produce

Gathering the harvest from outside is the priority
(see p. 338), but once you've got everything
vulnerable to cold weather in from the garden,
it's good to clear the greenhouse crops as well.

Tomatoes

If we've had a sunny September, most tomatoes
will have ripened well in the greenhouse and
been harvested, making October the time to lift
the plants. If there was even a hint of blight, add
the vines to the bonfire, not the compost heap.
Any fungal spores can persist in the compost
for 2 or 3 years and can reinfect tomato plants if
used as a mulch or for soil conditioning.

Basil

If the greenhouse falls below 5°C (41°F) on any
one night, basil will turn black instantly, so as
soon as you can, harvest all you have and make
basil oil or pesto and store it.

Eggplant, sweet peppers, and chilies

As temperatures fall, harvest peppers, chilies,
and eggplant growing indoors regularly. They'll
still be flowering, and this will encourage more
fruit formation.

Cucumbers

They will keep cropping into autumn, so close
vents and doors overnight to keep in the warmth.

In the Garden

Storing Garden Produce

Bringing in the food harvest before the cold and wet take their toll is a major preoccupation for October. Listed here in terms of priority, with the least weather-resistant first, are the edibles we concentrate on.

Eggplant, sweet peppers, and chilies

If you're growing chilis, peppers, and eggplant outside, harvest the whole plant. Dig them up and shake the soil off the roots. Hang them in a warm place to allow the fruit to continue to ripen.

Beans and peas

Harvest the last beans and peas before the frosts get them. Leave the legume roots in the ground, as nitrogen will be released as the roots break down. For the beans, the pods may be too huge and stringy to make good eating, but we still harvest them into baskets according to variety and leave them to dry out for a few weeks. We then shell them and put the beans into jars. Leave the jar lids off for another couple of weeks to allow them to fully dry out, and then store to eat through winter.

Florence fennel

This is one of the best autumn and winter crops, but it will get damaged in a hard frost. Cover it with fleece or a cloche so you can continue to harvest it from the garden. To protect it, mound up soil around the base of the bulb before covering to encourage it to swell and help prevent bolting.

Herbs

The hardy herbs such as parsley, coriander, and chervil will keep going whatever the weather, but the deciduous shrubs and herbaceous perennials need harvesting and storing before they disappear.

Lemon verbena Hang up stems of lemon verbena to dry before they shed their leaves. Cut good bunches, tie them together, and put them somewhere well-ventilated but warm. We hang ours in the greenhouse. If you have an Aga, hang them above that or in the airing cupboard. Leave them for a couple of weeks and then remove the crispy leaves and store them in a tin.

Tarragon There's nothing better than tarragon vinegar with its characteristic smoky flavor. It is ideal for winter salad dressings and is delicious in a hollandaise. Now is the moment to make it before the frost flattens your plants until next spring. Pick as much tarragon as you can and submerge it in a big jar of white wine vinegar. Leave it to steep for a month before straining into individual bottles. This keeps for years.

Mint If you have mint growing in pots, now is the moment to bring the pots indoors to extend their growing season by several weeks. If it's in the ground, harvest as much as you can. You can add the leaves to crab-apple or apple jelly, together with a sliced chili or two for an extra kick.

Thyme Most evergreen herbs are fine to pick year-round, with thyme being the exception.

It still looks good now but won't for long. Prune it back and hang the pruned stems upside down in a paper bag to dry.

Roots

To store root vegetables, you can make a traditional clamp (layers of vegetables with soil between each layer that's then insulated with a thick layer of straw over the top), but we use a simpler system, suited to beetroot and carrots (pictured on p. 339).

- Go to your local fishmonger, produce store, or wine merchant and ask if they have any wooden or polystyrene boxes or crates. These need to be at least 20 cm (8 in.) deep to hold a layer or two of roots, but go deeper if you have lots to store.
- Cover the bottom of the box with newspaper.
- Add 2 ½ cm (1 in.) of damp sand or moistened compost (you can use compost from this year's used growbags).
- Don't cut the beetroot tops off, but rather twist them. This avoids them bleeding, which results in less flavor and a spongy texture.
- Lay the roots on their side, virtually touching.
- Cover with sand or compost and move on to the next layer until you have filled the crate. It's fine to mix the carrots and beetroot in alternating layers. Kept cool, they will store well through winter.

Squash

If not done in September, lift up and place all the larger fruit at ground level onto tiles (or flattened fruit-juice cartons) to keep them off the soil. Leave them there—and the climbers on their vines—to ripen in the sun for as long as possible so that the skins can harden before storage.

Making squash hangers

For a quick fix, old tights make ideal hangers for squash, but they don't look particularly good. We make time to create hammocks from garden twine. These look like lovely plant holders—the twine tied in such a way that it flares out to form a circular hammock that holds the fruit and prevents it from slipping through. The instructions here are for a medium-sized squash (such as "Early Butternut"). For smaller squash, cut shorter lengths of string and reduce the spacing between the knots. For a larger squash, cut longer lengths and increase the spacing.

- Cut off eight lengths of string measuring about 50 cm (20 in.). You can use any number of lengths, as long as you have an even number.
- Gather the lengths at one end and tie them in a strong knot.
- Take two lengths of the string and make a knot about 5 cm (2 in.) from the top end.
- Do the same with the remaining pieces of string.
- Take two lengths of string coming from those knots—one from each adjacent side—and make another knot about 5 to 8 cm (2 to 3 in.) down.
- Repeat with the other pieces. Then, turn it upside down. You'll find you have created a rudimentary basket for your squash.
- Gather the lengths of string at the top and tie a loop to hang it up.

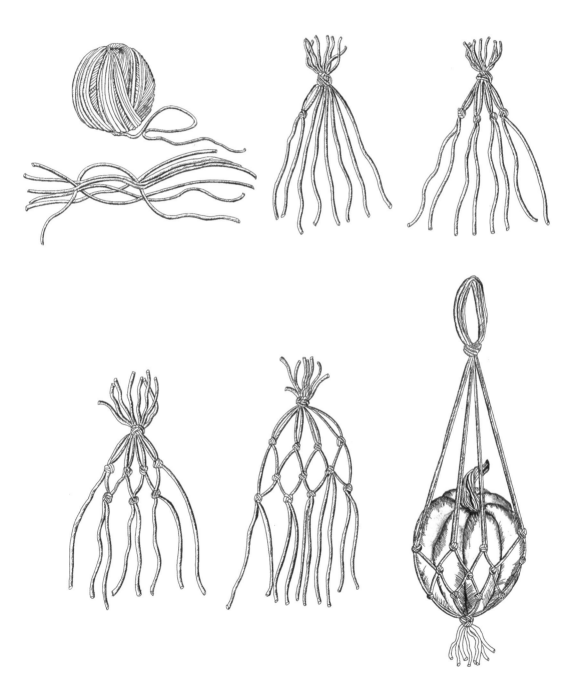

Planting Onions, Shallots, and Garlic

If you prepared a bed for autumn varieties of onions, shallots, and garlic in September (see p. 306), you can start planting in October. If you didn't, aim to prepare a bed early in the month (by incorporating plenty of well-rotted compost to improve fertility) so that you're ready to plant your sets at the end of the month and harvest in early summer. You can also plant in spring (see p. 121).

There are different types of garlic that can be planted at different times of year. The autumn varieties, which can be planted from now until Christmas, are softnecks like "Solent Wight" and "Albigensian Wight" (this one is also good for spring planting), or hardnecks like "Bella Italiano." To plant garlic, push in individual cloves no more than 5 cm (2 in.) deep and 15 to 16 cm (6 in.) apart.

How to plant onion and shallot sets
- Plant the sets with the tip of each bulb just protruding from the soil. You can do this straight into the bed toward the end of the month, but we prefer to insert the sets into small pots or module cells (one set per cell) first.
- Place them somewhere bright but cool (such as a greenhouse) and leave to root for 4 to 6 weeks to get them growing well before planting. Starting this way also helps to prevent birds from pulling the sets out of the soil.
- Depending on variety and size, plant onion sets at a spacing of 10 cm (4 in.) between each bulb, and 30 cm (1 ft.) between each row.

For shallots, leave a space of 18 cm (7 in.) between each bulb, and 30 cm (1 ft.) between rows.
- Keep the bed weed free, especially early on.
- You can add a cloche temporarily if you find birds keep pulling the sets out of the soil.

Planting Rhubarb

Whether you're dividing old plants or planting new ones, this can be done any time when the plants are dormant from September to March. In autumn, the soil will still be warm, allowing for good root development. If you wait until early spring, the plant will be raring to go and shoots will develop quickly, meaning they will require more moisture. For instructions on dividing rhubarb, see p. 308.

If you're starting from scratch, bare-root plants are the most effective and cheapest choice. When you receive your plants, pot them into 2-liter or 3-liter pots, depending on their size. Ensure each growing point/shoot is at or just below the soil surface. Grow them under cover for about a month until the roots have filled the pot and then plant them.

- Choose a well-drained area in dappled shade. Make sure rhubarb hasn't grown in that patch for at least a few years.
- Prepare the area by forking in plenty of well-rotted organic material.
- You need to allow at least 1 m (3 to 4 ft.)

between plants, as their stems and leaves will soon spread to fill the space.

- Plant the crowns no more than 5 cm (2 in.) below the soil surface, taking great care not to break any of the newly formed roots.
- Spread organic compost around the crowns anytime from now until spring.
- Don't harvest anything in the first season. Just mulch your plants—not too close to the crowns—and let them grow and establish themselves. Simply allow the sticks of rhubarb to die back in the first autumn so that the goodness goes back into the crowns.

Asparagus Care

- Cut down asparagus ferns as they yellow, reducing them to around 2 ½ cm (1 in.) from the ground. Removing the old foliage helps to keep asparagus beetles from overwintering in the bed and reduces the chance of other pests and diseases.
- Many modern asparagus cultivars are all-male because these produce a greater quantity of better spears. Female plants produce orange-red berries. If you are growing an all-male cultivar, remove any females now, and any seedlings.
- Carefully weed the bed.
- Cover with a deep layer of mulch—ideally, manure. This feeds the asparagus crowns and helps retain moisture next spring and summer.
- Mulch with grit over the top to keep the bed pristine.

Making Leaf Mold

Leaf mold is a hugely effective soil conditioner and expensive to buy, so it's well worth making your own in October or later in winter. If you make it now, you can be adding it to your soil this time next year. We use ours mixed into our seed compost too.

You need to gather leaves in one place so that they can break down. You can make a simple enclosure out of posts and chicken wire or, if you don't have the time or space, just add the leaves into the compost heap or pile them into jute sacks or even black trash can liners pierced at the bases with a few holes to ensure a little air circulation.

Rake up leaves and collect anything that has fallen (except large branches and evergreen leaves). Some leaves break down much quicker than others, so it is best to shred all the leaves before leaving them to rot down to help the process along. Do this by running the lawn mower over the leaves before you pile them into the enclosure or sack.

It's also vital that they are damp before you add them into your pen or sacks. If not, water the leaves. Dry leaves will sit there and do not rot down.

Cover the pen or close the sack and leave for 12 to 18 months. Put any filled sacks somewhere out of the way. The leaves will slowly rot down. Fungi start the process of breaking down the dead leaves, followed by bacteria. Check your heap every so often, giving it a quick poke to make sure it's not bone dry.

November
& December

Despite the vegetable garden starting to look and feel wintery, we're still able to pick something for almost every meal in November and December. It surprises me that there is such a range of produce out there that will grow happily for us, even now.

I can't deny that some of the winter-hardy plants are far more abundant grown under glass, so if you have a cold frame, greenhouse, polytunnel, or even a series of glass or plastic cloches, do use them. We grow a mix of salads and hardy annual herbs in our glasshouse here, but certainly in Sussex this protection is not essential. The most cold-resistant of these greens, such as parsley, mizuna, mustard "Red Giant," and American cress, may falter under snow or after several successive days of frost, but even without a cover, they won't die. They seem to hibernate and then, as soon as there's a bit of sun or a general thaw they come back to life.

Depending on the severity of the season's weather, the salad and annual herbs growing outside produce about 50 percent less compared to those growing inside. That's from now until March (here in Sussex), but after that the trend reverses. The indoor ones bolt as soon as you get a few sunny days, whereas those outside take over and often crop until May.

Out in the garden, we always have statuesque kalettes and crinkly forests of kale. Varieties such as "Redbor" and "Scarlet" have great color as well as presence and look particularly glamorous with a sparkling dusting of rain or frost on a sunny morning or even swathed in snow. These are by far the most

Previous page Late-season
salad "Black Seeded Simpson,"
"Merveille des Quatre Saisons"
and "Solix."
Opposite top "Rhubarb Chard,"
with late-flowering carnations
and kale "Redbor," which is still
giving splashes of color.
Opposite bottom Evergreen
rosemary thrives with us (almost)
whatever the weather.
Next page Kale "Redbor" is the
most splendid winter edible you
can grow.

splendid winter-garden vegetables. I think of them as the dowager duchesses of our vegetable bank, and the spring-cropping purple sprouting broccoli as their attendees.

Slightly the worse for wear but still edible are our chards (we give these the most sheltered spots over winter), evergreen herbs, and fragrant and tasty pelargonium leaves. We've found "Attar of Roses" keeps going until the first truly killer frosts, which more often than not arrive in early January.

There are benefits to winter growing beyond simply fresh greens for the kitchen. For one, there's no need to water the plants; the heavens do that for you unless the plants are growing under cover—and even, then they need very little water. There's also the benefit of a lack of pests. Slugs remain active if it's above 5°C (41°F) but hibernate below this, and their eggs don't survive exposed to cold. At this time of year, many of them die or bury themselves deep in the soil. There's no flea beetle either. In the main growing season, these beetles (which hop like fleas) pepper the brassica salad leaves such as arugula, mizuna, and mustard with tiny holes, but they are blessedly absent at this time of year. Also absent are the cabbage whites. I love the animation the confettilike butterflies lend the summer vegetable patch, but their caterpillars are of course devastating to cabbage-related plants, stripping the leaves of the more tender-textured brassicas such as "Cavolo Nero" down to a skeleton of midrib and veins.

As long as you don't have a large pigeon population, you can safely reveal all your brassicas now without fear of too many pests. Even if the odd caterpillar emerges from its egg, it will be eaten by birds. And robins, wrens, and tits will polish off the ash-like whiteflies that can still be a pain if you leave your brassicas enclosed. To help this process, put a bird feeder right next to any infested plants to draw in garden birds.

All in all, we find that our birds help keep our plants—and the pests that like to devour them—in pretty good order. That's how I want to garden.

Kale

I once worked as a trainee general practitioner in the Outer Hebrides in Scotland and was puzzled every time I spotted a small enclosure, often in the middle of nowhere, made from dry stone walls. I asked the locals whether these were for sheep and was told they were kale yards: tiny fields for summer potatoes and autumn/winter kale. In the winter months on the western-most coast of the UK, at least one day in three is pretty much guaranteed to be windy. Anything growing there in summer has to be robust, let alone in winter. Protected by walls, kale is about the only thing that can survive.

Seeing it there impressed me so much that I was keen to trial different varieties as soon as I arrived at Perch Hill and had plenty of room. In fact, that's a key point: kale does need space. That's why it is different from the salads, herbs, and other leafy greens such as chard that are perfect for small city gardens and large allotments alike. That said, there are some relatively compact varieties of kale such as "Dwarf Green Curled" and "Red Russian" (both reaching 60 cm [2 ft.] tall and wide) or even "Scarlet," which comes in at under 1 m (3 to 4 ft.). You can bonsai them too, repeatedly removing the leader to encourage them to branch. This way, they'll even fit in a pot, but you need to keep pinching the top to stop them growing and growing.

After experimenting with one or two varieties, I discovered that if you pick them right, kale is cut-and-come-again. If you snap off the leaves from the main trunk, you'll see another leaf bud forming just above the scar within a week or so. This takes a few weeks to get to a decent eating size, but as long as you have enough plants, kale will keep you supplied all winter long.

More recently, we've found the same applies to kalettes (also known as flower sprouts). Break them off the main stem and new buds will slowly form and another crop will come. If we start cropping these in November, we can usually get three crops from the elegant, walking-stick-like stalks before the end of winter.

Kale "Redbor," along with French artichokes, are the two most handsome plants for any vegetable garden—so, much so that they're worth including in an ornamental border design. "Cavolo Nero" is

A brassica bed, not at Perch Hill, but in the beautiful and abundant kitchen garden at Chatsworth House in Derbyshire. This shows you the patterns you can make with winter brassicas.

statuesque and handsome too. Annoyingly, the cabbage white
caterpillars seem to truly love it, so like all cabbages, they must be
netted, which diminishes their ornamental potential. As a general
rule, the summer bitterness of kale seems to drive the cabbage whites
to other brassicas but, sadly, they still adore "Cavolo Nero."

Although whiteflies are much less active now than in summer,
you may get a few overwintering. A well-positioned bird feeder next
to the infested plants will help to draw in garden birds that will feast
on the pests. Hopefully, they'll find them. If that fails, soak your kale
leaves for an hour or two in salty water then wash them in a deep
sink filled with cold water, rinsing them a couple of times. That
should leave them clean.

As well as the stalwart kales, we've recently added spigariello.
This is our new must-have. I was introduced to this leafy broccoli by
Belgian vegetable expert Peter Bauwens. He gave me a packet of seeds
a few years ago, and I'm now a big fan. Spigariello is classified as both
a broccoli and a kale—and correctly so. It has narrow, elegant curly
leaves that you can eat as a green all through the winter, apparently
without compromising the plant, and then in spring, tight, tasty
flower buds emerge like purple sprouting broccoli. These develop
further into edible flowers that look and taste delicious—with the
added bonus that the bees love to feast away on their nectar. It's a
three-in-one plant and has, in my view, got to be grown.

Kales don't just pack a punch in terms of stature, they are
supremos on the nutritional front. The leafy green reputedly has a
powerful healing effect, detoxifying the body on a cellular level.
One measure of the healthiness of food is its ability to inhibit the
effects of certain cell-damaging molecules known as "free radicals."
Free radicals are said to do all sorts of damage to the body on a
cellular level and are implicated in inflammatory diseases, such as
chronic fatigue syndrome, rheumatoid arthritis, cancer, heart disease
and brain diseases like Alzheimer's. To buy into the idea that
reducing free radicals is good for us was quite left field a couple of
decades ago but, after supportive scientific findings, it's now a more
mainstream concept.

Natural antioxidants are compounds found in food that can help
to protect against free radicals, and kale is often championed as an
antioxidant superstar because it contains high levels of vitamin C,
carotenoids, flavonoids, and glucosinolates—all top ranking among
the antioxidant crew. They behave as sort of free-radical vacuum and
are hugely beneficial to our health as a result.

Apart from being exceptionally healthy, cooked or raw, kale is also very tasty—all the more so in winter. In the summer, high temperatures and drought stress results in kale leaves that are sometimes bitter in taste, whereas in the winter, low temperatures and light levels, together with wet weather, make for kale leaves with a milder flavor that's better all round.

So it's now, in winter, that I want to eat kale the most. It's delicious raw, massaged until it softens in a tahini dressing. I also love it cooked, much like a seaweed dish you might find in a Chinese restaurant. Strip the leaf from the stem (which is tough and no good to eat), then shallow fry or roast the kale in a very hot oven to crisp it up (it will stay crispy even when cold). Top with the lightest sprinkling of caster sugar and some salt to bring out its flavor, and perhaps some roasted and chopped cashews. Do that and you've got delicious winter food, courtesy of the garden.

If in the past you have avoided or disliked kale, I say blame the chef, not the vegetable, and throw your recipe net good and wide to discover new ways to enjoy it. On a winter evening, when I'm thinking about cooking dinner, I'd be bereft without my bed of kale growing out there happily, whatever the weather.

Opposite The characterful broccoli-kale spigariello.
Below As in January and February, kale, chard, and salad become our outside stalwarts for winter.

Best of the kales

You've got to take your hat off to kale (Brassica oleracea Acephala Group). It's the trouper of the winter vegetable garden—still producing at this grey and freezing time of year. You can sow and grow it for baby-leaf salad pretty much anytime between March and September, but for full-sized, long-picking plants, sow 4 to 5 months before you want to pick. So for cropping now, we sow in late spring and early summer.

1 "Black Magic"
Recently bred, this kale is a more compact version of "Cavolo Nero" and stands at about 60 cm (2 ft.). We grow this in large pots and also in a repurposed water trough, as it makes for an elegant, edible container filler during winter (when there are very few cabbage white butterflies). Once picked, it tastes much the same as "Cavolo Nero."

2 "Cavolo Nero"
Also referred to as black Tuscan kale and "Nero di Toscana," this kale was hardly known in the UK before it appeared in the first River Café cookbook, more than 25 years ago. Back then, it was billed as an essential ingredient in many Italian winter dishes and has gone on to become a staple in British cooking. It is lovely to look at and delicious to eat. Its leaves are best when young and fresh. Keep picking

them regularly, because if they're left to grow too long, they become tough and bitter.

3 "Scarlet"
This one is similar to "Redbor," but a little shorter at 90 cm (3 ft.), so it is the one we tend to choose for our larger pots or troughs. With enough manure added to the compost in the container, it will thrive and crop for several months, be it winter or summer. I'm a massive fan.

4 Kalettes
Brassica oleracea kalettes (or flower sprouts), are a kale/Brussels sprouts hybrid, and are packed with antioxidants. If you have room, I really recommend you grow them. Unlike Brussels sprouts, they will crop at least two or three times if you pick the outer leaves by twisting them off the main stem.

5 "Pentland Brig"
Green and curly, this kale is the one that's most widely available at supermarkets. It's good to eat and ideal if you want to grow something familiar. But with plenty of more exciting kales growing here at Perch Hill, it doesn't really add much to our selection.

6 "Redbor"
This is the best-looking kale with statuesque, deep red, trunk-like stems covered in crinkly crimson leaves. My friend and colleague Arthur Parkinson
(who has a garden growing entirely in pots) grows "Redbor" just for its looks. He loves its fabulous color and leaf shape as a backdrop to tulips, daffodils, and wallflowers in spring, and he grows it with purple alliums, too. He pinches it out hard to prevent it getting too huge, but he is happy to let it run to flower as the bees have a field day.

7 "Red Russian"
Tender and more spinachlike than a classic kale, "Red Russian" is a beautiful plant featuring greyish leaves with a purple cast that deepens as the weather cools. It keeps producing for 6 months, retaining its gentle flavor and soft texture right through the year. Picked small, with leaves just a few centimeters long, it's delicious raw in salads.

8 Spigariello
Brassica oleracea spigariello is a new favorite of mine. You can eat the narrow leaves of this leafy broccoli from July right through the winter, and then in spring you can harvest its flower shoots like a tender-stem broccoli. Keep picking and it seems to keep producing for months at a stretch.

November & December

For gardeners that wish to claim a couple of months of down time, November and December can provide a handy break from the kitchen garden. And to my mind, it's quite okay to put your feet up!

Don't, however, take your eye off the ball completely. Listen out for the weather forecast and have a length of fleece or plastic extendable tunnel or cloche at the ready to protect your crops. We often still have vegetables out in the garden that are not 100 percent hardy, such as Florence fennel, beetroot, celeriac, and even carrots. Covered with a length of fleece or a cloche packed with straw, they will be protected from the frost.

For our inside crops, we have a great invention in our greenhouse: a thermal screen running on an electric motor, which I switch on and off according to the weather. Without it, we'd need to use bubble wrap on the inside of the glass.

On the odd warm day, we do sometimes do a bit of sowing, favoring plants that are happy in low light. However, don't be tempted to think, *Why not get cracking early and sow a few things this side of Christmas?* Seeds may germinate, but the resulting plants will be wimps and you'll find they collapse instantly if you forget to water them or if there's a savagely cold night just as they emerge. Wait until at least mid-February before you get going with general vegetable sowing.

If you're dead keen to keep busy, choose instead to research a growing topic on which your knowledge is sketchy. Read up about it and get prepared for action. Now is the perfect time to do this.

In the Greenhouse

Seeds to Sow Now

It's best to wait until early spring to sow most seeds. There are a few exceptions, which we try to remember to sow in the first week or two of November.

Fava beans

Sow fava beans into root trainers, selecting hardy varieties such as "Aquadulce Claudia," or if you can find the seed and have greenhouse border space, try the more rare "Martock," which is happy growing and cropping inside. It will give you delicious and tender fava beans to harvest in April. See p. 58 for fava bean sowing instructions.

Salads and pea tips

If you missed your chance to sow boxes of cut-and-come-again salads and hardy herbs in October (see p. 336), this is still worth doing in November. The same can be said of sowing pea tips (also see p. 91 and p. 305).

Forcing Rhubarb Under Cover

If you have plenty of rhubarb growing, you can force a crown to crop early under cover (you can also do this outside, see p. 62). There is a double advantage to forcing rhubarb: first, it brings the harvest forward and second, the stems you get are tender, sweet and hardly need any sugar during cooking. Traditionally, whole plants were dug up in the autumn and moved indoors to warm, dark sheds where they were encouraged to start cropping in the middle of winter. You can try this yourself, especially if you're already dividing a congested crown and therefore lifting the plant anyway (see p. 308). If you do lift the crown and bring it indoors, you will end up with rhubarb stems in January and February. If you force rhubarb outside instead, you'll have stems to harvest by March.

1   Lift a crown of rhubarb (ensure it is at least 3 years old) and leave it exposed on the bed until you've had a couple of good frosts.
2   Plant it into spent compost in an old compost bag and bring it inside into a warm cellar or laundry room.
3   Water it and then place an upturned container or trash can over the top of the plant to exclude all light.
4   After about 4 weeks, take a look. Some of the stems should be big enough to harvest. Pull what you want, then cover the plant again. A few weeks later, you should get another harvest. You can repeat this process a couple times.
5   In late winter/early spring, once you've harvested all you can, remove the outer sections of the clump, pot them into 2-liter pots of peat-free compost, nurture them under cover or in a cold frame for a short while, and then plant again. The inner section can be added to the compost heap.
6   Once the rhubarb is back in the garden, don't force these same roots for several years. Just let them recover and settle back in.

General Maintenance

If the weather is nice, we try to tick off lots of small tasks to get ahead for next year. It's a great way to get out into the garden for some fresh air, and all of these jobs are worth doing.

Pipes

Burst pipes are almost as inconvenient to deal with in the garden as they are in the house, so now is the moment to prevent the problem. If you can, turn off all of your outdoor water sources and drain the system. If that's not possible, insulate taps with lagging. If you're handy with a hammer and nails, build a slim, wooden cover around the standpipe so the lagging can stay in place all year. If not, pack with recycled bubble wrap or loose straw into a burlap jacket taped or tied around the lagging.

Tools

It's a good moment to do a sort-out of the garden shed and make sure your tools are cleaned and oiled so they don't rust over the winter. Sharpen blades of secateurs, snippers, and scissors, oiling them after they're sharpened before putting them away. Throughout the year, we place a bucket of oily sand in the shed (it doesn't have to be anything fancy, we simply add a slosh of sunflower oil to the sand) to plunge forks, spades, and hoes into after every use. That said, annual maintenance remains essential.

Shed

Have a good sort-out of the potting shed, washing all pots and seed trays so they are ready for spring sowing. Scrape all the dried-on grass from any mowers and strimmers. Ideally, get these machines serviced long before spring.

Greenhouse

Move all of the plants out of the greenhouse before giving it a good clean. Tip any old compost onto borders. Use a garlic candle (designed especially for greenhouses), which offers a nontoxic way of fumigating, ridding the space of any pests that were hoping to overwinter under cover. Wash the glass to allow in as much light as possible. Check for any visible pests before bringing plants back into the greenhouse.

To keep some cold out of the greenhouse over winter, attach bubble wrap to the inside of the glass for insulation. Ideally, use bubble wrap that is meant for the job, which is UV-stabilized and allows better light transmission than packaging wrap. At a pinch, recycled bubble wrap works well. Attach to the greenhouse with clips or staples if you have a wooden greenhouse. For an aluminium frame, attach with waterproof tape.

On mild winter days, ventilate the greenhouse to prevent problems building up—particularly, fungal diseases. Check your plants regularly and remove diseased foliage. Water plants on mild days if the compost feels dry, but aim to keep the water off the leaves to avoid fungal problems.

In the Garden

Planting Tulips with Crops on Top

Our main job for November is planting tulips, a task that applies to the vegetable garden as much as it does elsewhere. We grow swathes of tulips to add color among the salads, herbs, and kale in early and mid-spring, and November is the safest month to plant tulips to avoid tulip blight.

In the old days, we used to dig trenches and pour the bulbs in, but since we have moved to a no-dig system, we use a soil corer or trowel and plant the bulbs one by one to minimize disturbance to the microorganisms and invertebrates.

Even though it's getting late for transplanting salad seedlings out into the garden now, we do plant a batch of salads over the top. With color, leaf shape, and size in mind, we think consciously about making tapestries—striped, square, and checkerboard patterns—and we plant them out as early in November as we can, so the seedlings have a chance to settle in before the worst of the cold and dark really hits.

We alternate a bronze-leaved lettuce such as "Merveille des Quatre Saisons" with "Red Oak Leaf," and then a bright green such as "Cancan" for contrast. We grow the crimson mizuna "Red Knight" next to the more usual green mizuna, while "Red Frills" or "Red Giant" mustard alternate with the bright green "Wasabina." With this elegant arrangement of salad leaves forming the lower storey of our plants, and with plenty of flowers above, the palette and pattern potential is huge come spring.

You can plant tulips with crops that are hardy, such as the following:

Lettuce "Salad Bowl," "Solix," "Black Seeded Simpson," "Merveille des Quatre Saison," "Reine des Glaces."

Salad leaves Mizuna, salad arugula "Serrata," any of the mustards, spinach "Medania."

Herbs Flat-leaved parsley "Gigante di Napoli," coriander, chervil.

Leafy greens Swiss chard, the dwarf kales such as "Scarlet."

Leeks Go for beautiful varieties such as "Northern Lights" and "Saint Victor."

Planting tulips
- Using a long-handled bulb planter (these have a corer at the bottom), push the corer into the ground with your foot and remove a core of soil.
- On heavy soil, like we have at Perch Hill, we put a handful of old, used compost or grit in the hole, followed by the bulb.
- Move onto the next. As you push into the ground for the second hole, the first core pushes out of the cylinder in the bulb planter. Use this to replace the soil over your first planted bulb. Firm down and then move on to the next hole and bulb.

- Protect the tulips against rodent attack with chili flakes scattered densely over the soil.

Planting on top of tulips

Add lettuce, salad leaves, or other hardy seedlings over the top. Seedlings sown in gutters in September or October (see p. 304) are the perfect size for this. Use a trowel to dig a hole and then slide one seedling out of the gutter and into the hole before moving on to the next. Space them about 15 cm (6 in.) apart.

We also love leeks for their vertical shapes. Even though they are not cut-and-come-again, we always grow them and layer them in the same way with tulips. We select the purple-washed varieties ("Northern Lights" and "Saint Victor") and we try not to eat them all but allow some to flower in the spring. That gives you an extra show.

The best way to do this is to get the leeks started in gutters or in modules a little earlier than you usually would. We plant ours in October, then transplant leek seedlings in November over the top of the tulips. They will grow on slowly through the winter, look good, and reach harvestable size in mid- to late spring.

Winter Dahlia Care

Lifting dahlias

If you live in a frost pocket, you will need to lift your dahlias from your borders and pots for frost protection. Start this process once the frost has knocked back the top growth of the plants. Cut the plants back to about 10 cm (4 in.) from the ground and then dig them up. Remove as much soil as possible, then leave the tubers to dry off indoors for a week. Make sure to stand them upside down to drain any water out of the hollow stems. Wrap in several sheets of newspaper or pack into boxes of dry compost. Store in a dry, frost-free place.

Mulching dahlias

If you leave your dahlias in the ground as we do at Perch Hill, cut back and mulch them now. Reduce each plant to about 10 cm (4 in.), cutting just above a leaf joint. Label them clearly with a huge label so that you'll remember what and where they are. Mulch deeply, tipping a bucket of compost or green waste over the head of each one. Dome it over the crown. This will insulate the tender tubers through the winter and direct the rain away so there's less danger of rot. They will come back bigger, better, and earlier next year. It's so much easier than lifting and replanting. You can push the mulch aside once the weather warms up by late April or early May.

Soil Conditioning and Preparation

No-dig beds

Having now cultivated the soil in our garden for 20 years, we have improved our impenetrable clay. A few years ago, we moved to a no-dig system, and I can wholeheartedly recommend it. What this means is rather than digging down—and thereby destroying the soil structure, earthworm holes, and soil mycorrhizae, as well as spurring on the germination of weed seeds by turning over the soil—we are instead improving the soil with minimal intervention. You can also lay cardboard out over an empty bed or lawn and pile a deep layer of compost on top. The cardboard will rot down, having killed any grass or weeds, and you have a ready-made bed in which to plant.

Mulching

The soil is usually still warm in late autumn and also moist from rain, so now is a good time to mulch your garden with organic matter, adding it wherever there is bare soil. Spread your own homemade compost (see p. 244), leaf mold (see p. 343), or green waste, ensuring it is a good 4 cm (1 ½ in.) deep. It will help to condition your soil, retain moisture, and suppress the weeds.

Creating a bed for hungry crops

Having said we have a no-dig policy, we do sometimes dig a trench or pit to plant next year's hungry feeders, such as pole beans and zucchini. Over the winter, we slowly fill the trench with compostable material including shredded newspaper, egg boxes, and vegetable peelings and offcuts such as outer cabbage leaves. Come spring, we cover the trench back over with soil before planting the bean and zucchini seedlings. The bed provides the crops with nutrient-rich, moisture-retentive soil, which they love.

Feeding Garden Birds

Once rosehips, haws, and seedheads become thin around the garden and hedgerows, it's important to feed garden birds. We only started feeding the birds here systematically several years ago, but now have twenty or so feeders placed all around the garden.

On the ground, we have a cage with a medium mesh (to exclude squirrels and so on) over a fine mesh table (this allows water to drain away). It is for the ground feeders such as robins, wrens, dunnocks, and all the tits, which are happy feeding anywhere. Blackbirds are too big to get through the mesh, so we leave chopped-up apples on a bird table, and this seems to be a favorite with them.

We also have lots of hanging bird feeders. We make simple, nice-looking globes from dogwood or willow cut from the garden, and then we hang a suet-and-seed block inside. We place these in many of our smaller trees, as well as at our windows.

Between them all, these feeders attract life to the garden, which gives us pleasure and is most certainly the reason aphid infestations and slug and snail plant annihilations are becoming a thing of the past here.

Making a bird feeder

To make a feeder, you need just a few things, including an "S" hook and cylindrical suet block or cake that can be hung from it.

- Cut two lengths of pliable stem to about 1 ½ m (5 ft.). Dogwood is perfect for this in winter and spring as it's so colorful. Alternatively, use hazel or willow.
- Bend the stems gently to ensure they are as pliable as possible before you start working with them. It will prevent them from snapping when you move on to weaving

them in the next steps. To do this, bend them gently over your knee along the entire length of the stems.

- Make a circular ring from each pliable stem. One should have a diameter of about (25 cm) 10 in. and the other should be slightly bigger to allow the smaller one to fit inside (ultimately, you will combine the pair to make a globe).
- Weave in any twiggy bits to strengthen each ring, wrapping them around the stem, and finish off by tucking the ends in between the woven pieces.
- Place the smaller ring inside the larger one to

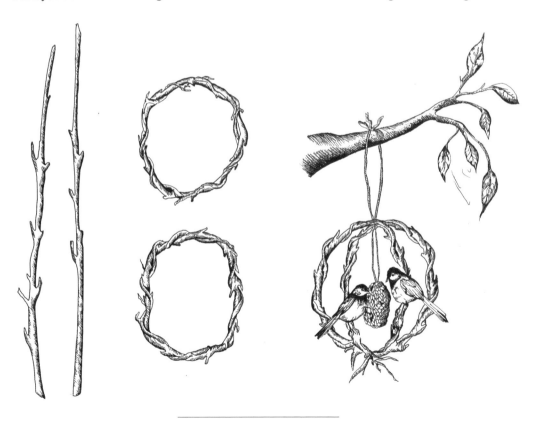

form a globe. Tie the top and the bottom firmly with flexi-tie or string across each axis. When you tie it at the top, include an "S" hook so that it hangs inside the globe for the suet block. Leave a loop of string at the top to hang the feeder.

Hanging feeders

Where you place your feeders is important depending on what birds you're keen to draw in. It seems that long-tailed tits are only happy feeding when there are decent-sized evergreens nearby for protection, whereas blue tits, great tits and coal tits are a little braver—though we do sometimes see a sparrow hawk or kestrel sweep down to snatch one.

Robins (mainly), sparrows, thrushes, blackbirds, and wrens are ground feeders but, as long as you keep your feeders full, they should get plenty from what drops down below the hanging feeders. Encouraging this means you won't be attracting rats and squirrels.

Goldfinches move in groups (called charms) of often five or ten birds and are quite shy. We tend to put thistle seed (their favorite) in feeders in a sheltered position, hanging them in a tree away from the house.

Sowing & Planting Guide

While the advice in this book is intended to inspire and guide gardeners across the country, and indeed the world, it is the result of my own experience at Perch Hill in East Sussex over the past thirty-odd years. These charts, meanwhile, are intended as a quick-reference guide, providing more general optimal timings and growing advice.

Vegetables

Common name	Plant group	Recommended technique
Saltwort	Hardy annual	Direct or module
Artichoke	Perennial	Module
Eggplant	Half-hardy annual	Module or seed tray
Beetroot	Hardy annual	Gutter or direct
Bean, cranberry	Half-hardy annual	Root trainer or pots
Bean, fava	Hardy annual	Root trainer or direct
Bean, French & pole	Half-hardy annual	Root trainer, pots, or direct
Broccoli (sprouting)	Hardy annual	Module
Brussels sprouts & flower sprouts	Hardy annual	Module or direct
Carrot	Hardy annual	Gutter or direct
Chard	Half-hardy annual or biennial	Seed tray, gutter, or direct
Pepper and sweet pepper	Half-hardy annual	Small pot, module, or direct
Zucchini, squash, and pumpkin	Half-hardy annual	Own little pot or direct
Cucumber	Half-hardy annual climber	Own little pot or direct
Florence fennel	Half-hardy annual	Direct or module
Kale	Hardy annual	Gutter or direct
Leek	Hardy annual	Gutter or direct
New Zealand spinach	Half-hardy annual	Direct, gutter, or module
Onion	Hardy annual	Module or direct
Parsnip	Hardy annual	Gutter or direct
Pea	Hardy annual	Gutter, root trainer, or direct
Pea tips	Hardy annual	Large box, gutter, or module
Sea beans	Perennial	Seed tray or direct
Spinach	Hardy annual	Gutter or direct
Sweet corn	Half-hardy annual	Module
Tomato	Half-hardy annual	Module or seed tray

Salads

Common name	Plant group	Recommended technique
American land cress	Biennial	Gutters, modules, or direct
Chicory	Hardy annual	Gutters or direct
Cress	Hardy annual	Small pot, module, or direct
Lettuce	Hardy annual	Gutters or direct
Mizuna and mustard	Hardy annual	Gutters or direct
Mixes	Hardy annual	Gutters or direct
Radish	Hardy annual	Gutters or direct
Arugula	Hardy annual	Direct
Spring onion	Hardy annual	Gutters or direct
Watercress	Perennial	Seed tray, gutters, or direct
Winter purslane	Hardy annual	Direct

JAN	FEB	MAR	APR	MAY	JUN	JUL	AUG	SEP	OCT	NOV	DEC

JAN	FEB	MAR	APR	MAY	JUN	JUL	AUG	SEP	OCT	NOV	DEC

Herbs

Common name	Plant group	Recommended technique
Basil	Half-hardy annual	Gutters or modules
Chamomile	Perennial	Seed tray
Chervil	Hardy annual	Modules or direct
Chives	Perennial	Gutters or direct
Coriander	Hardy annual	Gutters or direct
Dill	Hardy annual	Direct, regular sowing
Lemongrass	Perennial	Seed tray
Oregano	Evergreen subshrub	Seed tray
Parsley	Biennial grown as annual	Gutters or direct
Sorrel (French and red-veined)	Perennial	Gutters, modules, or direct
Sweet cicely	Perennial	Seed tray or direct
Summer savory	Hardy annual	Gutters or direct
Thyme	Evergreen subshrub	Seed tray

Edible flowers

Latin name	Common name	Plant group	Recommended treatment
Anchusa azurea	Alkanet	Perennial	Module or direct
Borago officinalis	Borage	Hardy annual	Seed tray, module, or direct
Calendula officinalis	English or pot marigold	Hardy annual	Module or direct
Centaurea	English or pot marigold	Hardy annual	Module or direct
Orychophragmus violaceus	Chinese violet cress	Biennial	Module or direct
Tagetes patula & tenuifolia*	Marigold	Half-hardy annual	Seed tray or module
Tropaeolum majus & minus	Nasturtium	Hardy annual	Seed tray, gutter, or direct
Viola tricolor	Viola, heart's ease	Perennial/Hardy annual	Seed tray, gutter, or direct

*Caution: Marigolds should only be consumed occasionally and in moderation

Potatoes

Common name
First early crop ("Sharpe's Express," "Winston")
Second earlies ("Charlotte," "Linzer Delikatess")
Main crops ("Belle de Fontenay," "Pink Fir Apple," "Ratte")

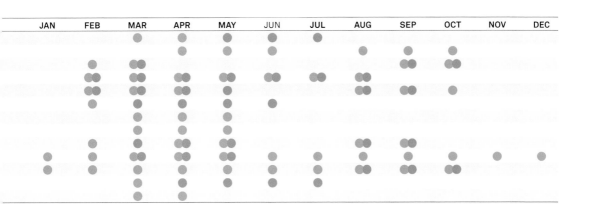

Index

Figures in **bold** refer to main entries.

insulating 50, 363
pests in 50, 119, 154, 157, 158, 363
planting in 138, 153, 160–62
sowing seeds in 54–61, 68,
   89–91, 116–18, 304–5,
   336, 362
thermal screens for 361
ventilating 363
watering plants in 303
see also tomatoes
groundsel 115
guttering
  planting 120–21
  sowing in 30, 46, 52, 57–8, 90–91,
   117, 305

H
hazel poles 50
hedges **97**, 309
herbs 18, 21, 25, 30, 35, **74**
  annual **78**
  evergreen **74, 77, 115**
  hardy annual **84–5, 120**
  harvesting **39, 78**
  perennial **77, 80–84,** 126
  sowing 49, 57, 68, 87
  teas *see* teas, herbal
  see also specific herbs
hoverflies 155
hyacinths 99, 100
hyssop 154–5, 192

I
insects
  plants to attract 155–6
  see also aphids
insulating
  greenhouses 50, 363
  pipes and taps 363
intercropping 152

K
kale 18, 21, 30, 35, **43,** 99, 100, 105,

154–5, 157, 241, **350–58;**
  planting 163–4; sowing 90,
  116; staking 201, 209–10
"Black Magic" 356
"Cavolo Nero" 117, 346, 350,
  353, **356**
"Dwarf Green Curled" 350
"Emerald Ice" 43
"Pentland Brig" 358
"Redbor" 25, 99, 117, 345–6,
  350, **358**
"Red Russian" 17, 21, 220, 350, **358**
"Scarlet" 17, 25, 117, 345–6,
  350, **356,** 364
"White Peacock" 43
see also spigariello
kalettes 30, 72, 90, 116, 117, 163–4,
  209–10, 345, **356**
kerching 39, 62
kohl rabi 21
komatsuna 35, **43**
  "Golden Yellow" 43

L
labels and labelling 52
lacewings 155
ladybugs 155
lavender 192, 232, 274
  "Miss Muffet" 158
layering 99, 100
leaf mold, making 343
leeks 12, 21, 30, 68, 72, 90, 99
  "Northern Lights" 25, 364, 365
  "Saint Victor" 25, 364, 365
lemon balm tea 228, 231, 232, 234
lemongrass tea 228, 231, 234,
  236
lemon verbena 81, 167, 213, 338
  tea 228, 231, 232, 234, **236**
lettuces 18, 22, 35, 39, **40–41,** 62,
  52, 157, 163, 285, 325; sowing 57,
  90, 304
  "All The Year Round" 40
  "Black Seeded Simpson" 40, 88,

  125, 364
"Cancan" 40, 364
"Cerbiatta" 40
"Merveille des Quatre Saisons"
  40, 88, 125, 170, 304, 364
"Red Oak Leaf" 40, 364
"Red Salad Bowl" 40
"Reine des Glaces" 41, 125, 170,
  364
"Salad Bowl" 304, 364
"Solix" 304, 364
lovage 35, 72, 77, 83, 126, 151

M
mangetout 18, 46, 305
  "Blauwschokker" 156
marigolds (calendula) 54, 105, 125,
  175, 188, 192, **194,** 207, 305
  "Indian Prince" 155, 194
  "Neon" 194
  see also tagetes
marjoram 117
mice 50
microgreens 38
mildew 82, 183, 194, 207
mint 18, 72, 74, 83, 105, 120, 122,
  126, 154, 169–70, 213, 338
  black peppermint 228, 231, 232,
  238
  Bowles's 83, 170
  Moroccan 170, 228, 238
  spearmint 83
  teas 228, 234, **238–9**
mizunas 29, 30, 35, 36, 38, 39, **44,**
  57, 62, 105, 159, 304, 345
  "Red Knight" 18, 44, 364
modules, sowing in 60–61, 90,
  117–18, 121
monarda 192
mosaic virus 64
molds 119
mulching 128, 151, 165, 366
mustards 12, 29, 30, 35, 36, **44–5,**
  105, 159, 364; as biofumigants

potash/potassium 162, 204, 206, 241, 273, 328
potatoes 21, 169, **176–9,** 335; sprouting 49, **61,** 93; earthing up 94,
 167; forcing **93,** 122, 169, 176, 178, 179; lifting 273, 303; planting 87, 115, 122–4, 152, 158; storing 169, 179, 249, 273; watering 167
 "Anya" 93, 178
 "Arugula" 178
 salad 138
 "Axona" 179, 249
 "Belle de Fontenay" 249
 "Charlotte" 93, 178
 "International Kidney" 179
 "Kestrel" 179
 "Linzer Delikatess" 179
 "Maris Piper" 9
 "Pink Fir Apple" 9, 61, 179, 249
 "Ratte" 9, 179, 249
 "Sharpe's Express" 178
 "Winston" 178
pots *see* containers
potting 119
separating seedlings 87, 91–2
primroses 72, **197,** 205
propagators, making 51
pumpkins 115, 273, 309, 311
 "Marina di Chioggia" **324**
 "Munchkin" 311, **325**
purslane
 summer 46, 90, 125, 170
 winter **46,** 306

Q
quinoa 148, 317–18

R
radishes 22, 30, 35, **46,** 120, 121, 133; sowing 57, 125, 152, 166, 306
 "Caro" 47, 133
 "Cherry Belle" 125, 133
 "French Breakfast" 125, 133

red spider mite 119, 303
rhubarb 18, 21, 99, **108–13;**
 dividing 308; forcing **62, 72,** 108, 112, 362; harvesting 111; planting 105–6, 342–3
 "Poulton's Pride" 112
 "Raspberry Red" 112
 "Red Champagne" 72, 112
 "Stockbridge Arrow" 72, 108, 112
 "Timperley Early" 62, 72, 108, 112
 "Victoria" 108, 112
root trainers 58–9, 117, 121
rosemary 18, 21, 72, 74, 78, **80,** 120, 122, 273, 274
 "Foxtail" 80
 "Green Ginger" 80–81
 "Miss Jessopp's Upright" 80, 158
 "Rosea" 81
 "Tuscan Blue" 81
roses 175, 188, 192, 197

S
sacrificial plants 157
sage (salvias) 18, 21, 25, 72, 74, **82,** 120, 122, 156, 175, 188, 191, 192, **199,** 249, 273, 274, 285, 317
 S. elegans 'Scarlet Pineapple' 199
 S. viridis blueflowered 54, 125, 138, 158, **199**
salad crops 18, 21, 29, 30, 35, 36, **42–6,** 49, 68, 99, 100, 312
 harvesting 38–9
 planting out 120
 picking 62
 preparing 39
 sowing seeds 57, 125–6, 362
 see also lettuces; rocket
salvias *see* sage
samphire 90, 125, 170
savory, summer 25, 96, 105, 154
scents, camouflaging 153
seaweed
 calcified 164
 liquid 87, 273

seedlings 67–8, 88
 planting **120–21**
 separating seedlings **91–2**
 thinning 126
seeds, sowing 50, 52, 88
 in containers 89, 336
 direct 96–7, 124–6
 in guttering 30, 46, 52, 57–8, 90–91, 117, 305
 in modules 60–61, 90, 117–18
 in root trainers 52, 58–9, 91, 117
 in seed trays 54–5
shallots 121, 214, **219,** 242, 306, 342
 "Griselle" 219
 "Jermor" 219
 "Longor" 219
shoo-fly plant 157, 318
slugs and snails 64, 157, 158, 165, 346
sorrel 18, 35, **84,** 105, 120, 122, 126
 French 72, 77, 84
 shamrock **47**
 wood **47**
sowing *see* seeds, sowing
spigariello 72, 353, **358**
spinach 18, 30, 35, 45, 49, 105, 120, 133, **143, 144, 148–9,** 317; sowing 57, 60, 91, 125, 275, 304
 "Callaloo" 148
 Chenopodium giganteum 148, 318
 "Hohei" 148
 Japanese 148
 "Medania" 47, 125, 143, 149, 364
 New Zealand 148
 perpetual 18, 140, 148
 red mountain 149, 318
 "Renegade" 149
 "Rubino" 45, 57, 125, 143, 149
 "Toscane" 149
spring onions 49, 60, 91, 159, 306
 "North Holland Blood Red" 219, 306
 "White Lisbon" 306
squash 18, 21, 157, 164, 241, 273, 309, 311, 320–27, 340; sowing

Acknowledgments

Thank you to Anita Oakes, Josie Lewis, Colin Pilbeam, Richard Lambden, Rebecca Cocker, and Jemima Reid for the hard work and cheerful help in making the kitchen garden and greenhouse look good every month of the year here.

For being encouraging reader-editors along the way, I'm so grateful to Kate Hubbard, Anita Oakes, Josie Lewis, Glenn Facer, Matthew Rice, and Becky Craven.

At Bloomsbury, thanks go to Rowan Yapp and Kitty Stogdon. And at PFD, to my long-term agent and ally, Caroline Michel.

Huge thanks to Esther Palmer for the practical drawings. Esther paints the watercolors that feature on all of our vegetable seed packets, which I dearly love—some have been combined into the endpapers of this book. And I'm so grateful for the airy and clear design of Glenn Howard and the fabulous photographs taken by my dear old friend and collaborator, Jonathan Buckley, which are as colorful of the vegetable garden as they are of our flowers.

Deepest thanks to Zena Alkayat, who went way beyond the call of editing duty on this book and *A Year Full of Flowers*. You've been an incredibly hard-working, clear and definite guide through the evolution of this book—and the last—and I very much hope the next. Thank you!

Sarah, Perch Hill

Many of the plants included in this book are available from companies specializing in vintage, heirloom, and unusual seeds and plants.

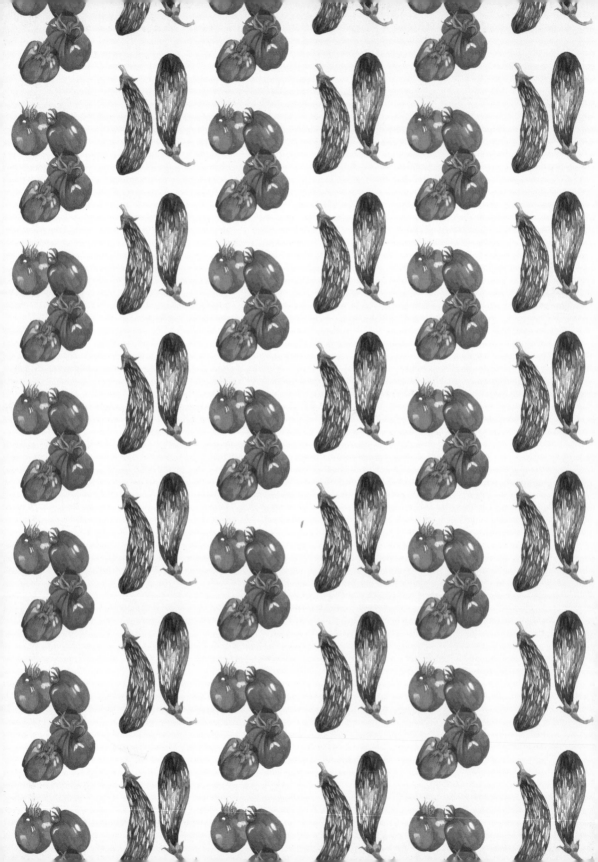